Joe
Enjoy the book!

Rockingham Forest -

Then and Now

Rockingham Forest -

Then and Now

Peter Hill

ORMAN PUBLISHING

Frontispiece : Cottingham (by Ron Mears)

First published 1995

© Peter Hill 1995

All rights reserved . No part of this book may be copied, reproduced or transmitted in any form, by any electrical or mechanical means, including information storage or retrieval system, without the permission in writing from the publisher, except by a reviewer who may quote brief passages.

British Library Cataloguing in Publication Data.
A catalogue record for this book is available from the British Library.

ORMAN PUBLISHING
2 Lovap Way
Great Oakley, Northants NN18 8JL

ISBN 0 9518199 2 5

FOREWORD

The Rockingham Forest was first established as a defined area by William the Conqueror who designated it a Royal Hunting Forest and built himself a castle from which it could both be enjoyed and administered. For the next 600 years it was a source of sport and revenue for successive Kings of England. The Forest was tightly controlled and the Kings interest carefully preserved by a complex administrative structure similar to that which still exists in forests which have survived to the present day such as the Forest of Dean.

In the case of Rockingham however, pressure from the large landowners in the area, spurred on by the quality of the soil and improved agricultural techniques, resulted in disafforestment and enclosure. This inevitably changed the landscape and led to the demise of the administrative arrangements for the Forest. While there are still a number of wooded areas, some of which date back to the original forest, they are contained within a complex of arable fields and pasture land and there is little recognisable forest left.

Yet the area has some very special qualities. Its gently rolling hills between the valleys of the rivers Welland and Nene alive with woods and farmland form a quintessentially English landscape, rich, varied, and cared for. A particular feature of the Forest area is the large number of landed estates, whose owners, while they may have hastened the demise of the Forest, have nevertheless looked after their land well. Not only have they nurtured the landscape for which they were responsible but over the years they have improved the economy and provided employment for many of those living in the Forest area. They were also in part responsible for a fine legacy of stone buildings ranging from palaces to barns. Nearly every village has a church worth visiting, as are many of the village pubs.

In recent years however, the staple industries on which the area has depended such as agriculture and steel making have been in decline with the latter now closed down for good. Local people are therefore having to look to alternatives such as tourism to fill the gap. The Rockingham Forest with its well documented history and evocative title provides an excellent focus for attracting visitors to the area.

It is therefore a good moment to reassert the identity of the Rockingham Forest and raise its profile in the public mind for the benefit not only of potential visitors but also of residents who may be unaware of the delights that surround them.

Accordingly I welcome this long-overdue book by Peter Hill which encompasses every aspect of the Forest from its origins to the present day. Of particular interest is the gazetteer with precise details of all there is to do and see. I hope it will reach a wide audience and encourage more people to visit the area and enjoy its many and diverse attractions.

Michael Saunders Watson
Rockingham Castle

Introduction

When you ask someone 'What is Rockingham Forest?' or 'Where exactly is Rockingham Forest?' you will be amazed at the many different responses! This is not surprising when you consider the traditional image, or simple dictionary definition, of the word 'forest'. This is even more the case when you drive, ride or walk round the area; and if you look at the way history and nature have shaped the composition of Rockingham Forest and determined its boundaries.

Rockingham Forest traditionally has its own unique 'spirit' and each community within the area shares this spirit, whether it regards itself as part of the Forest or not! Within the community there is a lot of individual talent and expertise, much of it hidden, that could be of general benefit - if only it is revealed and shared. With this in mind, the book was initially conceived as part of a project to encourage individuals, regardless of their age, background and interests, to come forward and meet together in their community, with a common aim of strengthening the spirit which is in danger of diminishing as the rapid changes representative of modern life take their toll. Here also is an opportunity to preserve and document the heritage of a community and its surroundings in some way: its history, attractions, walks, natural history, crafts, and traditions. As the older residents become fewer and fewer, it is vital to record their memories of a bygone age, before those memories irretrievably disappear. As the car becomes more dominant, it is essential to keep footpaths cleared - and to make their whereabouts known. As more and more housing erodes the countryside, areas of natural interest must be left intact - or even created.

Therefore, one aim of the book is to 'start the ball rolling', and raise a general awareness of what Rockingham Forest once was, and is today. Great efforts have been made in putting together what is hopefully a definitive record. This has involved countless hours of research, rambling, and conversation with members of the Forest community from farmers, naturalists, conservationists, rangers, and builders, to fellow historians, architects, art and craftspeople and the elderly.

It is only in recent years that the Forest's potential as a leisure or tourist attraction, spotlighting the wealth of historical, natural and activity interests within its boundaries, has been exploited. Many organisations of a varying specialist nature have made (and are continuing to make) significant contributions in promoting and conserving aspects of the Forest, and the second aim of this book is to unite and weave all these various elements together.

The third aim is to take the complex earlier and original material, and process it in an interesting, attractive way which can be understood by the average reader, without losing or omitting anything of importance. There is even scope for further research by others - which is certainly to be encouraged!

Hopefully, there is something of value in these pages for everyone, whether resident, visitor, passive reader, or active adventurer. Delve in and discover a new world! If you feel inspired, after reading the book, to go out and actively explore the Forest area and discover its many charms for yourself, or feel like doing something more for the community, you will certainly be rewarded and the book will have fulfilled a purpose.

Peter Hill
Spring 1995

List of Contents

	page
Foreword	v
Introduction	vi
List of Contents	vii
List of Illustrations	viii
Acknowledgements	ix
Part One: A History of the Forest	1
Part Two: A Forest Gazetteer	8
Part Three: Places On the Edge Of The Forest	92

Appendices

Tourist Information Centres	101
Museums	101
Walking in the Forest area	102
Horseriding in the Forest area	104
Cycling in the Forest area	104
Driving in the Forest area	104
The Rivers and Streams of the Forest	105
Local Nature Reserves	105
Wildlife Groups	106
Country & Pleasure Parks	106
Conservation Groups	106
Pocket Parks	106
Local History Societies	107
The Traditional Landowning Families of the Forest	107
The Medieval Deer Parks of the Forest	109
Lost Villages of the Forest	109
Monuments around the Forest	109
Leisure Activities	110
Markets	111
Annual Events	111
Refreshments	111
Bibliography	112
Further Reading: related books of interest	112
Glossary of Terms	114

List of Illustrations

Frontispiece: Cottingham

(between pages)

1. Rockingham Forest in the 17th century.   7 and 8
2. Letter and proclamation by James I.
3. Wadenhoe: Poaching Notice, 1819.
4. Fermyn Woods Hall Auction, 1910.
5. The changing face of Rockingham Forest.

6. Aldwincle.   16 and 17
7. Brigstock.

8. Old Corby.   22 and 23
9. Cottingham.

10. Deene.   26 and 27
11. Duddington.

12. Geddington.   36 and 37
13. Geddington.

14. Great Oakley.   42 and 43
15. Gretton House.
16. Kirby Hall.
17. Rushton, Triangular Lodge.

18. Kingscliffe.   52 and 53
19. Fotheringhay.
20. Nassington.

21. Rockingham.   64 and 65
22. Rothwell.

23. Stanion.   74 and 75
24. Wilbarston.
25. Thrapston

26. Weldon.   82 and 83
27. Woodnewton.

28. Kingscliffe.   90 and 91
29. Oundle.
30. Wansford.
31. Bulwick.
32. Nassington.
33. Apethorpe.
34. Wadenhoe.

ACKNOWLEDGEMENTS

I would like to thank my fellow local historians and those Rockingham Forest villagers whose suggestions and help have been invaluable in compiling this book. In particular I would like to mention Carl Hector, Ann Craske, Elizabeth Jordan, Ron Sismey, Sue Payne, Nicky Parr, Sue Hall, Bob Howe, Geoffrey Worrell, Tony Coales, Mick White, Geoffrey Fox, Pat Kimmons, Barbara Smith, Lewis Stanley, Tony Ireson, Julia Moss, Burl Bellamy, and Jeffrey Best. An extra special word of thanks must go to that great pioneer, instigator of local history in the area, and editor of Local History News, Ken Heselton, whose critical eye and suggestions made a significant contribution to the manuscript.

I would also like to acknowledge the academic imput (regarding architecture) by Professors David Henderson and James Curl of Leicester University; the co-operation of Professor Edmund King of Sheffield University on behalf of the Northamptonshire Record Society for permission to reproduce the map of Rockingham Forest in the 17th century; and to Rachel Watson of the Northamptonshire Record Office for permission to reproduce the James I documents (JAG 78).

My gratitude also extends to Commander Michael Saunders Watson of Rockingham Castle, for writing the foreword, and to John Sharman of Rockingham Forest Tourist Association, and Chris Wade of Rockingham Forest Trust, together with a Cambridgeshire Rural Strategy group for the use of some of their artwork for the cover, and to my daughter, Thea, for help with the final design.

A thank you is also due to those unnamed people who also helped me to provide an accurate record: farmers, naturalists, architects, builders, and demolition workers. The work of the Northamptonshire Records Office, and Local Studies Collection is also to be acknowledged, as is that of the librarians at Corby, Kettering, Northampton and Oundle.

Finally a big word of thanks to Northamptonshire ACRE for helping to get the project off the ground, and to British Steel, RS Components and ABR Foods for their part-sponsorship.

ILLUSTRATION CREDITS

I would like to express my gratitude to the following artists for permission to use examples of their work for this book:

Ron Mears : frontispiece, 11,13,15,16,17, 20, 21, 27.
Jeannie Loveday : 6, 7, 8, 9, 12,14, 22, 23, 26, 34.
John Paige : 18,19, 33.
George Harrison
(drawings reproduced by kind permission of John Worledge, and the granddaughters of George Harrison) : 10, 25, 28, 29, 30, 31.
Sue Payne : 32.
Unknown (c1908): believed to be by S.P.Pick : 24.

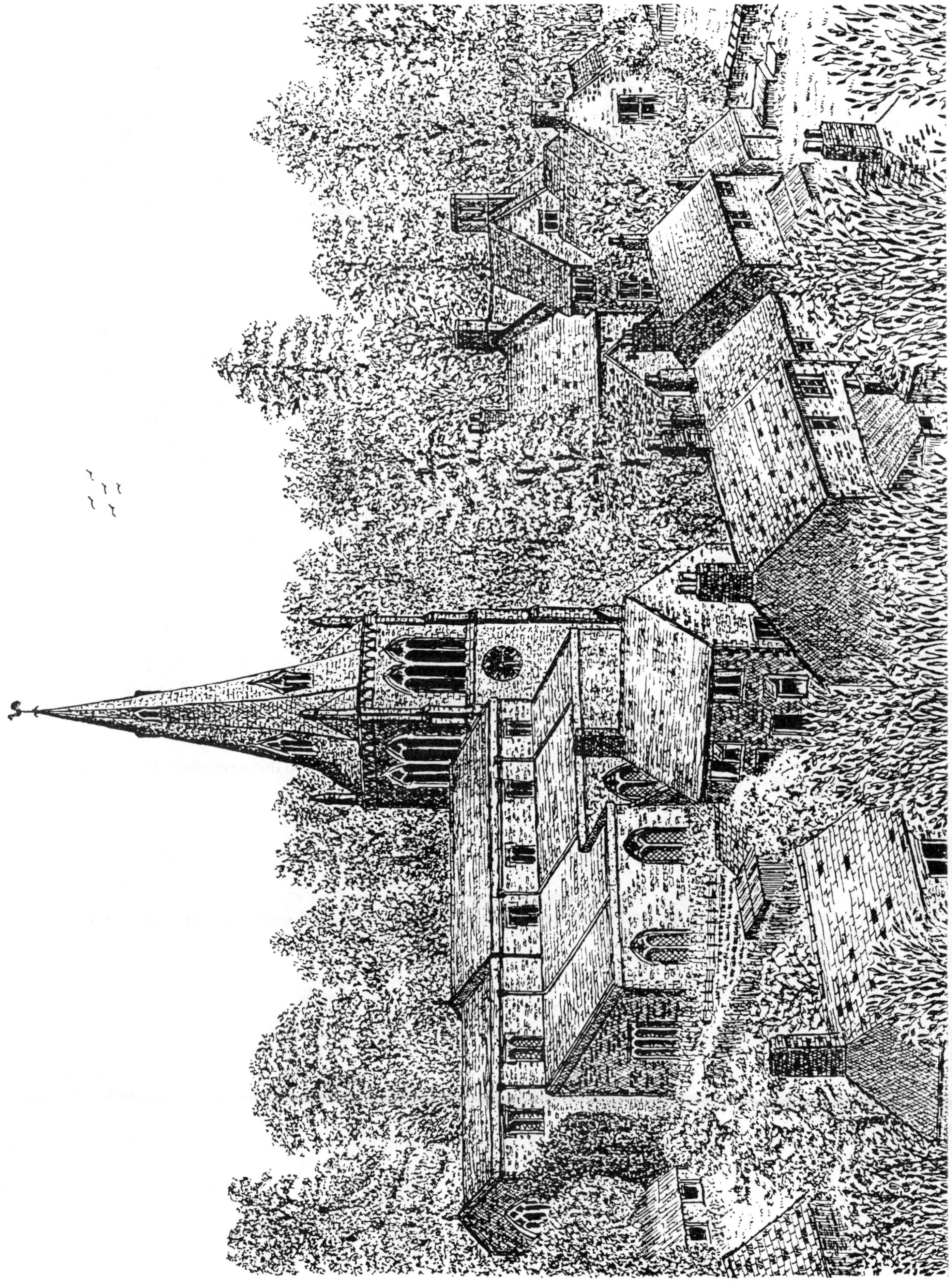

PART ONE: A HISTORY OF THE FOREST

'There are fallow, but no red deer in the forest. The fairest game is in the launde of Benefielde...Within its precincts there is good corn, pasture and plenty of wood.'
(Leland, John : 'Itinerary', 1534-43 pub. 1710)

'(In the 17th year of Charles I's reign...) Rockingham Forest is well nigh 14 miles in length, that is from the West End of Middleton Woods to the Top of Wansford Town. The breadth of it in the upper part from Brigstock to the Bend of the River Welland below Gretton is 5 miles. In the lower part from the Bank of the River Nyne (Nene) below Yarwell, to that of the Welland below Dudington is very near as much. And these as the Boundaries of the Forest now stand are the broadest Parts of it, but before that Liveden and other adjacent Towns were disforested, it was much broader .....Of the Forest, in general it is said, and that with great Reason that it is one of the largest and richest in the whole Kingdom.'
(Morton, John : The Natural History of Northamptonshire, 1712)

'The limits of Rockingham Forest are from Oxendon bridge to Stamford bridge. In length after the old Perambulation, it is about 20 miles, and 4 or 5 miles in breadth.'
(Bridges, John : A History and Antiquities of Northamptonshire, 1721 pub. 1791)

'Away south between the Nene and the Welland, stretches from Stamford and Peterborough the still vast forest of Rockingham, nigh twenty miles in length as the crow flies, down beyond Rockingham town and Geddington Chase. Deep tangled forest filled the lower clay lands, swarming with pheasants, roe, badger, and more wolves than were needed. Broken park-like glades covered the upper freestones, where the red deer came out from harbour for their evening graze and the partridges and plovers whirred up, and the hares loped away innumerable, and where hollies and ferns always gave dry lying for the night.'
(Kingsley, Charles : 'Hereward The Wake' 1866)

('The Forest of Rockingham once extended) from the south bridge of Northampton to the bridge at Stamford, 33 miles long, with an average breadth of 7 - 8 miles.'
(J.C.Cox: The Royal Forests of England, 1905)

Rockingham Forest. What kind of picture does it conjure up? The quotations above, made at different times in history, show different interpretations of the forest's extent, and changes in its appearance. Yet today, despite being a shadow of its former self, there are still pockets of the original place, unaffected by time, where it is easy to find yourself transported back into history, wallowing in a piece of *Olde England* - if you know where to go. This book will look briefly at that history in the first part, and look at places to visit in the second part.

Early origins.

It should be mentioned here that the term 'forest' does not mean the whole area was completely covered with trees: Rockingham Forest included (and still does) wide open spaces, smaller clearings, pasture, ridings, ponds, brooks and thick undergrowth. Both man (managing or clearing woodland, and using land and water for agricultural, domestic and industrial purposes) and nature (especially in the form of soil erosion, storms, climatic changes and disease), have had an effect on the eventual composition and size of the Forest.

It had certainly had earlier attractions, when it formed part of a larger forest covering nearly the whole county of Northamptonshire, and spilt over into the neighbouring counties. In the western area of the forest, around Kingswood, indications of Iron Age tribal settlement in the form of ditches and pits containing pieces of pottery have been found. Ironstone, conveniently near the surface, was used to make primitive tools and weapons. The top of nearby Rockingham Hill provided an ideal place for a fortress or for lighting warning beacons to other tribal settlements, and gave sweeping views for miles around, of the Welland Valley and beyond.

The Romans too found it an ideal place, working its rich and vast iron-ore deposits for their weapons, tools and equipment. All around the Forest area, extensive remains of Roman occupation have been found such as roads, bridges, villas, mosaic pavements, pottery, statuettes and hoards of coins.

The Anglo-Saxons certainly loved the region, settling in large numbers, and began clearing parts of the forest (assarting) for fuel; using its valuable timber to build huts for their new settlements; and clearing areas for the cultivation of crops, and grassland for grazing livestock. The whole forest is dotted around with villages of Anglo-Saxon origin, as can be seen in their names - Gretton, Cottingham, Rockingham, Blatherwycke, Wakerley, Duddington and Brigstock - to name just a few.

With the arrival of the Normans, officialdom took a hold on the Forest, with laws made by the hunt-loving conquerors (1066-1154) in their own interests, claiming it solely as their domain. Rich in deer and wild boar, it was exploited by hunting parties during periodic royal visits. William I sent commissioners to ascertain the extent of the Forest and to set its boundaries. The term 'Rockingham Forest' therefore came to mean an area designated for Royal Hunting, and hence it was subject to Forest Law.

It was considered an offence by anyone else (including the owner of the land) to chase and slay a creature within its boundaries. The king also owned all rights to grazing, mineral resources (such as iron ore), and timber. [It was possible for landowners in the forest to be granted a warren - at a price - for their own use, which restricted them to hunting foxes, hares and fowl only. Licences - with strict conditions - for deerparks followed later). Theoretically, the penalties were severe: for slaying any large game, an offender could suffer some form of mutilation, lose a limb, or even have his eyes gouged out. However, records show that no such punishments were carried out in practice, and that heavy fines were the norm.

Medieval administration of Forest Law.

The practice of royal prerogative for hunting, with the same stringent laws, continued with the Plantagenet rulers (1154-1485), and these were rigidly enforced. This was facilitated by a special administrative system. For this, the king appointed a *Chief Justice of Forests*, usually from the higher-ranking nobility, who had overall legal control and authority of a large region. From 1238, two such officials were appointed - one for forests south of the River Trent, including Rockingham, and one for those to the north. Below them, and acting on a local level were the *wardens* (Chief Foresters or Masters of the Game), high-ranking people, who were entrusted with custody of game and wood in a particular forest.

Answerable to them were hereditary *foresters-in-fee* (gentlemen keepers) and appointed *foresters* (or yeomen keepers). Their role was the most hazardous of all the forest officials: patrolling the forest on foot or horseback, on the look-out for poachers and trespassers whom they had to pursue and arrest. Inevitably, some foresters suffered injury or death over the years, especially in certain areas like Beanfield Lawn and Farming Woods (qv) as records show (particularly in the 13th century), though some came out of a confrontation quite lightly : in one case a forester was tied to a tree, later to be released by one of his captors! Often poachers would get away from their pursuers: there are frequent references of escape by being 'lost in the darkness of night' and 'thickness of wood'. Failure to carry out their duties properly also made the foresters liable to fines and an appearance in court. Similarly, they were not well-liked by the local populace, not only because they enforced the Forest Law, but because they could (legally) demand certain fees, as well as food for their upkeep! A career with job satisfaction?

Also, like other Forest officials, they were not all innocent themselves, often flouting the law for their own purposes. For example in 1246, a forester from Brigstock, James of Thurlbear, whilst dining with the Abbot at Pipewell Abbey found a poacher (who had earlier killed his brother at Beanfield Lawn) being harboured by his dinner host! The poacher was later imprisoned. In 1253, James himself was accused at court by some of the Forest villages, of 'hunting with a pack of greyhound (and) frequently assembling 18 men with bows and arrows in all the baliwicks of the forest, to do evil to the king's venison'.

There were other officials, who were not under the jurisdiction of the wardens, and who were not paid for their duties. The *verderers*, elected by the county court from the local gentry, were responsible to the king, and worked closely with the foresters. They acted in a combined role corresponding approximately to magistrate and coroner, attending the forest courts, and presenting the evidence of offenders appearing there. This evidence would often be in the form of bones, hide, antlers, a deer's head, an arrow or a sack, found at or near the scene of the crime, where they would be present at an *inquest* shortly afterwards, often headed by the warden, with representatives of the nearest four villages giving any information they could about the crime and suspects.

There were also *regarders*, who made general inspections of the forest every three years, to assess and prevent any damage to the woodland. *Agisters* acted in a 'rent-collecting' role, ensuring that money was paid by the owners of animals using the forest for grazing (see below). Landowners in the forest were legally bound to appoint their own kind of forester, *woodwards*, who performed a similar 'gamekeeper' role (and who were in later years responsible for the management and sale of Crown wood). Finally, another kind of official (who appeared later, in the 14th century) was the purlieu *ranger*, who had a kind of 'cowboy' role, driving any stray deer back into the forest.

There were two kinds of court to deal with Forest offences. The main medieval *Eyre* court met (theoretically) every seven years to judge and sentence those who had broken the laws of the Forest, mainly those pertaining to the theft, wounding or slaying of deer, but also any serious offences affecting the greenery, such as the destruction (even pilfering) of timber. [The *Eyre* court however fell into disuse as time went by, meeting only twice in Rockingham Forest during the 16th century, and again in 1635]. Whenever an offence took place, an immediate *inquest* was held by the warden, and the offender (if caught) was brought before local *courts of attachment* which usually met about every six weeks. Here imprisonment was imposed, to ensure that he was available to appear before the *Eyre* court. However, this could be waived for those with sufficient funds, on payment of a hefty financial penalty and and on giving an oath that they would be of good behaviour towards 'the King's Game, Vert and Venison of the Forest', until the *Eyre* court met to hear the evidence and pass judgement. The other role of the *courts of attachment* was to deal with minor offences against the greenery (for example, the theft of a small amount of wood of low value), where the verderers could act in a judicial role, imposing small fines. In time however, as far as Rockingham Forest was concerned, the name *swanimote* was given to these local courts. Originally the *swanimote* was a local administrative court, comprised of the verderer and a group of foresters and agisters, which met three times a year to organise communal grazing in the woods.

Defining Forest boundaries.

During the reign of Edward I, in 1286, a 'perambulation' of the Forest was made by various officials to ascertain and establish once again, the boundaries of the Forest, which included both private and royal woodlands. These boundaries could be identified, or defined at different places (often) by natural or 'permanent' markers: high objects ('marks') such as a tree; distances between forest and an adjacent building ('meres') such as a mill; and level characteristics ('boundaries') like a river or track. That year, the forest was found to be an immense 33 miles long and between seven to eight miles wide, stretching from Northampton to Stamford, and almost to Market Harborough ('Haverberge') in the west.

However as a result of grants and sales of land by the king, *assarting* (clearing tracts of land for agricultural purposes), and persistent lobbying by some of the nobles, another perambulation was made during the same king's reign, in 1299, when a large portion of the 'forest' area covered in 1286 and earlier, was left out! The boundaries fixed by the 1299 perambulation were to remain unchanged for well over 300 years.

Because the forest area was so large, it was for administrative purposes, divided into three areas of control or *bailiwicks*: Rockingham, Brigstock and Cliffe, each with its own keeper. Rockingham had overall control, being the seat of a royal residence, but each bailiwick was responsible for its own affairs. Because of the 1299 perambulation, villages that visibly should have (and previously had) been included as part of the Forest, were no longer listed as Forest villages. However, they were allowed the same privileges, such as representation at the *swanimote*, and rights of common. The listings of 1299 were as follows:

Rockingham Bailiwick: Rockingham, Great Oakley, Little Oakley, Cottingham, Middleton, East Carlton, Wilbarston, Gretton, Corby, Little Weldon. (Note the omission of Great Weldon, Deene, Kirby, Pipewell and Rushton).
Brigstock Bailiwick: Brigstock, Stanion and Geddington. (Omitted were: Newton, Grafton Underwood, Lowick and Sudborough).
Cliffe Bailiwick: Kings Cliffe, Apethorpe, Duddington, Fotheringhay, Woodnewton, Nassington, Yarwell. (Omitted were: Benefield, Deenethorpe, Glapthorn, Southwick, Bulwick, Blatherwycke, Wakerley, Laxton, Wadenhoe, Wansford, Cotterstock, Oundle, Stoke Doyle and Pilton). Cliffe was virtually a separate forest.

The bailiwicks also contained areas that did not belong to one particular parish: they were considered extra-parochial. In Cliffe they were Morehay, Westhay and Sulehay ('hay' meaning an enclosure or area fenced off for a particular purpose: usually hunting). They were placed under the care of a keeper who had a 'lodge' for that purpose. In later times, barns were added as the land was used for farming purposes. In addition to these areas, there were parks and lawns which also had 'lodges'. Parks such as those at Kingscliffe and Brigstock were for keeping deer, as was Beanfield Lawn, where the animals could graze peacefully out of harm's way - for the time being that is - until the hunt. There were also forest 'wastes' like 'Rockinghamshire' (a broad unenclosed plain) where deer mingled with domestic cattle from nearby forest villages, the latter animal more widespread than the former.

Surrounding the woods and enclosures in some places were 'walks' or 'ridings', such as Wydehawe and West Bailiwick. These were tracks which allowed access from one place to another, but these were also controlled by the forest officials.

Common rights.

The inhabitants of the villages in the Forest had, like any other village, certain common rights or privileges, though for these rights a fee was payable. These 'commons' meant that an ordinary man with little or no land could keep animals in the forest coppices and wastes: he was allowed *commons of pasture* (to graze his sheep), *agistment* (to graze his cattle), *pannage* (to let pigs feed on acorns and beech mast), and in many cases, *estovers* (to gather fallen or dead waste wood for fuel).

When 'enclosure' took place, many peasants were deprived of their livelihood - as a result of the land they had worked on for generations suddenly being converted to profitable sheep farming by the landowners. The villages of Rockingham Forest, untouched by these events, suddenly became very attractive to outsiders. Inevitably there were clashes with these 'vagrants' from outside, many of whom were punished (flogged and 'sent back whence they came') in front of the people of the village they had encroached on. There was even rivalry between the Forest villages themselves: in the 17th century, violent confrontations took place involving bodily assault and the destruction of greenery, especially around village boundaries. Fines would range from a penny to sixpence - a considerable sum in those days.

Though officially illegal, poaching was considered by Forest villagers a necessary supplement to their often meagre livelihood. It was often done in small groups and mainly at night, when there was less chance of being seen - and when superstition was at its height. Over-riding their own fears, they would play on the general belief in the supernatural, hoping that Forest officials would not venture out at that time (or be too busy indulging in the good life!). This was not always the case, as records show that foresters *were* on patrol, but were unable to catch poachers who vanished 'in the darkness' (see above). Some of the nocturnal expeditions however, did play on the imagination of Forest communities, and gave rise to ghost stories themselves! Beyond this, poaching remained a cause of violence, mainly against intruders from outside a village (or later, parish), and with rabbits becoming the main target, lasted well into this century.

Decline and disafforestation.

As the years passed, the forest laws grew lax. Fines, being a good source of revenue to fill the eternally-low royal coffers (as well as helping to pay certain forest officials and administrators), continued to be the main punishment for offences. Over the centuries, timber had been felled in large quantities, particularly for the purposes of shipbuilding for the Navy, though because of its inland position, Rockingham Forest was hardly affected. Other clearances as a result of population increase and further assarting for agricultural use, whittled away the extent of the forest. Above all, the unpopular policy of royal rights to the forest and hunting, which allowed kings to ride over the landowners' lands and woods, continued to be bitterly resented, though by the time of the Tudor monarchs (with the exception of Henry VIII), hunting was not so common as it had been. The landowners themselves hunted deer, and commoners poached in greater numbers, repeatedly flaunting Forest Law. In 1598, a directive was issued by the Chief Justice in Eyre asking authorised 'friends' in Rockingham Forest to keep an eye on the situation. The landowners dearly wished for disafforestation, i.e. freedom from Forest Law, and the right to do with their land as they pleased. As the 17th century progressed, they would at last see the beginning of the fulfilment of their wishes.

However, in the early years, the situation did not look promising. In fact, when James I, an avid hunter with obvious interests in the Forest, came to the throne in 1603, he set about trying to renew its ancient laws, including the imposition of severe punishments for offenders. He issued a proclamation to this effect straight away, and again in 1609 to all the owners of lands in the Forest followed by a letter the next year to the major landowners of Rockingham Bailiwick (Montagu, Watson, Hatton, Brooke and Tresham) cautioning them to apprehend 'evil disposed persons' who keep weapons and dogs with the intention of deerhunting.

Charles I who succeeded his father gradually took a different line. Desperate for money to fill the Royal coffers, he saw an ideal way of doing this by granting concessions and purchases. Soon after his accession, landowners around the Forest began to petition him: among them was Thomas Brooke of Great Oakley who in 1627 successfully obtained 'certain privileges and exemptions for himself and his tenants within the forest and the keeping of his own woods. Large tracts of woodland were sold: that same year, Christopher Hatton purchased Pipewell Woods, to add to others he already owned. The following year, the trees of Farming Woods, Morehay and Westhay were sold for £2,000 to Nicholas Pay, and those of Geddington Woods to Edward Montagu for £1,000.

However, the gate was not yet completely open. In his constant desperation for more money Charles resorted to a rigorous enforcement of Forest Law in which everyone would be affected, whatever their position. In June 1635, more purposeful swanimotes were held at Little Weldon (for Rockingham and Brigstock bailiwicks), and Kingscliffe, to try 'liberty takers'. At Little Weldon, 46 offenders appeared, and fines (from £2 to £20) were imposed for all manner of forest offences including chasing and killing deer, cutting trees and underwood and *perpresture* (building on land which 'encroached on the King's forest'). The latter pertained to a miller from Brigstock who had erected a windmill at Corby Woods, and to the son of Thomas Tresham, for maintaining a house built by his father at Brigstock Park 'contrary to Forest Law'.

That same year, the Eyre Court was revived in the Forest: this time, the major landowners found themselves subject to punitive heavy 'fines', that they could ill afford. These fines, up to £20,000, were imposed on members of the Salisbury, Westmorland, Hatton and other families. Two years later, Charles alarmed and angered a great many more people by extending the Forest area (with a formal perambulation made the following year) to its original and much wider pre-1299 boundaries, which meant that previously-excluded villages now found themselves subject to the conditions and penalties of Forest Law. As a result fines were imposed on several newly-included villages for failure to send representatives to the *swanimote*. The extension was also intended to force the major landowners to buy a pardon or disafforestation of their lands. This had the desired effect, but in reality the Crown received comparatively little revenue from these 'impoverished' buyers.

After intense protests, the king succumbed and gave up his attempt at maintaining the old Forest Law: a final perambulation was made in 1641 to establish the boundaries of the forest. This time, there was a complete reversal: the boundaries did not just revert to the smaller 1299 level, but shrank further because of newly-disafforested lands.

The years of the Civil War saw a further loosening of the laws, as the country was split and the traditional role and power of royalty was thrown into question. Indiscriminate plundering of the forest by both sides as a wartime necessity was a reflection of this and further fuelled the drive towards final severance from Royal interference and control. This cause was furthered by Oliver Cromwell in 1653, who was concerned about the state of the kingdom's forests. Following his proposal for the management of 'the King's forests, 'in a less offensive manner to the people', an Act was actually drawn up 'for the disafforestation, sale and improvements of the Forests'.

Indeed, during the Restoration, the new king Charles II, took little interest in the forests of the kingdom, except as a source of valuable revenue. He willingly leased or gave stretches of the forest away to those who petitioned him, with few if any conditions, provided the price was right. Wholesale disafforestation continued over the years, under successive monarchs, and the forest was whittled away further, until by the end of the 18th century (after the three Baliwicks were theoretically disafforested in 1795-96) only a small portion was still in royal hands. The resultant freeing of woodland had benefits for the livelihood of Forest communities, by encouraging timber-related crafts such as tanning and charcoal burning, as well as an increase in carpentry and (in some parts) wood-turning.

In 1817, an Act of Parliament was passed abolishing the Chief Justice in Eyre, and the forests of the realm were placed under a special commission. In 1832, another Act was passed officially enclosing and disafforesting Rockingham Bailiwick. By 1850 as a result of sales and enclosure, further large areas of woodland had disappeared, much of it being converted to arable land.

The coming of the railway also transformed the landscape, particularly in the Welland area, as did unprecedented large-scale ironstone quarrying, which took place well into this century, leaving many large hollows. World War II also played its part, with many flat areas in and around the Forest becoming airfields for the US Airforce. The long, straight landing-strips and the crumbling remains of associated buildings still dot the landscape. With agricultural and industrial changes, pollution of some of the waterways resulted in the building up of sediment, and other environmental problems, such as the disappearance of certain forms of wildlife.

Rockingham Forest Today.

Though its nature and size have changed, the Forest offers a lot today for resident and visitor alike. The key has been preservation - of selected areas of woodland, game, old buildings, and traditional walks. An interesting exercise was a perambulation made by the author and a group of other ramblers in stages, during 1993-94, following the 1299 boundaries as closely as possible, though much of the land is now in private hands. Despite a few minor obstacles en-route (some natural, some man-made!), the walks were pleasant - and a visual revelation. We were able to identify nearly all of the old place names and boundaries mentioned in the document, and found, surprisingly, that little has changed over the years. We often felt as if we were transported back in time, savouring the tranquil atmosphere, and feasting on the sights and sounds of nature as we passed through ancient pockets of woodland, or traversed fields and streams. A wealth of plant and animal life manifested itself: the latter including roe and fallow deer, muntjac, stoats, weasels, badgers, foxes, squirrels, rabbits, hares, even the rarely-seen dormouse, were all spotted during the walks. (Although we did not see any otters, they have since made a reappearance in some parts). We interspersed the walks with a wander along the quiet streets and lanes of villages whose older buildings have witnessed many an interesting scene and change over the years. If only the stones could talk!

Conservation, replanting and a return to 'methods of the past' are playing a vital role in the appearance of today's Rockingham Forest. In some parts, traditional habitat management, such as grazing, coppicing and pollarding, is being exercised by the Forestry Commission and The Wildlife Trust for Northamptonshire, to encourage the growth of new stems, foster breeding, and preserve rarer plants. Elsewhere, like other forested areas of the country, 'newer' plantations of fir trees co-exist with original woodland of hazel, oak, field maple, birch, ash, elm and small-leaved lime (the latter three being amongst the earliest species of tree in the Forest). Fewer of the older buildings are being demolished: by being rebuilt or renovated, they are not just receiving a new lease of life, but are retaining their old appearance. Many of those that formerly provided a community service such as a bakery, school or public house, have had that original role acknowledged in their modern name. In some cases, a visual reminder of the past has been retained in the form of an anvil, or inn sign-holder.

The Wildlife Trust, Forest Enterprise, and Northamptonshire Countryside Services, amongst others, are also creating or improving tracks, trails, ponds, glades, and facilities for visitors at many sites. In some cases, guides, new leaflets or explanatory notices have been provided,

Some areas have been set up as Nature Reserves or designated as Sites of Special Scientific Interest. Others have been made part of an experimental Countryside Stewardship Scheme, with the aid of consenting farmers. Here you can either explore the riverside, pass through watermeadows, or see ancient 'ridge and furrow' farmland - a corrugated type of landscape, produced by ploughing which improved the drainage and helped crop survival. You can wander around former ironstone or limestone quarries and gravel pits in which a variety of grasses and plant-life have taken root, and become an attraction to insects and birds. Some of these areas have been made into country parks, or wildlife sanctuaries.

The Forest has also seen the encouragement and introduction of 'pocket parks' in and around some of the villages and towns. These have been set up by local communities as a means of conserving some of the local landscape and its wildlife. Varying in size, form, and type of habitat, they are also pleasant places to visit and enjoy.

The Forest is also a great destination for day visitors and tourists. With this in mind, an association was formed by like-minded individuals in 1983, to explore ways and means of attracting visitors to the area, and by 1989, Rockingham Forest Tourist Association (ROFTA) was formally recognised by the Joint East Midlands/Anglia Tourist Boards as the promotional organisation for the area. Since then it has produced publicity and promotional material of both a specialist and general nature, and continues to develop new ways of helping visitors to enjoy their stay without spoiling the area.

The Rockingham Forest Trust, was set up in October 1993, to help maintain the countryside and to enhance the local environment: embracing and involving its communities, villages and craftspeople. Building on nearly a thousand years of Forest tradition, this is an exciting development with a key aim and the Trust is already starting initiatives that will benefit the area long-term. News concerning the Forest appears in a quarterly newsletter, appropiately entitled 'The Regarder'! The day of the Trust's launch also saw the formation of a new scheme based on the commitments of officials under the old Forest Law, whereby members (from the business sector) 'plight their commitments to safeguard the Forest' by becoming 'Guardians of the Rockingham Forest' and by contributing annually to the Trust.

The Forest area is criss-crossed with a vast number of footpaths and bridle-ways, and many of those which have long been over-grown have now been cleared and way-marked. Various local organisations have recently produced leaflets to encourage walkers, riders and cyclists and a list of those relevant to the forest area are listed at the end of the book. Several are included under each village heading in Part Two. For those preferring to drive, there are free touring guides (see the appendices).

After a ramble through the forest or surrounding area, there is no problem satisfying your thirst since most of the forest villages are well-endowed with pubs, many of which have restaurant facilities. The majority of these are of ancient origin, yet they are only a remnant of a far greater number that once existed in the Forest, as the gazetteer will show. This was not bad for an area where ale-houses were at one time considered a hang-out for poachers, outlaws and vagabonds!

Northamptonshire has traditionally been called the county of 'Squires and Spires'. The Rockingham Forest area can boast associations with many of them and is tightly packed with churches (though some only have towers instead of spires!), stately homes, and monuments. The region was an attractive place for farming, hunting and having a home, with its beautiful contrasting countryside and many waterways. Listed buildings can be seen everywhere - some surviving from medieval times. Thatch, cob, limestone and ironstone abound. Many of the stately homes with their priceless treasures, and vast grounds can be visited by the public at certain times of the year : all have something different to offer. Many of the churches are as fascinating as museums, containing valuable items of historical and artistic interest. They are well worth a visit - though in a few cases, a key may have to be obtained for access.

Some of the historical monuments and buildings in the Forest are in the care of either English Heritage, the National Trust, or Northamptonshire County Council. The latter is responsible for eight of these 'County Heritage Sites' (including stocks and dovecotes) in the Rockingham Forest.

Though many old English customs, like 'Plough Mogging' have disappeared in the Rockingham Forest area, just as they have elsewhere, the traditional May Day celebrations have been revived at Nassington, and are a very popular annual fixture. At Rothwell, a fair originating in medieval times is still held annually, though in a more modern form. There is a folk club held in the *Hatton Arms* at Gretton. In addition, traditional music from 'Empty Pocket' (Paul Rogers) is performed in the region, including 'Jack-in-the-Green', a celebration of Rockingham Forest in words and music. Historically-minded organisations from the Midlands and East Anglia like 'Livery and Maintenance' (15th century) and the 'Sealed Knot' (Civil War) have actively recreated battles and domestic life scenes, in period costume, in the grounds of some of the older buildings which are open seasonally to the public.

In some ways, the Forest is a microcosm of Northamptonshire's unique sense of independence, born out of a set of historical and socio-economic circumstances, which are yet to be researched and explored in depth. Though it is in danger, the special traditional 'spirit', atmosphere and way-of-life common to the villages in the area, still exists.

Rockingham Forest can still offer hunting - of a different kind. Join the thousands who, over the years have seen its marvels, discovered its legends and history, enjoyed its landscape, experienced its hypnotic atmosphere and received a genuine, warm welcome!

JAMES R.

Trustie and welbeloved Wee greete You well, letting you to Witt that as Wee are credibly informed there are many evil disposed persons towards our Deere and Game of our Forest of Rockingham that doe keepe Greyhounds and other Doggs Bows Crossbows Buckstalls Deerhayes and such like engines *to take and destroy our Deer* within and near unto the borders of the said Forest, contrary to the auncyente Laws and privileges of the same—By reason whereof our Keepers and Officers of the said Forest doe find themselves greatly grieved for presente remedy; whereof and for the better quiet and preservation of the Deer and Game within the saide Forest and near unto the confines of the same, Wee reposing especial truste and confidence in Your diligent and prudent care in this behalfe doe earnestlie will and require You from tyme to tyme to cause diligente search and watche to bee made, throughout all the Baylywyck of Rockingham in our said Forest and the borders thereof for all such offenders and all such Greyhounds and other Doggs Bows Crossbows Buckstalls Deerhayes and such like engines and *all takers of Pheasants or Patridges* with their Netts and Engines as you shall find within the said Baylywick and neare thereunto likely *to do hurte unto our Deer and Game of our said Baylywick* You doe take into your Custodie and doe binde all such offenders to their good behaviour and all such as You shall find to doe hurte to *our Deer or Game within the said Baylywick* with Greyhounds or any kinde of Doggs or by usinge of any such Engines you shall commit them to Prison there to remain until our pleasure therein shall be fully known—And this shall be Your sufficiente warrante in that behalf given at our Court at Wanested this 21st of June 1610.

To our trusty and welbeloved *Sr. Edward Mountacute Sr. Christopher Hatton Sr. Edward Watson Sr. Thomas Brooke and Sr. Thomas Tresham Knight* and to every of them——

JAMES RGX.

Certaine auncyente Lawes and ordinances of the Forest commanded by His Majesty to be published in the Parishe Churches within the Baylywick of Rockingham and neare and adjoineing unto the Borders and confines of the same.

1st. Noe man may chase or kill the Kings Deer and Game lyinge and feedinge within the Purlieues adjoininge to the said Baylywick except he have Freehold Lands to the Yearly value of XL shillings within the said Purlieues.
2. Every Purlieu Man muste begin his chase in his own Purlieu.
3. No Purlieu Man may hunt his Purlieues with any more company than his household Servants.
4. Hee must not use anie manner of Forestallinge with Quick Haye or with Dead Haye, neither Gun Crossbow nor any other Engine to take or kill the Deer withall but only chasing with his Dogge.
5. He must not hunt his Purlieues in the night tyme nor on the Sundaye nor in the Fence month nor oftener than three days in the week.
6. He must not hunt his Purlieu 40 days before the Kings General Hunting nor 40 days after.
7. He must not hunt his Purlieus when that the Forester is to serve any warrant near unto the borders of the Purlieus having notice given him thereof before.
8. He must repeal and call back his Dogge before they enter into the Forest neither may he pursue them into the Forest exepte they do first fasten upon the Deer and that the Deer do draw his Dogge into the Forest.
9. He may not hunt nor kill any unseasonable Deer.

To our Trustie and welbeloved *Sr. Edward Mountacute Sr. Christopher Hatton Sr. Edward Watson Sr. Thomas Brooke and Sr. Thomas Tresham Knight* and to every of them.

(Dash, Printer, Kettering.)

Above: a letter from the hunt-loving James I in 1610 to the four major landowners and Forest officials of the Rockingham Bailiwick, complaining about the abuse of Forest Law, and commissioning them to investigate and arrest the offenders.
Below: a proclamation printed shortly afterwards, for publication in all the churches in and around the area of the Bailiwick, setting out 'nine ancient laws of the forest' to counter the abuse of purlieu (private woodland) hunting. This was printed in accordance with the wishes of another letter sent by the King.

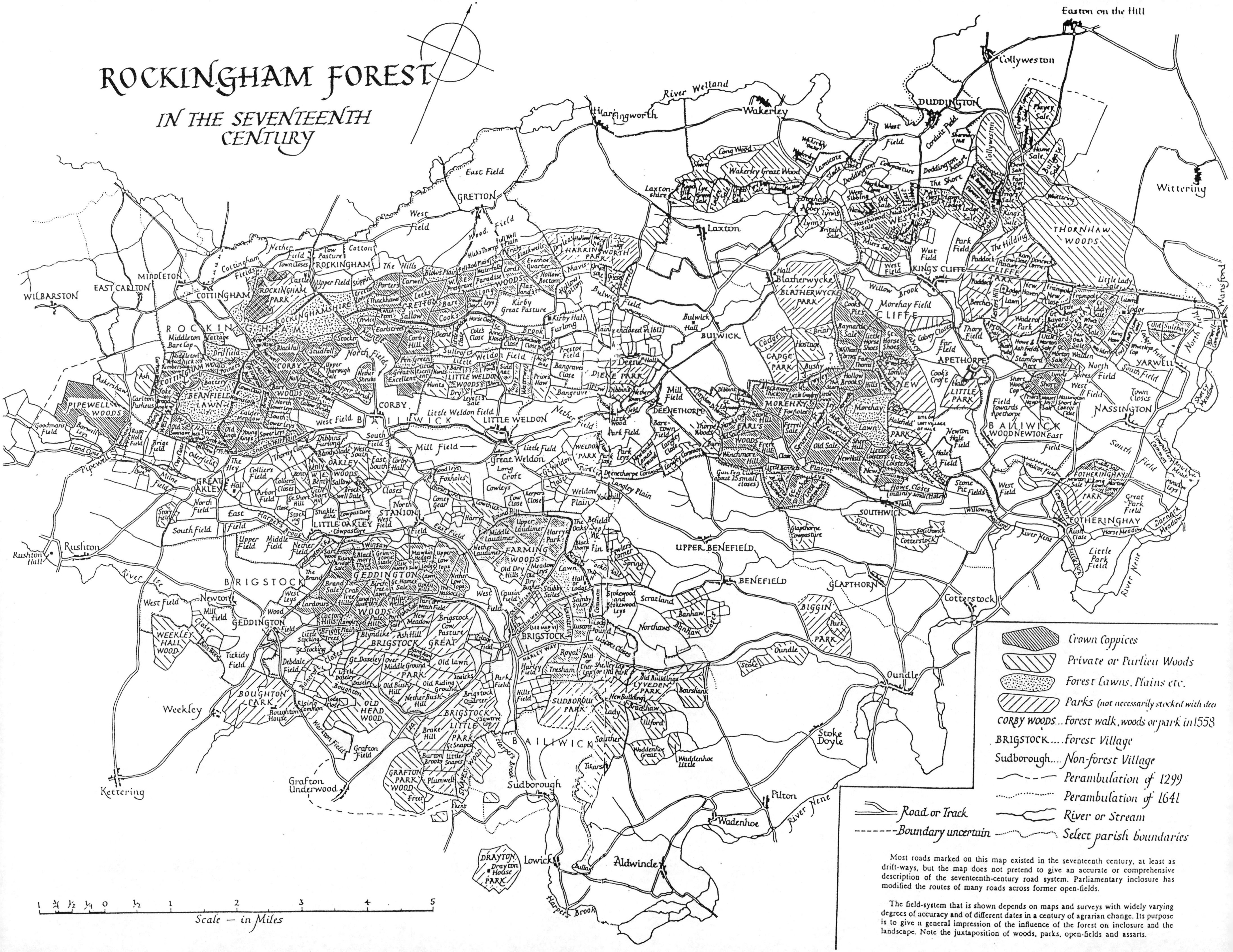

Most roads marked on this map existed in the seventeenth century, at least as drift-ways, but the map does not pretend to give an accurate or comprehensive description of the seventeenth-century road system. Parliamentary inclosure has modified the routes of many roads across former open-fields.

The field-system that is shown depends on maps and surveys with widely varying degrees of accuracy and of different dates in a century of agrarian change. Its purpose is to give a general impression of the influence of the forest on inclosure and the landscape. Note the juxtaposition of woods, parks, open-fields and assarts.

MANOR OF
Wadenhoe.

The Game on this Manor is intended to be preserved, And Notice is hereby given, that the Tenants and Gamekeeper are directed to lay Informations against all unqualified Persons and Poachers, who may be found attempting to take or destroy the Game; and all qualified Persons who shall be discovered sporting without having obtained leave, will be prosecuted as Trespassers.

"By order of the Lord of the Manor."

Wadenhoe, 16th August, 1819

Printed by T. Bell, Oundle.

A reminder that even after freedom from Royal control, poaching was still illegal.

Lot 5—*continued*.

THE FINE OLD DEER PARK

is heavily timbered and contains splendid avenues, many ancient and noble oaks and other forest trees, and many fine specimens of ornamental timber.

THE HERD OF FALLOW DEER is a particularly fine one, descended from those that ran wild in Rockingham Forest, and will be included in the purchase.

In the Park is BUSHY LAWN LODGE, occupied by the Head Game Keeper. It is very prettily situated and is a most substantial structure, built of the local stone, and contains sitting room, living room, kitchen, dairy and pantry on the ground floor, with four bedrooms on the first floor and three good attics above. There are two excellent cellars.

FARMING WOODS HALL.

SCHEDULE.

No. on Ordnance Map.	Description.	Quantity. A. R. P.
	PARISH OF BRIGSTOCK.	
352	Entrance Lodge, &c.	3 0 38
353	Engine House, Workshop, &c.	0 3 5
355	Farming Woods Hall, Stables, &c.	1 3 32
356	Pond	0 1 10
357	Pleasure Grounds	5 0 1
358	Pond	0 1 29
359	Pond	0 2 5
360	The Lord's Walk	1 0 31
361	Meadow Lawn	8 0 16
362	The Park	94 3 8
364	Part of Bushy Lawn	0 2 4
450	Nursery	2 0 39
465	Entrance Lodge	0 0 29
466	Stubby Stiles	15 3 36
467	Bushy Lawn	50 2 34
502	Bushy Lawn Lodge	1 3 15
504	The Lord's Walk	0 2 39
505	Gardener's Cottage and Butler's Cottage	0 1 17
506	The Lord's Walk	0 2 10
507	Kitchen Garden	2 3 6
		198 1 4
	PARISH OF BENEFIELD.	
Pt. 51	Part of Grounds	0 0 34
65	Plantation	0 1 20
		0 2 14
	Total carried forward to Summary, page 12 ... A.	198 3 18

The Grass keeping on Nos. 361, 362, 466 and 467 is reserved until 1st December, 1910.

Part of a 1910 sales catalogue of items from Fermyn Woods Hall (note the older name), near Brigstock.

The changing face of Rockingham Forest

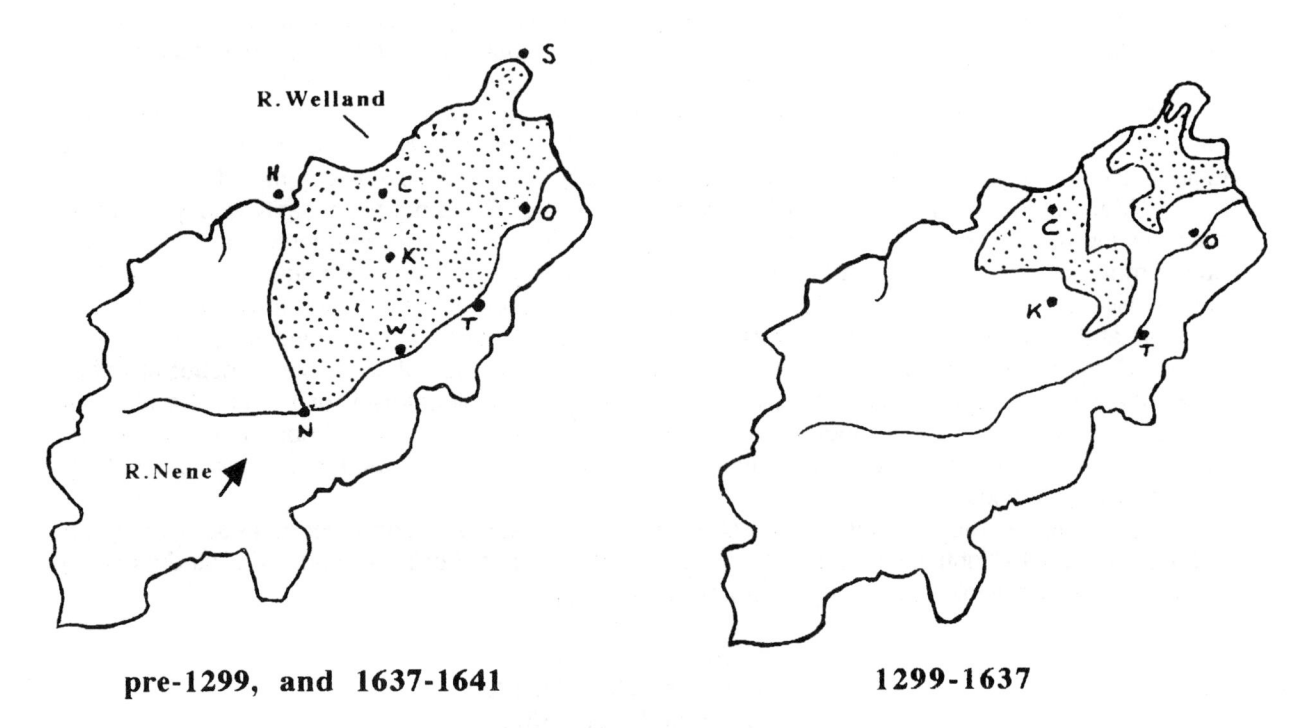

pre-1299, and 1637-1641

1299-1637

N = Northampton, K = Kettering, C = Corby, W = Wellingborough, H = Market Harborough, S = Stamford, O = Oundle, T = Thrapston

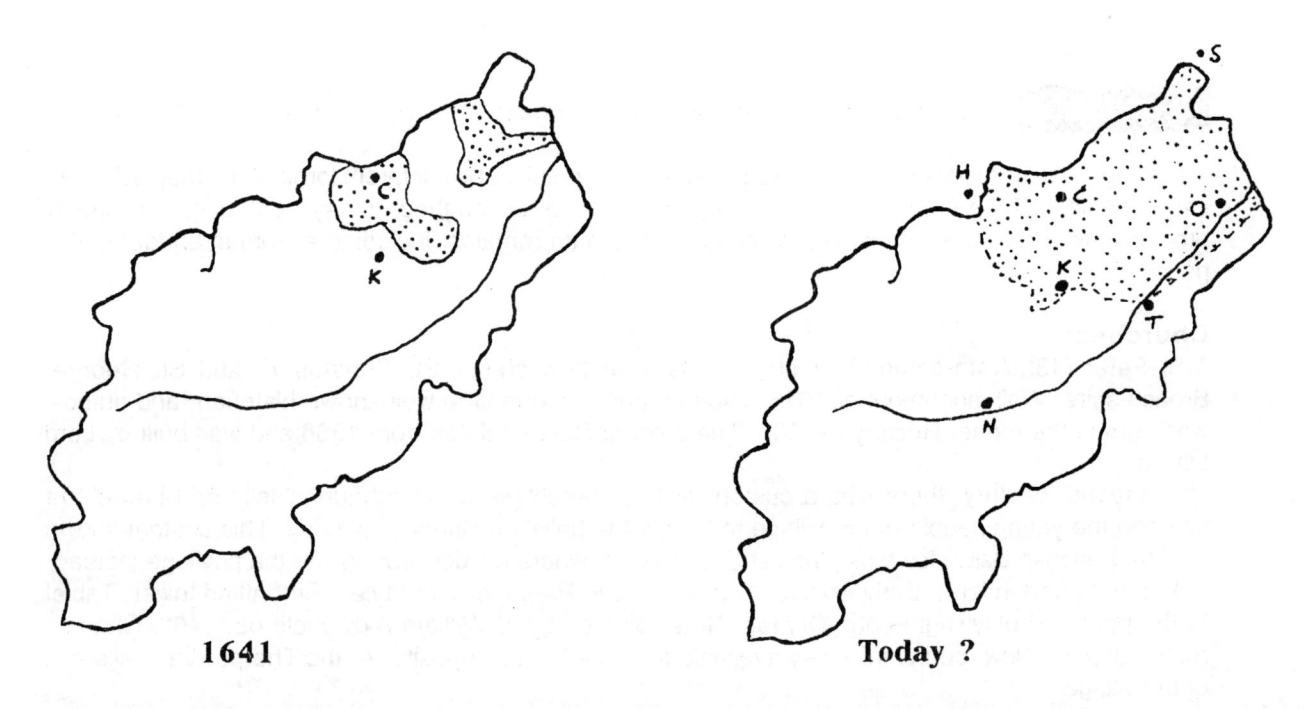

1641

Today ?

The boundaries of Rockingham Forest have never been permanently fixed, undergoing changes throughout the years, for administrative or judicial reasons or, more recently, for the purposes of tourism, leisure, conservation and development of the environment.
The drawings above give an approximate idea of the extent and boundaries of the Forest area at the indicated period of time. The boundaries of the county are in each case the modern ones, and do not take into account those parts lost when local government reorganisation took place in the 1970s.

PART TWO: A FOREST GAZETTEER.

A definition of what constitutes Rockingham Forest could be seen by some as a problem. For the purposes of this gazetteer, the list includes not just those villages/towns included in the original perambulations of 'Rockingham Forest' for determining the boundaries of the royal hunting area, but those geographically part of it, or on the periphery. Tourism has also had a hand in determining the modern 'boundaries', and prominent brown-painted roadsigns proclaiming 'Rockingham Forest' can be seen at various approaches to the region. The gazetteer therefore is an attempt to balance these factors, and embody the 'spirit' of the forest area. Inevitably, some places may be omitted!

Many of the buildings listed (with or without a datestone) are not necessarily wholly from that date, having had newer parts incorporated during the course of successive centuries. Equally, the house may be even earlier in parts, and a datestone merely recorded a change at that time. The original village schools which are still standing are listed, though in some cases they have changed their use and been replaced by more modern ones. The same applies to the original chapels.

Some Forest villages had an uncannily large number of pubs at some stage, especially after 1840 (the smaller populations of those days were certainly well-catered for!) - and the ale was stronger, almost soup-like. It must be stressed that some were just 'beershops', and not inns or alehouses. Many have long ceased to function and have disappeared, though in a few cases, they survive as private houses.

Prior to the 19th century, the churches of the Forest acted as social centres - something like today's village halls - until pews were added, taking up the space. For those churches listed as being of a certain style, the following dating criteria have been applied:

Norman: 1066-1087
Early English: 1189-1280
Decorated: 1280-1377
Perpendicular: 1377-1500

....

ALDWINCLE (origin of name: either Ælda's corner, or bend in the River Nene).

The village was formerly divided into two parishes, as a result of two different lords of the manor. Baulks Lane, leading off the village green, was originally a wide unploughed grassy track used for funeral processions. There are extensive prehistoric and Roman remains (including a Roman bridge) in the parish.

Churches:
* St Peter (13th/14th-century). A stained-glass window shows St. Christopher and St. George. Broach spire. Wall monument of 1616. Thomas Fuller, a one-time well-known historian and author, was born in the former Rectory in 1608. The present Rectory dates from 1866 and was built by Lord Lilford.
Until the 19th century, there was a custom at this church (as at neighbouring Islip and Lowick) of allowing the young people of the village to 'jangle the bells' on Shrove Tuesday. This custom known as 'The Pancake Bell', also took place at Sudborough, where women were given the privilege instead.
* All Saints (redundant). Early English, Decorated and Perpendicular styles. Embattled tower. Tablet to the poet and playwright John Dryden. Brass with effigy of William Aldwyncle ob. 1463. Chancel restored 1863. Now redundant - key available from the house opposite. At the Thorpe Waterville end of the village.
Baptist Chapel: 1823 (just off Main Street).
Former School: 1872 (now a pottery)
Former pub: the *Rose and Crown* (in Lowick Lane. Now called Tavern Cottage. It has an interesting - more modern - plaque on its front wall. There is no pub in the village today.
Other buildings of interest:
Main Street : No.78 and 'The Maltings' date from the 17th-century. Many other buildings are 18th-century.
At the other end of the village opposite All Saints Church stands Dryden's Cottage (The Old Rectory). The grandfather of John Dryden, the 17th-century Poet Laureate and playwright, was rector of the

church. The poet was born here in 1631, and there is a plaque to him in the church. Get the key here. The building behind the church is Aldwincle Manor.

Gardens: some of the gardens of the village are open to visitors annually as part of the National Gardens Scheme Charitable Trust programme. It gives the public a chance to see some of the fine gardens created around the country. Proceeds go towards national and local charities. For details of opening dates, phone 01295 710411.

Pocket Park: Formerly a quarry and area of old woodland, with rookery. Main Street.

Walks in the area:

*Spanning the road to Thorpe Waterville there is a bridge (Brancey Bridge) from 1760, just before which a newly-created walk is possible by the river, through a Site of Special Scientific Interest.
Beyond the bridge there is an interesting raised footpath along the road which is an area that is easily liable to flood. There are large areas of water here on the right.

* Another interesting walk from the village is following the Nene Way footpath (the sign pointing the way is at the roadside near St Peter's) to picturesque Wadenhoe. Follow the gently undulating landscape across meadow and through shrubbery down to the edge of the river.

* Titchmarsh (via the Nature Reserve). When in the Reserve, take the left hand route and at the exit follow the track, cross the main road and go straight on.

* Islip (via the Nature Reserve). In the Reserve, take the right hand route and follow it to its exit. You arrive at Islip Mill. Take the track to its right to get to the village.

* Islip (from the village). The green footpath sign is off Main Street to the right before the Green.

Titchmarsh Nature Reserve: the main entrance to this is actually in Aldwincle. From the village itself, you can reach it going down Lowick Road at the All Saints end. It lies on the left (signposted) where there is a car park. (An alternative route is to take the Sudborough Road and turn left at the Trout Fisheries sign.) The area covers 73 hectares of wetlands, pools and lakes and is managed by The Wildlife Trust for Northamptonshire. The River Nene forms one of the Reserve's boundaries and its tributary, Harpers Brook, forms the other. There is a footpath round much of the Reserve, with hides conveniently placed en route for bird enthusiasts. There is a specially-created Heronry, though this may not be entered by the public. As well as a vast variety of waterfowl, insects and plants can be found in abundance.

APETHORPE (Api's village)

A settlement of Viking origin. With its many thatched and quaintly-named buildings huddled together, the village has a charming 'chocolate box' look. There are some fine views of woodland on the periphery.

Church: St Leonard's. Earliest parts: 15th-century. Perpendicular style. On the site of an earlier church. There are traces of medieval wall painting. A large impressive marble monument with a domed canopy stands in the South Chapel to Sir Anthony Mildmay (d.1617) and his wife. The tomb is decorated with other figures representing various virtues and qualities. Two 17th-century helmets and a knight's tabard can be seen hanging above. The tomb was erected by their son-in-law, Sir Francis Fane, who later became Earl of Westmorland. Also in the church is the effigy of another knight (in plate armour), from 1442. An excellent (rare) early 17th-century stained glass window can be found in the same chapel as the Mildmay tomb, comprised of 4 panels depicting different scenes. The weathercock on the church steeple is believed to be from 1633.

Pub: the *King's Head*

Former pub: the *Westmorland Arms* (stood adjacent to the church. Demolished 1910).

Former school: 1846. Children now go to Kingscliffe.

Apethorpe Hall. (This is best seen from the Woodnewton Road). Construction was started in 1480 by Sir Guy Wolston. It passed to Sir Walter Mildmay (together with a large deer park in which the building is set) in 1550, and later to the Earl of Westmorland. It stayed with that family until 1904. Its large gardens date from the 16th and 17th centuries, and there was an avenue adorned with statues, a bowling green and a moat with an island. It has had Royal visitors: Elizabeth I stayed there in 1566, and James I stayed there five times between 1605 and 1619. It is not open to the public, but can be seen from the Woodnewton road as one approaches Apethorpe, on the left. A circular water tower (originally a dovecote) built in 1740, stands to the north of the Hall, and can be seen on the left, by walking along the track at the side of the pub (though you must look carefully in summer with all the dense foliage around!)

Other buildings and places of interest:
By pub car park, along Kingscliffe Road: A tall crenellated silo stands castle-like by the roadside.
Main Street: The two houses and Old Post Office next to the pub are 17th-century in origin, as is Wood Cottage which stands where the side street leads off, The large building on the opposite corner is The Post Office, early 18th-century with later additions. A little way past it along the side street to its right (Laundry Lane, which leads to Hunting Lane - no public access - in the grounds of the Hall) is a late 17th/early 18th-century building, Lilac Cottage.
Towards the church on the left : a large house on which there is a modern stone tablet with engravings of a tree, a wheatsheaf and an eagle, together with a rural piece of verse. The old school stands just past this. Just past here, on the corner of the road as it swings round to the left, and opposite the church, there is a whipping post, and a set of stocks, together with the only surviving stocks bench in the UK, which is either 17th or early 18th-century. All these are contained within a stone shelter. A war memorial stands outside the church. Set back to the right of the memorial and the church is The Manor House which is believed to date from 1711, and was the former residence of the agent for the Westmorland Estate.
Leaving the village: an early 19th-century thatched house on the right, and a little further on near the bridge, on the left-hand side, a 17th-century thatched house (with pigeon holes and ledges near the roof), adjoining an 18th-century dwelling. Once over the bridge spanning Willow Brook, the road splits in two directions: one leading to Woodnewton, the other to Nassington.
Local crafts: Art (including etchings): Crispin Heesom, 2 The Terrace, phone 01780 470547.
Walks in the area:
From Apethorpe, there are public footpaths to Kingscliffe (a contrast of field, woodland and quarry), the old Morehay Walk area, and a 'circular' walk around outlying areas, passing by a pond (locally called 'The Pond'!) and Cheeseman's Lodge (mid 18th-century) which lies some way out of the village and is believed to be originally the residence of the Park Keeper. (The lost village of Hale is in the vicinity. The track also skirts Tomlin Wood.)
All these walks start from the track beside the pub. At the signposts, turn right and head across the fields for Kingscliffe; turn left for the other walks, skirting the grounds of Apethorpe Hall and passing a large pond en route. All are well sign-posted with black/white arrow markers. Perhaps an O/S map is needed for the Morehay walk, which if you are feeling very energetic, can be extended, in several different (long-distance) directions. (There is no longer a keeper's lodge at Morehay but the wood in the vicinity bears the name, Morehay Lawn. The panoramic views across the forest are breath-taking in places, especially at the end of Morehay Lawn, which lies along the track.
*****Lost village:** *Hale* (corner, nook). A small village that disappeared at the time of the Plague 1348-1349. The Domesday Book recorded only three tenants. Bridges described it in 1728 as having ruins and 'Three long streets are still visible in Lord Westmorland's park'. It had a church: St Nicholas. A Chancellor's Inquiry in the reign of Edward III stated that 'no-one lives in Hale and has not since the pestilence'. Halefield Hall is said to have stood in Apethorpe Park.

BLATHERWYCKE (settlement where bladderwort grows)

A quiet, sleepy settlement with a charm of its own and an interesting history. A one-street village with a fine bridge and lake. The village was once larger, but part of it was deserted in medieval times. No longer possessing any shop, post office, school or pub, it is a village with many datestones.

Church Holy Trinity (redundant). Early Norman (late 11th-century) south doorway and tower. Early English and Decorated windows. Brasses (16th-century). New porch was added 1868. Church partly restored in 1855, and again in 1893. A section of the church is devoted to memorials, monuments and floorslabs of the Stafford/O'Brien families (lords of the manor). There is an ornate stone monument from 1595 to John Stafford in knight's garb, with wife and children, and a wall tablet erected by Sir Christopher Hatton. A wall plaque (benefactors table) referring to one of the old charities from 1684, informs that a perpetual sum of money was left 'to buy six of the oldest men in the village a plum pudding on Christmas Day.' The church, protected by nature, nestles in a swathe of greenery in quiet surroundings, with a neo-Gothic ruin beside it covered in ivy.
Lost church. At one time, a nearby church dedicated to St Mary Magdalene, co-existed with Holy Trinity. It ceased to be used around 1448. No remains exist although there are earthworks in the grounds of Glebe Farm, to the left of the first lane leading off the Kingscliffe Road (locally known as Jackdaw Lane and at one time, Maudlin's Lane) to the A43. Several human remains were found during building work.

Former school: c1830 (for 20 children) with schoolhouse. It was built on the site of an earlier school.
Former pub: the *Horse and Jockey* (now Glebe Farm, on the left of the road to Kingscliffe).
Other buildings and places of interest:
<u>Stone bridge</u>   Medieval in origin, there are datestones on one side, recording when parts of the bridge were repaired: 1656, SOB 1726, 1826, 1890. On the other side there is a later datestone: 'NCC. Repaired 1931'.
<u>Main Street</u>: on the bend of the road to Bulwick, house with datestone: 1831 SOB. Just before the bridge, on the same side (almost opposite the Gate Lodge) beside the brook stands the former school. Behind this, at the end of a drive is The Old Rectory (Bridge House) from 1836. This has a roofed nesting box attached to the upper wall.
The Gate Lodge (1878) stands at the entrance of a drive which leads to where <u>Blatherwycke Hall</u> once stood. Built in 1720 near the site of an earlier manor house, it was originally the domain of the Engaine family. The estate passed to the Stafford family with whom it remained for generations. One of them later married a member of the O'Brien family and the joint surname 'Stafford O'Brien' became synonymous with the Hall and village. A large thriving Grecian-style building, it was demolished in 1948. The Gate Lodge and the large stable block (1770) within the grounds are all that remain.
<u>Blatherwycke Lake</u> is supposedly the largest fishpond in the UK and was formerly a reservoir for Corby Steelworks. Willow Brook, a tributary of the River Nene, feeds into it. The small pond on one side of the bridge was once used for sheepdipping, fishing and cart washing.
<u>Kingscliffe Road</u>: passing out of the village, several houses can be seen with 19th-century 'SOB' datestones. The road skirts the edge of the lake for some way and is an ideal spot for bird watchers. Some way along the road towards Kingscliffe, and at the end of the lake, is a disused mid-19th century mill.

Snippets:
* The former Village Hall built in 1900, was demolished 1959.
* The churchyard has been documented on two or three occasions, and particular reference has been made to the strangely-placed tombstone (the inscription facing the wall) of a black servant, Anthony Williams, who had worked at the Hall and who had drowned in the lake in 1836 whilst trying to save his master who had fallen from a boat whilst fishing. The inscription (awkward to read) is a piece of poetry:

> *'Here a poor wanderer hath found a grave*
> *Who death embraced whilst struggling with a wave.*
> *His home far off in the broad Indian main*
> *He left to rid himself of slavery's chain.*
> *Friendless and comfortless, he passed the sea*
> *On Albion's shores to seek for liberty.*
> *Yet vain his search for aye with toiling brow*
> *He never found his freedom until now.'*

* The village was also the scene of a strange burial from ancient times. Two coffins were discovered, with the upper parts of a female skeleton in one, and the lower parts and an urn in the other. It has remained a mystery why this was so - though similar burials have been known to have occurred elsewhere.

Walks in the area:
* Bulwick (see above)
* Kings Cliffe. You can either follow the quiet road (see above), or take the interesting track past the church. Along here, look out for the statue of a Greek archer in a field to the right! You also pass the side of the lake for a while, where various kinds of waterfowl congregate. The view of the sun on the lake at sunset is superb. Most of the walk keeps to the edge of fields, but at one stage you pass through the yard of Alders Farm, and walk alongside Willow Brook, before crossing it as you get nearer your destination.
* Fineshade Abbey and Woods. Take the road to Kings Cliffe and at the second turning to the left off the road as you leave the village follow the Public Footpath sign over the field. When you get to Lynn Wood with 'Fineshade Abbey' in view there are arrow markers in four directions: one goes straight on to Fineshade Woods, two lead across the A43 (one of which continues to Town Wood and Wood

Hollow) and the other to Kingscliffe.

* An ambitious walk for those who like distance and adventure is to Apethorpe or Southwick, via Hostage Wood. For some walkers an Ordnance Survey map is a must. There are arrow markers, but it is easy to lose your bearings and you could end up anywhere! At the end of the large Hostage Wood on your left go straight across the farmland towards a derelict farmhouse, to the left of which is a wooden bridge (arrow-marked) over a small stream.Go straight across and follow the sometimes muddy Bridle Path to the next field. Here, head for the green clearing among the trees in the near distance, at the end of which is a grassy track which you follow uphill past the rectangular wood of Morehay Lawn (at present marked by a derelict brick building) until you come to Tomlin Wood where there is a post with arrow markers in four directions. For Apethorpe go straight on; for Southwick head right. Superb views, peace and a unity with nature are the rewards.

* Circular Walk via Kingscliffe and woodland. This a fine 'circular walk' and takes about two and a half hours. You begin as for the Apethorpe and Southwick walk . When you get to the four- directions marker post at Tomlin Wood, go left, skirting the wood to the top and round the corner for some distance until a clearing with a post either side appears. keep going until you reach two houses and a road. Turn left, and at the right of the houses, follow the arrow markers along a path that gradually descends to Kingcliffe which you will see down below. When you get to the end of the field where the black wooden Public Footpath sign stands with a stone wall behind, turn left until you come to an outbuilding with a road leading off to the right opposite it. Go down this, over the stone bridge and keeping on the left side of the road, turn left at the stile a little way on.You are now on the route back to Blatherwycke, arrow-marked for most of the way, following the second walk listed above, in reverse.

BRIGSTOCK (*bric stoc* : secondary settlement by the birch trees).

The village was of great importance in the history of Rockingham Forest, being its largest village, a Royal Manor, and at the head one of the three Bailiwicks. It has considerably expanded to what it is today with newer housing making an appearance. It is the meeting place of an annual Boxing Day Hunt. There are several 17th-century (and earlier) houses still standing. A village which, like its surroundings, needs time to explore!

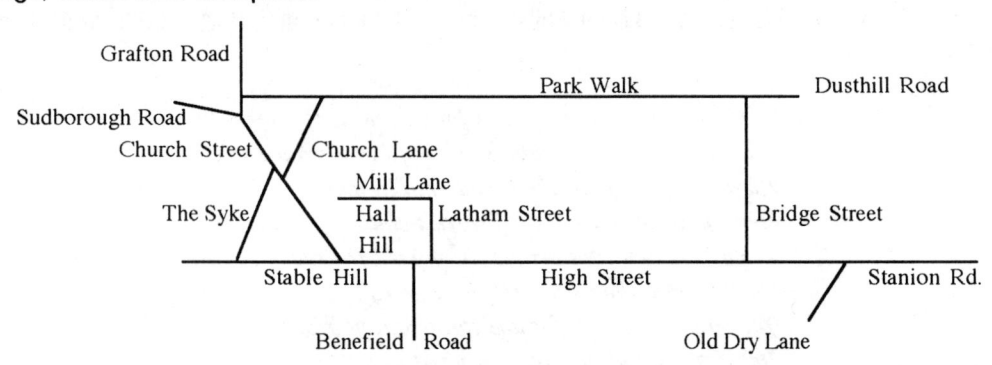

```
            Grafton Road
                 |
                 |                  Park Walk              Dusthill Road
     Sudborough Road _____
         Church Street \   Church Lane
                        \     Mill Lane
         The Syke  /    Hall  Latham Street           Bridge Street
                        Hill
     _____
              Stable Hill        High Street              Stanion Rd.
                       |                            
                  Benefield Road              Old Dry Lane
```

Church: St Andrew. Fine Saxon work from the late 10th/early 11th-centuries, including a semi-circular stair turret (similar to that at Brixworth), with a crude Saxon window at the top of the tower. Leading to the turret within the church, is a unique low, narrow triangular-headed doorway (and door). The chapel to the Lyveden family dates back to 1233. There is a marble monument to the first Baron Lyveden (whose name is associated with the lodge nearby). The clock dates from 1742. The church is a favourite haunt of bats (as a notice inside testifies!) There is supposedly an underground tunnel leading from beneath one of the church doors to the Manor and was used between 1160 and 1300. The bells (from 1600) were at one time rung three times a day to help lead travellers through the dense woodland of the Forest.

Congregationalist Church: 1799 (in Mill Lane).

Former Methodist (Wesleyan) Chapel: 1845 (in Park Walk. Now the Women's Institute).

School: 1873 (Latham Street). There were two other schools (in Back Lane and the High Street) during the 19th century.

Pubs: the *Green Dragon*, the *Old Three Cocks* (a former coaching inn).

Former pubs: the *Golden Lion* (opposite the Market Cross), the *Angel* (High Street near the butcher's shop), the *Lord Nelson*, the *Black Horse*, the *Fox and Hounds* (Bridge Street. It burned down in 1938), the *New Inn* (High Street, nearly opposite Bridge Street. It closed down 1975. Now a private house); the *Mason's Arms* (on the site of the old village pound in Benefield Road).

Other buildings and places of interest:

Old Dry Lane: The tall narrow building on the corner is known locally as 'The Matchbox'. It was formerly a clothing factory (Wallis and Linnell, built around 1873, for just over £1334). It was constructed in this manner so as to let in as much natural light as possible.

Bridge Street: on the left-hand corner, Fotheringhay House (of late 17th-century origin). Opposite, on the right-hand corner, is the 19th-century Old Bakehouse. Horsebrook Cottage on the right is named after the brook that it once overlooked and which ran under the mid 18th-century stone bridge here. The bridge,'Bottom Bridge', is high up with a single cutwater and pedestrian sanctuary, and the brook is such a trickle, that one wonders if such a construction was ever necessary, but at one time the water of Harpers Brook which was wider and deeper than today, flowed here before it was diverted to its present course. Near the end of the street on the left is thatched Park Cottage (early 18th-century), with a long chimney breast down its side. It was used from about 1857 as a clothing factory of Wallis and Linnell, before the 'Matchbox' was built.

Dust Hill Road: This was part of the old cattle drovers' track to Geddington, known as 'Clay Dick'.

Park Walk: Hill Farm Herbs lies on your right. This was originally a dairy farm, delivering milk to Corby and surrounding villages until the 1950s. It has been tastefully converted into an indoor and outdoor shopping area with a fascinating array of herbs, spices, garden plants, dried flowers, preserves, candles, cards and books to choose from. There is also a tea room and an Old English garden containing some of the plants, which attract several species of butterfly, and is a blaze of colour in the summer sunshine. The farm is open from March until Christmas Eve, and at limited times from Christmas until the end of February.

Church Lane: Tucked away on the left by the pavement en route to the church is no.16, a beautiful small thatched 17th-century cottage with 'eyebrow' dormers'. The trees beside the cottage are used as a rookery, and you are bound to hear the birds' raucous cry or see them circling around! Opposite is a home for the elderly, which stands on the site of a former fellmonger's yard and a blacksmith's.

Church Road: No.1, on an ancient site, has a green Domesday plaque on its front wall. This was the former Market House, in its present form from the mid 17th-century. It is of cruck-frame construction and has some unusual interior features. (It is however not open to the public).

Hall Hill: a large square area, where the market was held for centuries. The Market Cross dates from 1466 (in the reign of Edward IV) and is inscribed on both sides with the initials of Queens of England, together with the dates of the inscriptions, beginning with Elizabeth I (ER.1586), Anne (AR.1705), Victoria (VR.1887) and finally, Elizabeth II (ER.1953). By 1623, however, its market had declined in importance, and no longer exists. Brigstock House (Greystones) is of 16th-century origin. Thatched no.12 is early 18th-century, and next door, Home Farm House, from the same era has what may well be a medieval octagonal flue on top of its chimney stack.

T-junction of Stable Hill and High Street : On the upper wall of the house facing you (no. 2, a former post office) is a large stone tablet depicting either a horse or a sheep, and two dates, 1588 and 1730.

Stable Hill: Stable Hill Cottage is a thatched house of 16th-century origin. A little further down on the other side near the corner is 'Jeffs' which has a datestone of 1748.

Mill Lane: The Manor House has parts from around 1150 (Hall Hill), though in its present form it is mainly late 15th- and early 16th-century, with several additions made later, particularly in the 1850s. It was once a Royal Hunting Lodge favoured by King John on his frequent visits here, for the fine sport in the Forest, and at one time he held his court in the house. Sir Edward Montagu, Chief Justice of the King's Bench (Henry VIII) was born here in the late 15th-century. The building was associated with the family until 1859, after which it passed to other owners until the 1930s when it became a convalescent home for film stars!

Latham Street: Brigstock Mill, part 18th-century, was last worked in 1910. It stands on the site of a watermill recorded in the Domesday Book. The wheel and gears are still intact. *Latham's School* was founded in 1620 by the Reverend Nicholas Latham of Barnwell. He became a generous benefactor in the region and was associated with other buildings (still standing) in Barnwell, Oundle and Weekley. He grew up in Barnwell. In 1873, the school was rebuilt for 200 children by the Duke of Buccleuch. The school originally stood near the Market Cross.

Benefield Road: On the left, stand a group of thatched cottages built in the late 18th- and early 19th-centuries for villagers who worked on the estate of Fermyn Woods Hall, which lies some way up the

road (Lyveden Way). They later acted as a silk factory. If not tired, walk up the hill where you will find on the left Tresham Lodge which was once known as First Gate Lodge, because of the wooden gate which used to span the road at this point, to prevent deer escaping from the Deer Park of the Hall.
At one time the building was smaller, and was covered in ivy, giving it a 'story-book' appearance. (There was also at one time, a 'Second Gate Lodge' further along the road towards the Hall).
High Street: Opposite the alleyway, Farm Close, is Pytchley House (no.11), an early 18th-century building which once acted as the Duke of Montagu's Militia HQ, and was also The Old Forge. A few doors away stands no.15 which is of 17th-century origin.

Pocket Park: Off Lyveden Road, near the footbridge to the Country Park, spanning the by-pass. A wooden post with a sign and routed colour design of a cowslip marks the entrance.
Local crafts: *Stoneware/Earthenware: Pots and Prints, 12 High Street. Contact Jenny Dunbar (01536) 373353. *Art/Printmaking: Rosalind Stoddart, 5 High Street. (01536) 373469.

Snippets:
* The area around The Syke (an old word for a 'meadow beside a stream') was prone to flooding at one time, and in the late 19th and early 20th-centuries children would fasten cocoa tins to the soles of their boots to cross at that point!
* In the dip along Lyveden Road, there was a pump. This area was known as 'Cackle End' because it was a meeting place where the women would fill up their vessels with water and gossip!
* On the left of the Stanion Road (leading to the A6116 from the village), you will pass Training Kennels. It is here that the village windmill once stood: a short-sailed structure with a tall stone base.
*There were large medieval deer parks around Brigstock, especially to the south west where little ploughing took place. These lay on either side of the road to Grafton Underwood and consisted of the Great Park (created early in the13th century), to the east and skirting Geddington Chase; and Little Park, (created mid-14th century) to the west. Containing several acres of woodland, they covered a widespread area, as far as Drayton Park near Lowick, and bordered on Geddington, Boughton Wood, Grafton Park Wood and Slipton. In 1603, the villagers created a disturbance, when a landowner, Sir Robert Cecil threatened to sell off some of his newly-acquired woodland. He began making clearances in preparation, thereby depriving the villagers of some of their 'traditional' fuel, timber, pasture (and probably venison)! Fortunately the matter was settled amicably with no bloodshed, despite 'a troop of lewd women' from the village being let loose to disturb Cecil's workmen as they carried out his orders!
* **Hale :** is a 'lost' village which has only been mentioned in one known source. Like its namesake (which existed near Apethorpe), it had a church called St Nicholas (the last incumbent of which was listed in 1389). In 1617 it passed from William Montagu to Sir Edward Montagu. It is not recorded thereafter and its site - even existence - has been a subject for speculation. However, a Brigstock historian has done a considerable amount of research and believes it to be have been sited close to the Harry's Park Wood area (Old Dry Hills) which can be seen to the north of the village, east of the A6116. A footpath, to Weldon, passes close by (see 'Walks' below).
* It is inevitable that a large Forest area like Rockingham Forest, would have attracted outlaws in medieval times, and so it is no surprise that the name of Robin Hood occurs among these - as in so many other parts of the country. No historical evidence exists, but it makes a good story! He is said to have taken refuge in Brigstock church, but being betrayed by some of the villagers, escaped during a siege by soldiers sent by Ralph de Hanville, an official of the manor in Henry III's reign. During the attack, the priest was killed by an arrow whilst he was at the altar! This 19th-century poem by C. Montagu-Douglas-Scott relates the tale:

> *Bold Robin Hood to Brigstock came,*
> *In the Farming-woods he lay,*
> *And he feasted himself on his sovereign's game,*
> *So long as he chose to stay,*
> *For the sheriff was dead, and the verderer fled*
> *At the sight of bold Robin away.*
>
> *Bold Robin he entered the Church one morn -*
> *'Twas Blest Saint Mary's Day -*
> *And the people they stared at his bow and his horn,*

As kneelèd him down to pray;
And there by the door knelt fully a score
Of his merry men keen and gay.

The dark-eyed priest the Mass intoned,
(A buck in his larder lay)
And up in the belfry a little wind moaned,
As a little wind moans today;
When sudden, without was a stir and a shout,
And Robin was up and away.

The arrows came rattling onto the walls
As Robin he rushed outside;
Thro' a window one flew - and the good priest falls
At the feet of the Crucified;
The women they scream and the men blaspheme,
And each and all would hide.

But Robin he marshalled his own merry men
With a blast of his bugle horn,
And he fought his way to the woodlands then
Thro' the stooks of the golden corn;
And the arrows around him lay thick on the ground
Like a harvest of ills forlorn.

And lo! an armed knight was down,
Who in swift pursuit has led:
"Now carry me back to Brigstock town,"
Sir Ralph de Hanville said;
"So sore am I hurt thro' my stout mail-shirt,
That I fear my days are sped.
"And carry me into the Church," said he,
"Full soon I must confess;
The priest will be there devout in prayer
For the sum of our success,
Since I promised him well o' the red monie
If Robin we should possess."

Straight into the Church Sir Ralph they bore;
He moaned at the least delay;
On the Altar steps in a pool of gore
The dark-eyed rector lay:
"A judgement, and right," said the wounded knight,
And he passed unshriven away.

Walks in the area:
*The track from Brigstock towards Weldon through Harry's Park Wood will lead you to the **The Bocase Stone**, which according to one theory, was the site for swanimotes (see Chapter 1) or even a place where people claiming forest rights could be listed. Another theory - certainly a good story! - was that the ancient Bocase Oak which stood close by, was where Robin Hood hid his weapons to help his men avoid capture, during one close encounter with their adversaries. Yet another theory is that the place was used as a meeting point by archers, foresters or hunters. (The word 'Bocase' may well be associated with 'practising with the bow'). Whatever the case, it was certainly an important site, for its own commemoration stone (from Charles I's time) was placed along that bridleway. The inscription reads: IN THIS PLAES GREW BOCASE TREE. Perhaps the easiest way to get to it, is to

park in Brigstock (if you park in the place suggested for the walk round Brigstock, you are near): go up Old Dry Lane (near 'The Matchbox'), cross over the main road (A6116), to the track almost opposite. Proceed along this and keep going, straight over the cattle grid, ignoring all turnings. Once in the park, you will pass 18th-century Bushylawn Lodge on the right. Eventually a large farm house (Bocase Farm) with stables will appear (same side). A little way past this, the Bocase Stone will appear on your left. Look hard - sometimes it is hard to find! (Use stout footwear).

*Adjoining woods are Laundimer Woods and Old Dry Hills. There is another pleasant walk along by the latter, (where the lost village of Hale may have existed) which eventually, after a considerable distance, leads to the Weldon-Benefield road. On the right of the track, as you reach this road, was the former site of 'The Stone Chair of Weldon', a huge boulder (now in a local barn) said to have been used as a place of punishment for miscreants who were chained to it and left to starve' ! Begin this walk as for the one to Bocase, but just before the cattle grid, take the track to your left (currently with a protective bar across it).

* Geddington: there are four routes possible, from different parts of the village, all of them rewarding. The first three however, although signposted with black and white arrow-markers for much of the way, can vary in difficulty according to the season, and a keen eye and sense of direction, with the aid of the OS map, are necessary. The first route begins in Park Lane between two houses (nos 3 & 5) at a wooden 'Public Footpath' sign, through a gate, and along a short narrow grassy track. You then cross over the fence via a stile and turn right uphill. The other three walks are from Dusthill Road which leads off Park Lane by the bend. The first of these begins from the green metal 'Public Footpath' sign on the left hand side. The second begins further along the road and follows a hard track. The third is much more straightforward, and is a continuation of Dusthill Road which becomes a grassy track winding all the way down to your destination, skirting peaceful Geddington Chase - a true relic of the old Forest, with sunny glades and plenty of wildlife. Stout footwear is recommended for all these walks because of the nature of the often muddy and undulating surface. (The author recently led a group on a combination of these walks which tested the footwear - as well as the fitness, endurance and patience - of all the participants!)

Brigstock Country Park, across the main road from the village, was officially opened 1986 on the site of former sandpits (Beeby's). Much of the sand and gravel was used for building and enlarging the town of Corby as it is today. Several of the pits have been filled with water and stocked with fish. There are also ponds with reed mace and bulrush, where you may well find newts, and a coot or two in the vicinity. It is a favourite haunt of rabbits as the many burrows dotted around will testify. There are many pleasant walks around the park, and special care is taken to ensure that dogs do not foul the paths (as well as 'scoopers', there is a dog track). A Rockingham Forest Interpretation Map can be viewed here. There is a Ranger's Office where information is available; maps, badges and booklets are on sale; exhibitions and displays can be found and fishing permits can be obtained. There is an enclosed children's play area, toilets and ample car parking. Special events and Family Days occur throughout the year. Conservation volunteers also do a great deal of work around the park throughout the year, and new helpers are always welcome!

*Fermyn Woods (Farming Woods)
The best place to enter the woods is from Brigstock Country Park.
There is a short specially-created walk (for which a free leaflet is available from the Ranger's Office, or one of the special boxes placed at the entrances). Deer (Fallow and Muntjac) and squirrels are a common sight, but are easily disturbed. The wide ditches at the side of the path have been known to host large bank voles. There are several bird boxes fitted to the trees. Coppicing and forestry are carried out here and oak, ash, hazel, beech, sycamore, field maple and several conifers may be seen, as well as a few silver birches.

* There is a walk to Lyveden New Bield (see below) from the park (follow the black and white arrow markers, and the track hugging the side of the woods and fields, and look out for the building in the near distance). En route, you pass quite close to Stephen's Oak Riding (see under Sudborough).
* For the more ambitious, it is also possible to walk to Aldwincle (and Wadenhoe) via Lady Wood and Souther Wood (woods to the east of Fermyn Woods, from which they are divided by a large stretch of farmland). Take the Lyveden track as above, as far as the wide track you meet at the end of the forest edge, but instead of crossing and going straight on, turn right onto it and head towards the woods, following arrows and green/yellow bridle markers until you reach a Public Footpath sign on your left. An excellent long walk, but good waterproof footwear recommended!

ALDWINCLE: St. Peter's Church and the Old School

BRIGSTOCK: St.Andrew's Church

* **Fermyn Woods Hall:** off the ancient Causin Way (the Brigstock to Benefield Road). It is a large impressive building when seen from the road and was originally a 14th-century hunting lodge for the Head Archer of Brigstock. The present building dates from different periods since then, the earliest parts being early 17th-century including a gateway engraved with the Tresham crest, which came from nearby Lyveden Old Bield. It is not open to the public. A former deer park stands outside as does a cistern in the grounds, which has a date inscribed on it: MDCCCXXIX (1829). An octagonal-shaped Pump, or Well House dating from the same period stands close to the road. It has a lion-head spout, gargoyle heads on its corners and the original handle still intact.

*Harley Way, an ancient road, is the turning off the A 6116 before the Country Park turning and there is also a footpath to the road from near the Ranger's Office. Narrow in places, it winds its way from Brigstock to Oundle and splits the woods in two sections at one point. Along this road, gliding takes place and it is quite common to see gliders hovering around overhead. A club meets regularly in a field off the road. This area is rich in archæological remains: a Neolithic axe has been found as well as coins, pottery, metal objects and the site of a Roman Temple (not far from the entrance to the gliding club). Watch out for deer!

* **Lyveden New Bield:**
Unroofed hunting lodge/summer house, built of Weldon stone in 1604-5 for Sir Thomas Tresham. It is in a cruciform to symbolise The Passion, and contains many symbolic, religious carvings. There is a water garden close by. It is under the care of the National Trust and may be visited all the year round. A small car park is along the Brigstock/Oundle road (the ancient Harley Way). The roof-less building lies about half a mile away up a farm track. During the Civil War, the Parliamentarian army passed through and the commander, Major William Butler (son of Neville Butler of Barnwell) had the timbers 'sawed' out (sic) of the timber walls and with them built a house at Oundle'. (This was 'Cobthorne' in West Street). For the more energetic, there is a footpath behind the building, across the fields to Fermyn Woods and Brigstock.

* **Lyveden Old Building:**
This lies off the Harley Way, but closer to that road than the New Bield, and also built by Sir Thomas Tresham, on the site of an earlier Manor House of 1460. Today it is a private residence. The area between here and Lyveden Brook is also notable for being the site of the **'lost' village** of Lyveden, which was once the centre of a large-scale medieval pottery industry. The village became totally deserted by the 16th century when Tresham used the site as part of the grounds of his house. Across the Harley Way en route to Banhawe Wood and Benefield, is the site of a moat. Lyveden is thought to be one of four villages of that name and there is evidence of other former settlements in the area, which actually comes under the parishes of Pilton and Benefield.

BULWICK (bull farm). Pronounced 'bullick'.

Once a double settlement (Henwick - 'hen farm', stood adjacent to the village, just on the other side of the brook), Bulwick is an interesting village long associated with the Tryon family. In some respects it is still a double settlement with a detached part, signposted Red Lodge Lane, further along the road to the A43.

Church: St Nicholas. Earliest parts: 13th-century. Tower, c.1400 with octagonal spire and crocketed gables. Set in the spire is what is jokingly referred to locally as 'the tallest tombstone in the county' - when repairing the spire in 1724, the stonemason, a member of the celebrated Ireson family, needed a slab of a certain size, and used the tombstone of Hannah, a female relative! Medieval relics. Alabaster monument (1612) to Henry Fowkes and his wife, kneeling in prayer and wearing contemporary dress (finely detailed). Memorials to members of the Tryon family (former lords of the manor). The church was restored 1863.
There are records of a 'chantry' (to Mary and St Anne) founded in the churchyard, as a chapel for two priests. There was also 'a guild in honour of St Anne'.
Pub: the *Queen's Head*. Part of the building dates from 1675, the other from 1683 (both date stones can be seen on the front wall).
Former pub: the *Carbery Arms* (in Blatherwycke Road, now Carbery House. 18th-century. Named after a Laxton family).
Former school (with adjoining Schoolhouse): 1831 for 80 children.

Other buildings and places of interest:
Main Street:
The thatched house standing on the corner at the side of the track by the church is 17th-century. Set back to the right at the end of the track, is the Rectory (1827). At the rear, there is a round 18th-century dovecote, which may be visited, with the consent of the house's occupants.
The Post Office, and further along on the same side, 'Inchmore', a long building with its gable end facing the street, are both 17th-century in origin. Next to the old school (almost opposite the church) is a house with the datestone, 1658. The Mill House, further along is 18th-century.
Blatherwycke Road:
Facing the triangular green ('The Pound') is an early 18th-century thatched farmhouse, 'Top Farm'. Nearby, 'The Farmhouse' which dates from 1626, has an interesting barn from the same period.
Red Lodge Road (traditionally known as Henwick Lane or The Ridings) is detached from the main part of the village, and signposted 'Red Lodge'. Two thatched cottages stand on the left, 'Thatch Cottage' and 'Pheasant Cottage' (named after a family that lived there), both of 17th-century origin. Further along on the right is a large thatched building from the same era, Home Farm. Ahead of you at the entrance to a driveway, is the 17th-century Gate Lodge to Bulwick Hall which lies at the end of the drive. This was rebuilt and enlarged in 1676 for the Tryon family, originally from Harringworth. It later passed to the Conants. It is not open to the public (except: see below). 'The Gardener's House' (early 19th-century) stands close by.
Gardens: some of the village gardens (including the Rectory and Bulwick Hall) open annually to the public as part of a national scheme (see under Aldwincle for details).
Snippets:
* It is hard to imagine now, but until 1863, three very small cottages with a smithy stood right by the entrance of the church, where the memorial gates are today. It must have been over-crowded!
* The area was the scene of much iron-working activity by the Romans, on a scale similar to that at the Forest of Dean. It is rich in other remains too: in 1876, a village vicar had amassed a collection of over 100 Roman, Saxon and medieval coins. A remarkable later find was a 14th-century seal of the Pope!
* In a gory 19th-century incident at the Mill, a miller (Geoffrey Sarrington) trapped his hand badly in the machinery, and freed it, by cutting it off - with a blunt knife!
* Reginald Fitzurse of Bulwick, was one of the four knights responsible for the death of Thomas à Becket in 1170. After the deed, he spent the rest of his days in misery as an outcast in the Holy Land!
* A strange 17th-century tale, 'The Bearded Lady of Bulwick', is recorded in an early 20th-century poem:

> *At Bulwick, where the willows grow,*
> *There lived a lady long ago*
> *Whom everybody feared;*
> *They thought she had the evil eye,*
> *But this they all could testify,*
> *She had a horrid beard.*
>
> *She scolded all her servants well,*
> *And made the Hall a very Hell,*
> *Bedreaded far and near;*
> *Yet every Sunday-morn she went*
> *To Church, and took the Sacrament*
> *At least three times a year.*
>
> *There was a rumour, - how it grew*
> *Of course nobody ever knew;*
> *Thus rumours have a way, -*
> *That this old crusted harridan*
> *Had fought a duel, and pinked her man,*
> *In Charles the Second's day.*
>
> *'Twas said her beauty had been great*
> *At some nigh prehistoric date,*
> *In far-off London town;*

Howbeit, one day in coach and four
She drove up to the entrance door,
And there, a hag, got down.

The Hall she had inherited
From one, a cousin never wed,
A wealthy man and mild;
Her husband too had passed beyond,
(Of brandy he was overfond)
Nor had she any child.

At Bulwick where the willows grow,
This lady lived so long ago,
So long has disappeared,
That nothing else of her is known,
Than this - she was a horrid crone,
And had a horrid beard.

Walks in the area:
* The track which runs close to the Rectory, leads to Blatherwycke. This is a short, but rewarding walk.
* Deene. Follow the short, grassy track (traditionally known as Goram's Lane) at the rear of the pub. Cross the stile, passing a mound on the right (into which is built a former icehouse). Keep left of Willow Brook. The walk crosses the A43.
* Apethorpe. A tricky walk, with an OS map really needed, but very worthwhile. Walk along the road to Blatherwycke and take the track at the footpath sign on the right as you leave the village. At one point the track meets the bridleway to Morehay Lawn, which is also a rewarding walk.
* To Lodge Coppice, Hollow Wood and Dryleas Wood: three remnants of the Forest which lie beside the brook and large fishpond of Harringworth Lodge. Walk along the short road signposted Red Lodge, and turn right before the Gate Lodge. The road passes over the A43. At the bend, leave the road and turn right onto a track. Follow the arrow-marked posts through a number of fields. The end of the walk brings you to the 'Jurassic Way'. You can follow this (left) to Gretton, or right to Harringworth.

CORBY, (Old Corby) (Kori's village).

It is hard to imagine the industrial and steel town of Corby as a small rural village - but it was, and a fine one at that, with a network of inter-village walks, a ring of woodland, a thriving weaving community and a unique tradition. The village actually lies outside the modern town centre close to the railway station, supermarkets and former steelworks.

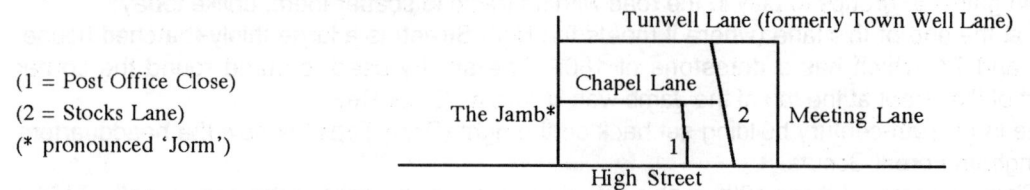

(1 = Post Office Close)
(2 = Stocks Lane)
(* pronounced 'Jorm')

Tunwell Lane (formerly Town Well Lane)
Chapel Lane
The Jamb*   2   Meeting Lane
1
High Street

Church: St John's (formerly St Peter's). Earliest parts: 13th-century (Early English) from which time the tower dates. The broach spire was added in the following century. Twelfth-century font with dogtooth pattern. There are fragments of medieval glass in some windows. Interesting clock. There is a datestone (1625) on the porch of the south doorway, together with a sundial. 15th-century chest tomb, possibly to John Neville (Latimer), a one-time lord of the manor. The church was restored in 1900. Its name change the same year was due to the fact that there was a clash on feast days with the similarly-named church at Deene for which the Corby rector was also responsible. The church at nearby Stanion is also St Peter's.
Former Congregational Chapel : 18th-century. Altered in 1835. It stood in Meeting Lane.
Former Methodist Chapel : 1847. The building stood in Chapel Lane.
School: built in 1834 by William Rowlett, a generous wool merchant originally from Corby, who had made good down south. It was enlarged in 1881 by J. Alfred Gotch. In Meeting Lane.

Original village pubs (still standing): the *Cardigan Arms*; the *Nag's Head* (now the *Nags*); the *White Hart* (the original pub which stood in front of the present building was known as 'Top House', and a row of houses which once stood between the pub and the railway line was called 'Wade's Row'); the *White Horse* (the original building stood a short distance away, close to a farm).

Former pub: the *Black Horse*. It stood as part of a long row of buildings near the *Nag's Head* in that section of the High Street which curves round towards the church.

Other pub of interest: the *Knights Lodge,* which stands outside the village, in the newer part of Corby, near Kingswood and west of the town, at Tower Hill Road. The building stands on what was the original Kettering - Uppingham Turnpike Road, but is now blocked off (since 1965), near the course of the present road (A6004). It was formerly a Keeper's Lodge for Benefield Lawn. Built in 1610 by Sir Christopher Hatton on the site of earlier buildings, there have been sitings of a ghostly monk from Pipewell Abbey, accompanied by a chill in the air, inside the pub on many occasions in the past!

The growth of Corby:
Although Corby is now seen as an industrial conurbation, the original village still exists side by side with its larger descendant, and offers the visitor a small glimpse into its past. A former Viking settlement, it retained a custom of Scandinavian origin, using a 'stang' (pole) that featured many years later in what was to become a traditional event. Due to its close proximity with Rockingham Castle and surrounded by forest, it did not escape royal attention. This was certainly the case around 1220, when Henry III granted the lord of Corby manor, Henry Braibroc, the right to hold two annual fairs and a weekly market. One of these fairs still exists, and as the **Pole Fair**, is held every 20 years in the village. Before every fair, barricades are erected across the various entrances to the village and anyone wishing to gain access must pay a toll to a gatekeeper. Refusal to do so means being carried to the stocks - the men on a pole, the women in a chair The next fair is due to be held in 2002.. Further royal attention followed in 1585, when Elizabeth I granted the village a Charter for 'services rendered' (supposedly in gratitude for being rescued by Corby men, whilst lost in the forest, but more likely it was a gift to her favourite courtier, Sir Christopher Hatton!)

The charter gave privileges such as exemption from certain tolls and duties, and was re-confirmed by Charles II in 1670. Handloom weaving and farming became the main occupations in the village until early in the 19th century when a national slump resulting from the Industrial Revolution, caused a collapse in handloom weaving, which in turn led to hard bleak times for many villagers. However, from the 1870s with the coming of the railway, brickmaking, and ironstone quarrying of the rich deposits in the area, the village began to see better times and a period of growth which transformed it into what it is today. In 1993, on gaining borough status, it had its first mayor.

Other buildings and places of interest in the village:
The Jamb: a small street (whose name derives rom the French word for leg, *jambe*, on account of its shape). It was in The Jamb area that buying and selling used to go on, the Pole Fairs took place, and where news or gossip would be exchanged. Many of its older buildings have sadly disappeared. Children would gather in groups to play in the road with no traffic to scatter them, unlike today!

High Street: at the end of this lane (where it meets the High Street) is a large thinly-thatched house, now nos. 75 and 77, which has a datestone of 1609. The smithy used to stand round the corner opposite. Part of the street at the top of the Jamb was known as 'Cock Row'.

The Nook: the large 19th-century building set back on the right ('Tree Tops') is now the headquarters of the Rockingham Forest Scouts.

Post Office Close: A group of three 19th-century stone houses on the right of the narrow path. Tallow candles were once made here at the rear of the old post office.

Remnants of Rockingham Forest: can be found south of the village (off the A427 and St.James Industrial Estate) in Oakley Purlieus; and near the town centre of 'new' Corby in Thoroughsale Wood and Hazel Wood. These provide excellent **walks** all the year round and contrast strongly with the industry, commerce and busy roads of the town. There are benches thoughtfully placed along the tracks and a large amount of wild life is still abundant in the area.On the edge of Thoroughsale Wood, along Willow Brook Road, is a former 19th-century gamekeeper's lodge.

Pocket Parks: both in 'modern' Corby (1) close to St.Brendan's School, off Occupation Road (2) 'William Mawdsley Pocket Park' close to the rear of the Kingswood Comminuity Centre.

Snippets:
* A questionable tradition has it that Robin Hood used Corby as a base, during his visits to the Forest!
* A boundary stone once stood about a mile outside the village on the road to Cottingham. On each side was inscribed a symbol : a key signifying Corby parish, a cross signifying Cottingham.

Corby & District Ramblers: offer a variety of walks. Contact: Eileen Cronin, tel: (01536) 60361.
Hotels: the Rockingham Forest Hotel is situated at the northern end of the town on the Rockingham Road, by the Sports complex (close to Rockingham Castle); the Carlton Manor is at the south eastern end, on the Stanion Road. Both are in an ideal position for exploring the Forest area.

COTTERSTOCK (Corther stoc: assembly place).

Formerly a two-manor village, with a medieval seat of religious learning, Cotterstock lies by the Nene and once had a flourishing milling concern.

Church: St Andrew's. Early English with Norman remnants and Saxon herringbone work. Tower, late 12th/early 13th-century. The large chancel was built for a college of priests in 1338. Elaborate 15th-century crenellated porch with carved beasts. 14th-century stone benches. Medieval coffin lids. Brass to one of the provosts (1420). 15th-century glass, and octagonal font. Church restored in 1877.
Former pub: the *Gate*.
School: 1876.
Other buildings and places of interest:
By the river Nene: The former Cotterstock (Corn) Mill was at one time a a hive of activity, with trade coming from miles around. Now peace reigns, except for the busy water gushing through. In 1968 it was badly damaged by fire and has undergone rebuilding. Round the bend on the same side is Cotterstock House, which dates from the early19th-century.
Village Cross: once adorned with medieval graffiti, it is said to have been uprooted three times: it now stands on a spot it has occupied since 1897. The stocks once stood close by. Behind the green is Dovecote House, former Manor House, with a datestone of 1722. The house is now named after its early 19th-century rectangular dovecote.
Church Farm (17th-century): behind the church. This was built on the site of the former 14th-century religious college for priests, established by John Gifford, provost and lord of the manor. The college was dissolved in 1538. There is an early 19th-century square dovecote to the rear.
Main Street : Old Vicarage (1651) stands on the right. Not far away on the same side, and set back from the road is Cotterstock Hall (1656-8), also known as Holt's Manor, which was the second of the two former manors of the village. It has a small claim to fame, in that the poet Dryden stayed here (for the last two years of his life) during which time he is supposed to have written his 'Fables In Verse'. A little further along, is a third driveway to the Hall. At the entrance stands Gatehouse Cottage, complete with thatched cockerel clambering up the roof. It is late 18th/early 19th-century in origin. To its left is the Blacksmith's Cottage and The Old Post House (both 1864) with the old school in between them. Across the road from the latter is the former village pub, the *Gate* (early 19th-century).
Snippets:
* The area was popular with the Romans : remains of a villa, two mosaic pavements, and other items were unearthed during the 18th century. Fourth-century coins have also been found.
Walks in the area:
* There are two walks into Oundle, both following the river (on different sides) for part of the way. One begins at the bridge by the Mill, the other on the left of the street in the village opposite Cotterstock Hall.

COTTINGHAM (home of Cotta's people).

The villages of Cottingham 'cum' Middleton are virtually joined together. Sadly, many of the village's fine older buildings disappeared in the 1960s, but there are pockets of the past to be found along narrow lanes and tracks, and some fascinating relics and remnants to be seen - if you know where to look! The view of the church, and surroundings, leaving the village along the Corby Road, is superb.

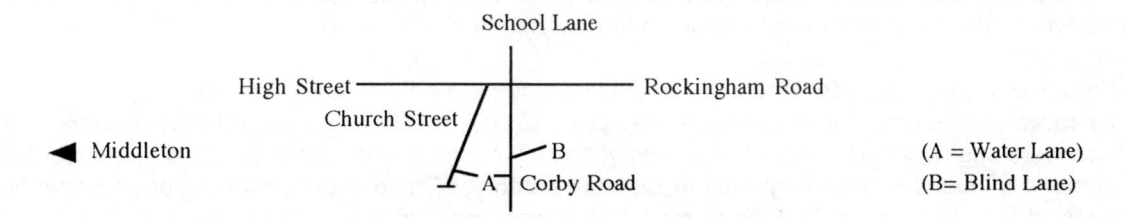

```
                            School Lane
                                |
         High Street ───────────┼─────────── Rockingham Road
                   Church Street /
 ◄ Middleton                    /─ B                    (A = Water Lane)
                              ─ A ┐ Corby Road          (B= Blind Lane)
```

Church: St Mary Magdalene. Earliest parts: 12th-century. The tower is 14th-century and there is a broach spire. The capitals on the tops of the pillars of the north arcade have fascinating unusual medieval carvings of ladies and knights. The church was restored in 1880. At the belfry end is a wooden board from 1670 with the will of William Downhall: At the front end of the church is a plaque to a former lord of the manor Thomas Medlycott (d.1761) and his wife, erected by their daughter, Barbara, who went on to become (with her own daughter) a major landowner in the region. The key is available from the rectory opposite.

Pubs: the *Spread Eagle*, the *Royal George*, the *Hunting Lodge*.

Former pubs: the *Crown* (stood on the corner of School Lane & High Street), the *King's Head* (stood in High Street), the *Three Horseshoes* (believed to have been in Church Street).

Methodist Church: 1878 (1808). In Corby Road.

Former School: 1871 (School Lane).

Other buildings and places of interest:

Church Street:
At the beginning of the street, no. 2 is late 17th/early 18th-century in origin. No.4, from the same era, was formerly a post office, undertaker's and from at least, 1860, a shop. It is of an interesting design both externally and internally, and has a wide arched-doorway to the right of which was the old Village Reading Room. There is a possibility at some future date of this being used as an exhibition/display area - once again providing public enjoyment as it must have done so often in the past. No.14 is from the same era. Between them, stands no.8, which is believed to have once been a small brewery. The Old Rectory lies at the far-end and dates from the mid-1600s. By the ivy-covered walled area near the steps leading up to the church, is a former washing place for horses and carts. A water-filled trough still lies, partially-hidden here. 'The Dale' lies beyond the church at the end of the road (see under 'Walks').

Corner of Corby Road & Rockingham Road (this area where roads meet is aptly known as 'The Cross'):
Here in the green area, once stood the village water supply and a large well-head with the sign: "Erected by the copyholders, 1854, William Thorpe, John Spriggs, Bailiffs'. Close by stands no.3 with a group of time-ravaged outbuildings from the same era .This has been variously, a bakery, a fish and chip shop and home of a donkey! Behind it, is the rear of the *Royal George* outside which there was formerly a path.

Corby Road: This was once the main shopping area, with as many as three shops flourishing: not bad for a small village! The Old Bakehouse (next to the present and only existing shop) is 17th-century. 'Greystones' (no.12) is 18th-century. Its right-hand section, viewed from the front, housed a butcher's shop, which used an outbuilding as a slaughterhouse. There is also a ruined dovecote in the garden. On the opposite side of the road to the chapel, stood a blacksmith's.

Water Lane (leads to and from the church): Stoneways (1863) has interesting carved figures (which came from a hall in Leicestershire) at the top of its front wall. Walking up the lane from the Church Street end, you can see the outline of the original oak crucks used in its construction. In a field to the right, near the end of the lane, are the remains of a lime kiln.

Blind Lane (links Corby Road with Rockingham Road). Here there are some fine 19th-century buildings, including Jasmine Cottage (opposite the pub) formerly a stonemason's house, with a grindstone outside, and to its right, where its old wooden nameplate hangs from an outbuilding with an old firemark at the top, is a house from 1846. Both houses were connected with stone craft during the 1800s.

High Street (on the way to Middleton):
The Hunting Lodge pub, restaurant and hotel was originally the stable block. This belonged to the late 17th/early 18th-century Manor House or Bury House. This was also once known as The Berrystead or Cottingham House and it lies to the right of the pub (facing you as you enter via the driveway). At one time it marked the boundary between Cottingham and Middleton.

Rockingham Road. On the right-hand side, on the way out of the village, is another former Wallis and Linnell clothing factory (as at Brigstock). It is now a shoe factory.

Nature Reserve: a newly-acquired site, lying outside the village, alongside a (green signposted) bridleway off the A427, before the Middleton turn-off Many 'derelict' trees and varieties of flowers.

Snippets:

* There was once a house for lepers in the village during Henry III's reign (1216-72).

* There was formerly a custom of distributing apples to children after Afternoon Service on Xmas Day. These were originally cast down from the belfry, and later in front of the Rectory, close to the orchard.

* There is a legend in the village that in the 18th century, a maid was thrown out of an upper floor window of Bury House, and that the sorrowful figure can sometimes be seen wandering around!

OLD CORBY VILLAGE: The Jamb

COTTINGHAM as it was: from Corby Road, looking towards 'The Cross'

* The stump of the old village windmill (now incorporated into a private home) stands in Windmill Close amongst newer housing. It can be seen when approaching the village from the top of the Corby Road.
* Cottingham once had a watermill which burnt down many years ago. The remains of the mill race can be seen in the field on the left, just before the bridge over the Welland, on the road to Bringhurst.

Local crafts: Museum Casts/International. Display and design construction, and manufacture of costume figures, replica food, historical and archaeological reconstructions, for sale or display, (mainly in museums) in UK and world-wide. Contact Sue Hall or Chris Owen, 4 Church Street. (Tel: 01536 771127).

Walks around the area:
* There are two different walks to the River Welland. One is via Mill Road, near the beginning of Middleton, turning off just past the modern school and football ground, on the left (signposted), and following the track across the grass and over a small stream until you come to a gravelly track at which you turn right, and walk down until you reach the river. You can continue over the bridge and walk down the (now grassy) track, looking out for a stile in the hedge (on the right) which will take you gradually uphill to the fascinating hamlet of Bringhurst.

The other route to the Welland (a different part) is to walk along Mill Road towards Bringhurst. There are stopping places and a stile on the left as you near the river. This area can get flooded very easily after heavy rains and can be difficult to negotiate by car or on foot!

* Though the High Street of the village naturally merges with Main Street of Middleton, there is a more rewarding, spectacular - uphill - walk to the latter, via the footpath beside the church. Go up the steps towards the church gate, turn right, and follow the path beside the churchyard to 'The Dale', a large natural grassy, limestone hollow, where some stone quarrying once took place. Some of this was used, amongst other things, for building the church. Many typical wildflowers grow here such as rest harrow, scabious, and cowslips as well as the rare meadow saxifrage. It is now a **pocket park**.

Turn right through a metal gate, and keeping the hedges on your right, walk uphill and along the ridge towards Middleton which lies below. The occasional views of the Welland Valley are really spectacular.

DEENE (valley)

A 'late' one-street village from the 13th century. Long associated with the Brudenell (Cardigan) family, Deene centres around the grandiose Park and magnificent stately home.

Church: St Peter (now redundant). Thirteenth century. Restored 1869. Recessed broach spire. In 1724, the south aisle (repaired 1728) collapsed killing two local workers. Brudenell chapel with memorials to the family : one white marble altar tomb has recumbent figures with bronze seahorses. For many years, villagers from Deene sat on the north side, those from neighbouring Deenethorpe on the south side.

Former pub: the *White Hart*, later known as the *Sea Horse Hotel* (a seahorse was the crest of the lords of the manor, the Brudenell family, since Henry VII). This impressive large building (earliest parts 17th century) with its distinctive oval window, still stands, though at the time of writing is derelict. It was once a thriving place filled with many guests as well as locals. There was a popular skittle room on the floor above the bar. It is reputed to be haunted every New Year's Eve at midnight by a 'grey lady' !

The building is currently in the hands of 'Greenbelt' who hold an annual Christian festival in the Park.

Former school : 1872 (The pupils were specially clothed by the Brudenells). Now the Village Hall.

Other buildings and places of interest:
The oldest buildings, like Blacksmith's Cottage and Home Farmhouse are 18th-century in origin, but some may have been rebuilt on the site of earlier dwellings. On the front wall of one of the newer buildings, next to the former school, is a fine tablet depicting a standing horse and deer (the latter holding an arrow in its mouth) - the arms of the Brudenell family.

Deene Hall (behind a high wall). Set in Deene Park, this impressive building is mainly 16th-century, incorporating a fragment of a medieval house. It came into the possession of the Brudenell family (beginning with Robert) in 1514. Thomas Brudenell, who had been an ardent Royalist during The Civil War and imprisoned in the Tower, was created Earl of Cardigan in 1661. A descendant who lived at the Hall, the seventh Earl, fought in The Crimean War, leading the ill-fated 'Charge Of The Light Brigade' immortalised in the lines of Tennyson's eponymous poem. The Hall has a fine interior courtyard/quadrangle. One tradition has it that Henry VII slept here after the Battle of Bosworth. The author noted, during a private visit, a large colony of tiny frogs leaping gymnastically around the path at the side of the house one idyllic summer's evening! The Hall is open to the public on certain days between Easter and August.

Deene Park has beech and elm trees gracing its slopes as well as some rarer trees. The vast lake completes an attractive scene. There are also 'swallow holes' in the park for flood waters on the land to flow into and disappear. At one time the Park was rich in both fallow and red deer. A walk across it is possible (see under Deenethorpe). The gardens are open annually as part of a national scheme (see under Aldwincle). It has been designated a 'Garden and Park of Special Historic Interest'.
Local crafts: *Art (horse & field sports): Rosemary Coates, West End Flat, Deene Park (01780 450).
Snippets:
* Deene Rectory, built in 1811, stood at the rear of church, until it wasdemolished in 1971.
Walks in the area:
* Deenethorpe (see below). Starts at the footpath to the left of Blacksmith's Cottage.
* Bulwick (qv.)

DEENETHORPE (village of the valley)

Once a thriving 'picture book' village with a population in the mid 19th-century of over 250, it lay in a beautiful setting with several thatched buildings. In fact, it was a larger village than Deene.Today the pub, school, shoemaker's, baker's and shop have all gone and it is a sad, forlorn shadow of its former bustling self, with little left to see, except a few remaining crumbling, ivy-covered vestiges of its past.

Former pub: the *Cardigan Arms* (formerly the *Nag's Head*, was in the old centre of the village, near where phone box stands). Demolished in the 1960s due to an unsafe gable, it was a fine old, long, thatched building with a 'stable' door. Now, only a heap of rubble marks its spot. It was regularly used by US airmen from the nearby airfield during the 1940s.
Former school: 19th-century. Demolished in the 1960s, it stood at the end of the village, on the right, as the little 'MainStreet' peters out into a track, towards what was later to become the airfield.
Other buildings and places of interest: Along Main Street (no name plate) is Deene Lodge Manor Farmhouse (on the right). The last building on the left before the road peters out is thatched mid 18th-century Matchbox Cottage with a matching thatched well.
Snippets:
* Despite its present sleepy appearance, the village has had its share of action and incident. At the back of the village are the runways and derelict control tower of a wartime airfield and base. Here the US Airforce 401st Bombardment Group were stationed in the Second World War. On one occasion, a bomber from the airfield crashed in the village damaging some of the houses and shattering windows at Deene Hall. On the other side of the airfield is the Weldon to Benefield Road along which is a lay-by with a monument to the Group.The airfield is now used by The Flying Fortress Club (lessons given).
* One of the turn-offs into the village from the A43 (ie.opposite the road into Deene) which today is lined with more modern houses, is traditionally known as Burbage Lane . It was named after Thomas Burbage, a prosperous villager who lived close to the former pub, and who became associated with the building of almshouses in West Street, Oundle.
* The village was the early home of James Pain, a farmer's 'fairman', who later moved to Great Oakley, where he married the miller's daughter. His son, also named James, went on to become a celebrity in the region, as founder of the largest ironstone-works of its kind in the country, and local benefactor.
Walks in the area:
* Deene (via Deene Park).There are three short roads leading out of the village to the A43 and Dene. (The first leads to the ornate, castellated mid 19th-century Porters Lodge and Gatehouse of the Hall. The third leads near to the road into Deene which crosses the small St.Andrew's Bridge). For an interesting walk, however, take the middle one and cross the main road to the black Footpath sign. The walk is arrowmarked on posts, though you must look out for them <u>very</u> carefully. Watch where you put your feet: the ground is watery and marshy, and the 'track' is sometimes non-existent! A barbed-wire fence lies to the left, and the Park lake lies to your right. Leaving the watery area, head through a small area of woodland to a stile at the fence lining Deene Park. Proceed uphill, following arrow-marked wooden posts for some distance. Turn right, and pass over stiles and a wooden footbridge to a farm-track at the end of the village. An adventurous, fun walk with fine views of the Hall and Park.
* Brigstock (via Airfield). Follow the road through the village past Matchbox Cottage, and carry on as it becomes a track. There is then a long walk over the runways of the former wartime airfield to the Benefield-Weldon road (part of which is named Yoke Hill) on the other side. Cross over and keep straight on for a distance, with the trees of Harry's Park Wood to your right, past the Bocase Stone and Fermyn Woods Park, across the A6116 to the Footpath sign and down into Brigstock. Arrow-marked

most of the way. A long, exhilarating walk.
* Upper Benefield. A footpath leads off to the left mid-way along the 'main street' of the village, across fields, over a small part of the airfield, and through a short spinney. Part of the walk is almost parallel with a road running to the left. The end of the walk brings you out near the village pub.

DESBOROUGH (origin either 'fortified place' 'holy place' or 'placewhere deer kept')

Now a large town, its colourful older ironstone buildings stand out amongst the new. It has proved to be an area rich in archaeological finds. A settlement has stood here since the Bronze Age, and several relics from that era have been found. Fom the later Iron Age, Celtic finds have included the famous, decorative 'Desborough Mirror' now in the British Museum, which also houses a marvellous gold Anglo-Saxon necklace found in a garden. For many years the town was famed for weaving, and later, the shoemaking industry.

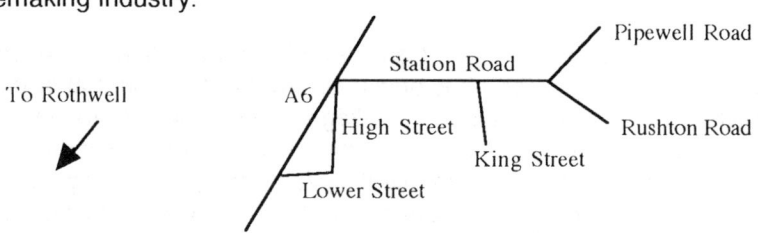

Church: St.Giles. Broach spire. Earliest parts: 13th-century (though built on the site of an earlier Saxon church). Memorials to former lords of the manor, the Poulton family. Piscina made of parts of a medieval shrine. Ornate canopy (Tudor). Painted wall plaque with the Ten Commandments and other religious wording. The large churchyard has some interesting tombstones, some of which are metal. A footpath to Rothwell runs alongside the church to 'The Damms', a field of some historical importance (see below).
Baptist Chapel: 1858 (in Gold Street).
Schools: 1841 (National) ; 1878 (Board)
Pubs: the *George* (18th-century); the *King's Arms* (18th-century).
Former pubs: the *Swan* ; the *Talbot* ; the *Angel* ; the *New Inn.*; the *Black Horse.*
Other buildings & places of interest:
In the cul-de-sac, opposite the church: Church House (18th-century); and next door, White Hart House.
Gold Street: the former Manor House (late 17th/early 18th-century).
The Damms: in the field behind the church lie earthworks where a battle is supposed to have been fought between the Saxon inhabitants and the Vikings.
Nature Reserves: Two sites are under the care of The Wildlife Trust for Northamptonshire: (1) Tailby Meadow, which features a rare type of grassland in the form of a 12-acre hay meadow, named after the former owners. With 15 species of grass and a variety of wildflowers, the reserve attracts many butterflies and dragonflies during the summer. It is signposted from Rushton Road, and is situated on the edge of the town, off Broadlands (park in the Leisure Centre Car Park). (2) The Plens, is a former ironstone quarry containing a variety of habitats for different kinds of wildlife. There are remains of a railway track. Situated north of the town. Access is via the railway bridge leading to Pipewell. Stout footwear recommended.
Local crafts: *Living Silk Needle Painting: Joyce Jaycock, 11 St.Giles Close. Tel. 01536 760993.
*Copper Repousse Pictures: Hazel Gardner, The Copper Gallery, Lower Street. Tel. 01536 762333.
*Collage/Prints: Elizabeth Glover, 9 Dovedale. Tel. 01536 710478;
*Art (watercolours of local scenes): John Sharman, 30 Leys Avenue. Tel: 01536 760582.

Walks in the area:
*Stoke Albany. The walk begins at the entrance to the The Plens Nature Reserve (see above), and is arrowmarked most of the way (turn <u>right</u> at the entrance). Leaving The Plens, a walk uphill over grassland brings you to a high stile, another (shorter) field and a minor road which you cross, into yet another field. A straight walk brings you, after passing through a gate, and a short field to the Desborough-Stoke Albany road, where there is a farm on the opposite side. Turn right and follow the road for a considerable distance, past Bowd Lane Wood on your right (part of a former manorial park), down into the village.

DUDDINGTON (farm or settlement of Dudda's people)

A fascinating village with a wealth of old buildings, Duddington is generally reckoned to be one of the most attractive places in the county, let alone in the Forest. The buildings have a special charm and the setting around the Welland is particularly inspiring. At present, some streets have no name plates.

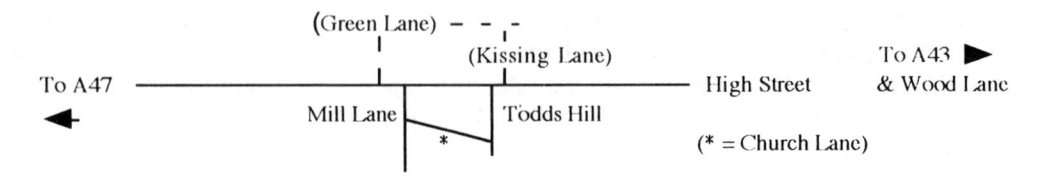

```
                    (Green Lane) - - -
                           |     (Kissing Lane)                    To A43 ▶
  To A47 ─────────────────┼───────┼──────────────── High Street    & Wood Lane
   ◀                  Mill Lane │ Todds Hill
                              \*/                  (* = Church Lane)
```

Church: St Mary. Earliest parts c.1150, on the site of an Anglo-Saxon building. Unusually-sited tower. Octagonal broach spire. Main door (c.1220) has original ironwork. It is said that in the Middle Ages that gangs of forest raiders were liable to attack the village at any time. At the sounding of a warning the villagers could rush for shelter in the church behind this invincible wooden structure. There are traces of medieval painting inside. Thirteenth-century font, with a hesp originally used to help keep it locked against theft or misuse. Royal coats-of-arms on the wall include those of Henry VIII. Jacobean altar rails and communion table. Several monuments and floorslabs to the Jackson family (major landowners and later holders of the manor). Restored 1844.

Former school: built 1891-2 for both boys and girls and opened 1893, according to the stone on the front wall (prior to this there was the school next door and before this the village had an earlier school from around 1667). It is an ornate building inscribed with a coat of arms. On the gate to the playground is a sign: 'Any person who omits to shut and fasten this gate is liable to a penalty not exceeding forty shillings'. A plaque on the wall nearby threatens prosecution to anyone using the grounds who is not a schoolchild.

Pub: the *Royal Oak*

Former pubs: the *Crown*, the *Windmill* (early 19th-century, now a private house, 'The Old Windmill'. It is almost opposite the village green).

Other buildings and places of interest:

High Street: (left-hand side, opposite the Royal Oak) Dial House (1722), built by the village tanner. Just before this, there are two 17th-century houses. Past Dial House and set back from the road is Home Farm, which is 17th-century with later additions. At the rear of the building there is a dovecote: a late 18th-century or early 19th-century, rectangular two-room structure with a pyramid-like roof. Public access to this is possible, but at present (1995) a visit has to be pre-arranged with the Burghley Estate Office.

The large building next to the farm is the Manor House, which has an early 16th-century gable. From 1585 the Burghley and Cecil families held it until 1798 when it was acquired by Thomas Jackson whose family had farmed and owned land and property at Duddington since the beginning of the 17th century. His son sold it to John Monckton in 1843. There is a datestone above the door: 1633. The house stands virtually in the centre of the village.

The Old Post Office (built 1842 and used as a post office two years later). This building also served as a girls' school, with the boys using a nearby converted thatched cottage. Such was the problem of being a fairly large village!

Todds Hill (the narrow road at the side of the Manor House. No name plate at the time of writing):
On the left stands the original village poorhouse, a fine but now forlorn L-shaped 17th-century building (originally two houses) currently in need of repair. The present Village Hall, next to it, was partly rebuilt from older rubble, and stands close to the church. Church Lane, also currently with no name plate, joins at this point from the right, and the corner house with mullioned windows, Cromfield Cottage, is another building of 17th-century origin.

Mill Street:
At the top of the hill (once known as Stocks Hill), on the corner facing the triangular 'green' (on which stands a fine horse chestnut tree), is the aptly-named Stocks Hill House, a fine large building dating from 1601. The main entrance shows that the house was altered in 1858. Opposite the green, and down a narrow driveway is Todds Barn (1815).

Deene: St. Peter's Church from the lake.

DUDDINGTON: the bridge over the River Welland and the old watermill.

Midway along stands Church Farm (17th-century) and before this another 17th-century house.
The Water Mill stands at the bottom of the road on the left near the bridge. It originally dates from around 1664, but has undergone various stages of alteration and repair, which have been recorded via various inscriptions on its stones such as 'John Wyles 1745' (above the arch seen from the wall by the stream) and '1793 TS'. Its original function having long since ceased, it is used today as offices. On the opposite side of the road stands the 18th-century Mill House.
The graceful **medieval bridge** spanning the River Welland until the 1970s carried the growing traffic of the A47, which now passes overhead nearby. It has returned to a scene of tranquillity and provides, with the nearby mill, a pleasant safe place to stand, reflect and admire the view. It has four arches and two cutwaters, and was repaired/widened in 1919. On the bridge itself there is a boundary marker, separating Duddington from Tixover in neighbouring Leicestershire (the Welland acts a border for both the county and Rockingham Forest).

Snippets:
* On a historical note, Elizabeth I during her reign, granted a charter to the villagers that included a toll-free concession 'wherever they may pass' throughout the kingdom.
* Interesting one-time local place names include Spider Eye, Long Stockings, Noses Holt, Peter's Hook.
* The old Green Lane (off the High Street, opposite Mill Street, beside Beaumont House, which dates from 1828) and Kissing Lane (off the High Street, opposite the Manor House) are still accessible to the pedestrian, and worth a short walk. (No name plates for identification at present, though a black and white arrow marker is visible for the latter).
* Finally, Duddington could be named 'the village of clocks' - see how many you can find during your walk!

Walks in the area:
* There is an excellent walk to Kings Cliffe through extensive woodland of Rockingham Forest. Begin from the pub, cross over to the path which runs right, along the A43. At the end of the path, cross the busy road, and at the the Public Footpath sign, follow the track (which is known locally as Wood Lane) and keep going straight, following the black/white arrow markers, all the way. There are little 'horseshoe'-shaped diversions in places where it gets muddy, and waterproof footwear is advisable. The route is now part of the Jurassic Way. For a diversion en route, quite near the beginning of the walk up the track, there is a green marker to the right. This leads you to Fineshade Woods (qv.), where further excellent walks are possible.

* Also at the bridge end of the village, you can get to the village of Tixover, with its strangely isolated church. Cross over the bridge and follow the path, part of which was the old road. A key is available for the church (with a notice to the effect) from a house on the right near where the village ends. It is mainly 12th-century and has an interesting 17th-century marble monument within. From Tixover you can also get to Barrowden via a bridleway, part of which follows a curve of the Welland.

* Ketton. Though not in the Forest, this can be a glorious, quite lengthy walk on a summer day and is highly recommended. It has recently been made part of the Jurassic Way. It is also well-signposted, and there are a number of stiles for access. Begin at the footpath sign on the right, just past the bridge. Since you are now in Leicestershire, the footpath signs hereafter will be in the standard green and yellow of that county. You follow the Welland for a stretch, before ascending a slope, and following a short woodside track. Crossing a short field, you come to a minor road at which you turn right. Just past the large group of buildings (Tixover Grange) there is a signpost to the left which will points your way across a sloping field and a long track to Ketton. Towards the end of the track, keep to the left of a cluster of trees which obscure a farmhouse. Once over a stile, head in a north-west direction to another stile beside the narrow road. Do not turn left here - but keep straight on, along a shady track between houses and a large meadow. On reaching the road turn left. This is Geeston, one of the two 'satellites' of Ketton (the other is Aldgate). Here you will be able to go along part of the Hereward Way (signposted in green and yellow), another of England's fine cross-country, long-distance paths. Here on the other side of the Welland, you will be able to explore the area around Ketton, which has many 17th-century buildings, pleasant back-street lanes, tracks, and stream crossings. Ketton is well-known for its stone quarries which lie just outside the settlement, off the A6121 to Stamford.

EAST CARLTON (settlement of free peasants or Karli's settlement)

Many years ago there was also a West Carlton (with manor), but inter-marriage and circumstances united the two manors (on each other's doorstep) under the name, 'Carleton', later East Carlton. Originally with just one short street, East Carlton has always been a small village, now considerably enlarged (on the park side) by newer housing as a result of the coming and growth of the Steel Works at Corby.

Church: St Peter's. Early English style. Tower. The south transept has monuments and tablets to the Palmer family from the 17th century to the present (including Sir Geoffrey Palmer, d.1673). Rebuilt in 1788 (there is a tablet above one of the doors). 18th-century communion rail. There is a wellhead outside.

East Carlton Countryside Park : the grounds of the former Carlton Hall (rebuilt 1873), which stands on the site of an 18th-century house (itself replacing a 17th-century building), and was built in the French style. For years the Palmer family were lords of the manor of East Carlton (later members were <u>not</u> associated with the biscuit company, Huntley and Palmer, as is frequently reported!) It lies surrounded by around 100 acres of field and woodland, and is open (free of charge) to the public 24 hours all the year round. There are fine views of the countryside. There are lots of things to do: two walks/nature trails of varying distances have been laid out. There is a duck pond with several breeds of waterfowl, an Alpine garden, and over 14 kinds of tree (including one of the largest boled lime trees in the UK) can be seen, some of which (such as those lining the entrance) have identity plaques on them. There is an enclosed children's playground and a picnic/barbecue area. In summer, there is a children's camp and occasional family fun days. The former stable block (1768) now houses a working blacksmith's, various craft-making rooms upstairs, a cafeteria and a museum/steel-making Heritage Centre. Outside are reminders of the once-thriving local steel industry, in the form of an old locomotive and gigantic drag-line bucket, both popular with active children!

Other buildings and places of interest:
Row of almshouses (1688) by Sir Geoffrey Palmer (now divided into five private dwellings). There is a stone tablet above the centre door inscribed 'Hospital of the blessed Jesus in Carlton' and 'Rebuilt and more amply endowed by Charlotte Palmer, Anno Domini 1868'. These buildings originally stood in the grounds of the Country Park across the road (near the entrance, where the coach park lies on the left) and were later transferred to their present site.

The Coronation Hall: depicts King George VI and Elizabeth, his wife (the Queen Mother) above the door.

The Swallows a house facing the footpath sign to Middleton, looks older than its datestone of 1870, with its mullions and Tudor window, and may well be on the site of an earlier building.

A little way past this, as the village comes to an end is Little Mead Farm from 1863. The large red brick building on the opposite side is the Old Rectory from 1872.

Local crafts: Glass figure making, hand-made joinery, cake making, flower arrangements and knitwear can currently be seen inside the craft workshops in the Country Park. Commissions undertaken. There is an adjoining blacksmith's forge outside, where you can see the smith at work.

Snippets:
* The village originally had two manors: In the 15th century, the Palmer family acquired the East Hall after William Palmer married Anne a member of the Ward family who owned the East Hall. (His son,Thomas acquired Holt from the Trussell family, by marriage. Later this passed to the Nevills whose name became synonymous with that village). By 1471, they possessed both the East and West Manors. The West Hall was allowed to run down and was virtually non-existent by the 18th century. Sir Geoffrey Palmer (knighted in 1660 in recognition of his services to the Royalist cause for which he had been imprisoned by Cromwell) purchased the estate of another 'Carlton': Carleton Curlieu near Kibworth, Leicestershire.
* Church Lane was once known as Wire Lane.

Walks in the area:
* Excellent possibilities. The country park has several entrances, the main one being through the mid19th-century gates off the main road opposite the church. There are footpaths into the grounds via the rear of the stable block following the green Public Footpath sign: this route is interesting because it passes Home Farmhouse and some of the old outbuildings, including a late 18th-century square dovecote on the left. The path comes out into a picnic area of the park, and a path (right) to Middleton.

* Other entrances are via the footpath to Middleton, also signposted, opposite the large house.
* To the left of the large house (The Swallows) and Ninestones (no 10) is a stile and footpath to Wilbarston. Interestingly, this 'footpath' was originally the road/track to Wilbarston. It first of all follows a hedge on the left, through a gap and goes uphill towards a ruined brick building (near the pylons) and down across a stream en route. You arrive at the edge of the village, by the Village Hall. It is now part of the 'Jurassic Way' and is arrow-marked.
* Continuing down the hill, past the Old Rectory, you can either turn right and walk round a field opened up to the public with the farmer's consent, as part of the Countryside Premium Scheme, marked with a green plaque at the two entrances (another is further down the road). This is an experimental scheme with the consent of the farmer, that permits public access to a stretch of countryside for enjoyment (providing of course that no vehicles, tents or guns are taken in). You can also continue down the road to the small 18th-century stone bridge crossing the stream. (Some way along on the left of the stream, there used to be a watermill). The quiet road eventually leads to a crossroads for Ashley, Middleton and Drayton.

EASTON ON THE HILL

Time is needed to explore the history-encrusted streets of this large settlement. A treasure chest of the past awaits the curious visitor who is willing to walk and observe. There are many 17th-19th c. datestones.

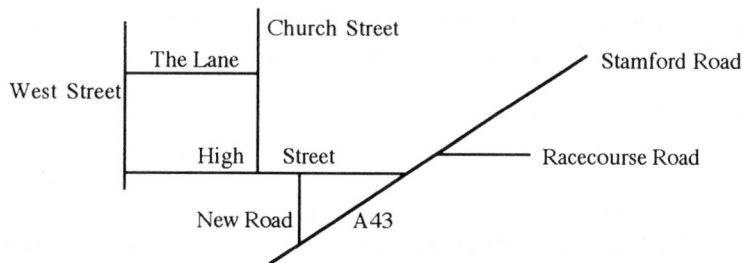

Church: All Saints. Early English style. Earliest parts are 12th and 13th-century. Tower with four tall pinnacles (15th-century). Some medieval paintings, glass, tiles, floorslabs, coffin lids and masonry. Seventeenth-century seating. There is a sundial on the south porch:1797. Chancel restored in 1888.
Pubs: the *Oak Inn* (1820), the *Exeter Arms* (has a datestone inscribed 'Ino.Susa Jackson 1765'). Both pubs on the Stamford Road; the *Blue Bell* (in Church Street)
Former pubs: the *Slaters Arms* (in The Lane), the *Retreat* (stood in Stamford Road), the *Carpenter's Arms Inn*, the *White Horse*, the *Princess*, the *Crown Inn*.
Methodist Chapel: 1874 (in Church Street, on the site of an earlier 1827 chapel. Now Chapel House).
Former schools: (1) In the 17th century, Richard Garford, a village benefactor, gave money for a boys school, probably held at first in the church and certainly later in the Old Priests House. In 1766 it moved to a building (datestones 1724, 1729) in Church Street (now no. 61), close to the church. (2) The school moved in 1868, to a newly-constructed building with an ornate spiral tower, cupola, clock and bell added in memory of the original benefactor. It stands on the corner of New Road and is now used as the Village Hall. The Old School House is next door, facing the High Street. (3) A Girls/Infants School was built in 1829-30 for 130 children. Stands on Stamford Road, opposite the High Street.
Other buildings and places of interest:
Stamford Road: Crown Inn Cottage (the former pub) with a crown plaque on its wall. On the same side, the last two houses before the High Street begins are no.6 (from 1761) and no. 4, Rock House (from 1834).
High Street (Stamford Road end): Early 18th-century barn with triangular air vents. Two houses from the 17th century appear on the left, nos.54-56 with a blocked stone doorway and a light blue (later) datestone of 1823. Next door, with its black iron sign-holder, is an early 19th-century building, the former *Carpenter's Arms Inn* (now no.52), and another 17th-century house, no.40 (Mask Cottage). Nearly opposite the junction with Church Street are two more 17th-century houses: nos.30 and 32. On the right-hand corner of Church Street is a really amazing house (with three datestones on the front: 1607, 1674 and 1792 - and another on the chimney! An old saying in the town is that the '1607' datestone with an 'R' and 'M' on either side, is the number of miles to Rome!
The remainder of the High Street is just as intriguing with yet more 17th-century buildings: including on the right, the *Bluebell Inn*, (with an extension building date on its chimney of 1797). Opposite, is a

fine T-shaped house (no. 20) with stone mullioned windows, and a sundial with the date, 1649. This was once yet another inn, the *Princess* . Set back a little way past here with its gable end facing the street, is no.18 and tucked away from the street near it, is no.12. Further on towards the corner of the High Street is no.6, the former smithy. A chain is still hanging on the outside wall by the forge where the horses were shod. Finally, completing this fine group of buildings from the same era, is Yew Tree Farm House (no longer part of a farm) right on the corner.

West Street:
Almost opposite The Lane (the turning on the right) is a large 17th-century house. Near the bend on the other side is Tailors Cottage which is of more recent origin but which has a (reset) datestone of 1636 and next door, a house from 1857. A little further on is a real gem managed by the National Trust: **the Priest's House**, an early 16th-century (Pre-Reformation) dwelling with religious connections. It was later known for a while as The Old Rectory, and also housed the original village school until 1766. Today, it contains a small museum of village bygones upstairs, and is well-worth a visit. At present the key may be obtained from the Glebe House (once known as Lutine House) next door, an imposing 18th-century building which has a white sundial above front door: 'Fear The Lord Always'. Across the road is the smaller and older (17th-century) 'Glebe Cottage', no.45, situated in an idyllic setting.

Track continuation of West Street: worth a visit, though some distance down the sloping road (not for vehicles) is The Gamekeeper's House, an attractive, compact building with an ornate gabled porch and crowned chimney tops. The Marquis of Exeter, lord of the manor of Easton-on-the-Hill , had his coronet and the date 1845 engraved on the upper front gable.

The Lane (from West Street end):
The first building on the right is a 17th-century house (Vine Cottage) with barn. The first building on the left with a slightly crooked shape is partly 17th-century and was formerly part of a pub, the *White Horse.* Next door is another of the old village bakehouses. Beside this is a house (no.3) dated 1742, with a rectangular dovecote from the same century, at the rear. The final building of interest is at the end of this short street, on the right is The Manor House (17th-century), with a later 'coach house' opposite.

Church Street:
No. 23 has mullioned windows and a datestone of 1688 (the former village workhouse stood in the vicinity); no. 19 (Ivy Cottage) has two datestones, 1622 for the original house and a rebuilding date of 1816. No.11 (partly built in 1677) has mullioned windows. The right end of the building is called Branstone House and has a datestone on its gable of 1680, and the other end is now the Post Office. The white house close by is also from the same era.

Pocket Park: on the edge of the village at Spring Close, close to the Stamford Road. A small sloping meadow with a stream and a variety of trees. A pond is being restored. In the rockface under the suitably named Rock House, between a willow and a yew is Clay Well, beneath a stone dome and grill. There is a distinctive four-faced monument to the Polish paratroopers who were stationed here during World War II, before taking part in the Battle of Arnhem.

Snippets:
* The High Street was formerly known as Bell Street ; Park Lane was Gas Walk.
* In the 18th century, the village was celebrated for its locally-quarried limestone.
* The unusual lay-out of the village has been attributed to the fact that it once had three manors.
* The village could also be known as 'The Village of Datestones' due to its large number of these. See how many you can find!

Walks in the area:
*There are cross-country footpaths to Tinwell, Stamford, Wothorpe and Collyweston Bridge.
* There is a Site of Scientific Interest to visit along Racecourse Road, just off Stamford Road. The road is so-named for the horseracing which took place nearby in the 18th and 19th centuries.

FINESHADE ('Finn's Head')

Approaching the crossroads can seen (from the A46) a stable block (1848), the only remaining (later) building from what was once the Priory of Fineshade (also known as the 'Church of St Mary of Castel Hymel'), which became **Fineshade Abbey**. It was built just north east of Castle Hymel which did not stand for long, being demolished early in King John's reign, when a John Engayne the Elder formed a priory for the Augustinian order of monks, which held part of the manor of Kirby. The antiquary John Leland passing by en route from Deene to Collyweston in 1538 made the following observation: *'Almost yn the Middle way I cam by Finshed, lately a priory of Blak Canons, leving it hardly on the righte hand, it is 4 miles from Stamford. Here in the very place where the Priory stode was in times past a Castel called Hely. It longgid to the Engaynes and they dwellid in it'.* In 1542 during the Dissolution, it passed to Sir Robert Kirkhay as a private residence, which it remained until 1956, when only the stable house was retained and used as a home.

On the main road, opposite the driveway to the grounds is a large old house dated 1881. Further along on the same side, and just before the crossroads, stands Bottom Lodge, remnants of an early 19th-century building, together with a ruined dovecote.

Fineshade Woods offer a specially-created and signposted leisurely 'circular' walk for which there is a leaflet at the Fineshade (Top) Lodge forestry offices, where forestry literature is also available. It is the main building of the 'village' and is generally 19th-century, with earlier parts: there are datestones of 1761 and 1771. Beyond the woods there are excellent walks to Kings Cliffe, Duddington, and Blatherwycke. The latter two can be rather muddy in places during wet periods and practical footwear is advisable. The adjoining woods are : Westhay Wood, Buxton Wood, Lynn Wood and North Spinney. There are also cycling facilities and a route about which, again, there is a leaflet, and areas are set aside for a car park and The Caravan Club. There is an annual husky race after Christmas. In autumn these particular woods are rich in varieties of fungi that do not seem to be as widespread elsewhere in the Forest. Mycologists take note!

FOTHERINGHAY (The island of the people of Forthere).

Long connected with royalty (the House of York), and a religious seat of learning, this small village is something special with its peaceful atmosphere and idyllic setting by the Nene, with Willow Brook flowing nearby. Fotheringhay breathes history. A place to explore slowly and to enjoy.

Church: St Mary the Virgin and All Saints. Fifteenth-century architecture and an elaborate, painted pulpit (restored to its original colours). Imposing tower with octagonal lantern crowned with pinnacles. From 1411 onwards, it was an ecclesiastical college and church combined and was extensively rebuilt. (The college had been transferred from the castle, where it had been set up 13 years previously by the first Duke of York and his son). The college was dissolved in 1549 and the collegiate choir (chancel) was emptied in 1573, with its woodwork and glass going to other local village churches. Today, there is an historical exhibition, documenting 'Fotheringhay Through The Ages' and its royal connections. Memorials and tombs of members of the House of York are to be found within, and there are books and other memorabilia on sale. A 'Chapel of All Souls' furnished by The Richard III Society has been installed as a memorial to the House of York.

Pub: the *Falcon Inn* (early 19th-century). A popular local haunt (booking is advisable for the Egon Ronay-recommended restaurant).

Two previous inns: the *Old Inn* and the *New Inn*, both standing near the west entrance to the castle and opposite each other in Main Street. The former (used around 1400-50) disappeared and its site occupied by five cottages. The latter (now known as Garden Farm) has a 15th-century gateway with references to Edward IV and four generations of the Neville family etc. It was built between 1461-76. Both inns were used for the overflow of visitors to the castle.

Former school: no longer exists. Leland wrote: 'There is a school in the town erected by Henry VII'.

Gardens: some of the village gardens are open annually as part of a national scheme (see Aldwincle).

Other buildings and places of interest:

The bridge : Spanning the Nene, the present structure has four arches and is 18th-century (1722) using stone from Kingscliffe quarries. It was first recorded 1498, and was first rebuilt in 1573. This area around the river is a restful place to be especially in the warmer months: fishing, picnicking, walking, boats passing through and mooring along the banks.

The site of the castle faces the river. Access is over the bridge (coming from the Oundle end), and where the road bends left into the village, turn right and walk down a track at the rear of a farm. The site is signposted and there is an information board for your orientation. Originally built around 1100 by the son-in-law of William I, only the earthworks (mound) of the castle remain plus a token piece of masonry. It was the birthplace of Richard III (1452). Two of his ancestors died in battle: Edward Duke of York was slain at Agincourt in 1415. Richard, third Duke of York, died at Wakefield in 1459. (There are memorials to both men in the church). Richard himself also died in battle - at Bosworth in 1485. The author has noted a single white rose regularly laid on the masonry on the anniversary of his birth, 2 October). The castle was also host to Mary Queen of Scots, who after a four-month period of imprisonment there, was executed (in the Great Hall) on 8 February 1587.

Main Street: The former inns lie on opposite sides (the 'Old' on the left, the 'New' on the right). Next to the 'New' (Garden Farm), is Garden Cottage, a small thatched 17th-century building. The former Vicarage (part 17th-century) stands on the corner of the road to Nassington. Behind the pub is a 17th-century thatched house. The Post Office building dates from the 18th century. Opposite the pub, is a stone gateway inscribed: 1711. Further along is 'Thatched Cottage' (c.1800).

Local crafts: Ironwork : Fotheringhay Forge (& Woodburners), still in use and worth a visit. Stands close to the pub. Open Monday to Saturday 10am until 4.00pm. Tel. Barry Keighley, 018326 212 for details.

Refreshments: Village Hall, set back at the far end of the street on the right, offers teas on Sunday afternoons during the summer season.

Snippets:
* A market place with a cross once stood to the east of the church, and an annual fair took place at the feast of St Michael's. A maypole was erected annually on the site during the 16th century.
* There were two deer parks in the village. The smaller ('Little Park') stood close to the site of the castle. The much larger park was created early in the 13th century and stood immediately west of the road to Nassington.

Walks in the area:
*There is a fine walk (past the rear of the castle site) across the water meadows, and crossing the Nene to Eaglethorpe and Warmington. A must for nature lovers.
*A little way out of the village on the road to Nassington, off to the right, is a walk to Elton via Middle Lodge, Willow Brook , the old railway track and the Nene.
* Nassington. A rewarding walk, along a quiet lane and track, passing over a stone bridge across Willow Brook, and walking alongside Park Spinney and fields,which include part of the former deer park. The walk begins at the first turning on the right, as you leave the village, on the road to Woodnewton. Signposted/marked.
* Woodnewton. Take the same turning for Nassington, but leave the road at the first signpost on the left, over a field. A pleasant walk, well-signposted, with two small wooden benches (perhaps former stiles) thoughtfully provided! Follow the markers along a track and then the edge of a field which you cross to the wooden bridge over Willow Brook on the other side. A short walk from here brings you into the village.

GEDDINGTON (Geytington: the settlement of Gæte's people).

A major forest settlement with long-standing royal connections, Geddington is a place worth exploring with its fine bridge (in an idyllic setting), narrow alleyways, old buildings and tracks through woodland.

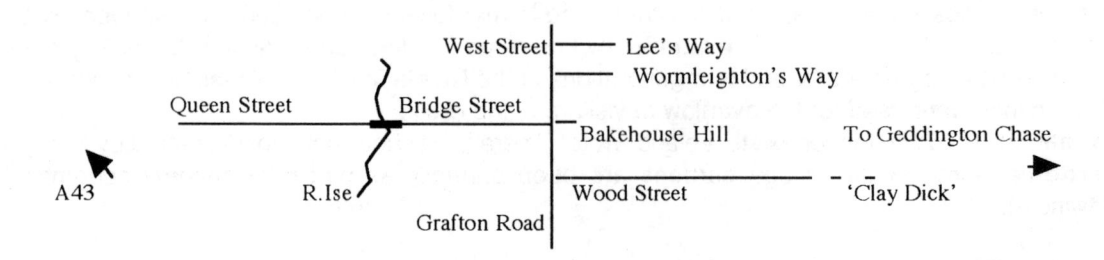

Church: Mary Magdalene. Earliest parts: Saxon (possibly 10th-century), which include unusual internal arcading. Ancient aumbrey. 'The King's Door' (once associated with the royal hunting lodge that stood behind the church) was added in the 12th century. Fourteenth-century tower with spire. Screen: 1618 (given by Maurice Tresham of Newton, whose coat-of-arms and initials can be seen). Colourful, ornate stone altar piece: at the base of either side are the figures (in personified form) of the River Ise and a king's jester. Tresham monuments from Newton, including alabaster slab. Floor and wall brasses, including Henry Jarmon and wife in contemporary dress (c.1480). Medieval slab of a priest holding a chalice.The church underwent major restoration in 1857.

Congregational Church (former Union Chapel): 1876 (on corner of Chapel Lane).
Pubs: the *White Lion*, the *Star Inn* (formerly the *Swan*), the *White Hart Inn*.
Former pubs: the *Duke's Arms*, the *Royal George*, the *Angel*, the *Royal Oak* (now the post office).
School: 1849. The Infants school was built in 1894.

Other buildings and places of interest:

The Eleanor Cross. Constructed in 1294, the cross was one of 12 erected at resting points en route to Westminster Abbey, for the body and funeral procession of Edward I's wife Queen Eleanor who died prematurely in December 1290, whilst staying at Harby in Lincolnshire. This was the fourth resting place. The cross is the best-preserved of the remaining three (the other two being at Hardingstone on the A508 London Road into Northampton, and at Waltham. There was formerly a well at the base, and the stocks also stood at this point. A pageant 'Edward and Eleanor : A Village Remembers' was held in the church by villagers in 1990 to commemorate 700 years since the event occurred. A video was made of the occasion. 1994 marked the 700th anniversary of the erection of the cross, and the village celebrated in style, from June to December with a series of events including a street party, flower festival, music recital, commemorative service, and another pageant (held in the village square), 'The Spirit of Eleanor'.
Opposite the cross on the right, stands the former blacksmith's, The Old Forge. The turning past it, Bakehouse Hill, leads on to a 17th-century building now known as the Old Bakery (no. 6), top left. This short road bears right into Church Hill which has more buildings from the same era, next to the Old Forge.

West Street. The thatched house adjoining the pub is believed to be 17th-century in origin, as are nos. 2 and 4. Leading off on the right of the street at different points are two narrow thoroughfares, both with fine old thatched houses at the beginning of each: no.1 Wormleighton's Way dates from the early 18th century, and no.1 Lee's Way is 17th-century in origin. Next to the former All Hours shop is a one-time farmhouse (no.40) which also dates from the same era. The big house at the end, West End House has a datestone: 1822. Opposite this is the 19th-century Old Vicarage, which also once acted as a private school. Amongst its illustrious pupils were William Gladstone, the famous Liberal Prime Minister.

Bridge Street. On the left hand corner is Eleanor House Teashop and Restaurant - highly recommended - at the rear of which is a blue painted sundial: 1767. Ahead of you, now with bollards across each entrance to slow down traffic on its narrow roadway, stands the magnificent medieval **Bridge.** Originally built in 1250 and straddling the River Ise, it has five arches, large cutwaters and pedestrian refuges, and formerly carried the main road to Kettering and Stamford! The centre arch has a keystone from when part of the bridge was rebuilt: 1784. At its narrowest the bridge is 14 feet. Here there is also a ford which traffic can use as an alternative, and which is a favourite haunt of large numbers of ducks (who get a good meal here!) and local children who love to splash around, in warmer weather. It is a relaxing place to breathe in the peaceful atmosphere and sample a piece of the past unchanged. The river has in the past been favoured by crayfish.

Queen Street. Looking at the houses on the left-hand side: no. 3 near the bridge is a house of 17th-century origin, and was once another of the village bakehouses. The thatched Post Office was once the *Royal Oak* pub and also dates from the same era. Some of the more interesting buildings of the village are partially hidden in this street, and tucked away behind the Post Office at an angle to it, is thatched no.13, from the same era. Along the road a little way on behind a wall is another partially-hidden building (no.25): yet another Old Vicarage with Gothic windows. A little further along is a wonderful assortment of 17th-century cottages (nos.19-25) huddled together at different angles and elevations, making a picture of cosy domesticity from a bygone age. The thatched house next door may well be from the same era. Its neighbour to the right (no.39), opposite the *White Lion* pub, is early 18th-century in origin.
Cross over. The house before the pub, Jesselton Cottage, dates from the late 17th/early 18th-centuries. Further down, opposite the Post Office, and just before the chapel, is another partially-hidden building, The Croft, recently re-thatched, with a church-like gateway at the side and a datestone: 1748, probably from the rebuilding of an earlier house - indeed it contains evidence of medieval work and is reckoned by some villagers to be among the oldest buildings in the village.
For a short detour, turn left at the chapel into Chapel Lane and proceed along the path. This leads into a small park with a small stream and pond, and contains a newly-created enclosed area for dog-walkers,

called The Meadows. If you go on across the busy main road ahead, you can walk across the meadow, close by the river, to Newton - but it can be very muddy. Alternatively, if you want a short rest, go down the turning opposite (by the Post Office) which leads by the Village Hall, to a larger park and cricket ground.

Grafton Road. Just past the teashop, on the corner of the road is no.2, a thatched 17th-century house, next to which (facing the church gates) is Church Farmhouse, from the same era, with a large timber-framed gateway. Yet another 17th-century house (no.6) is beside this. Across the road leading up to the corner of Wood Street is the former school, and on the opposite corner, the later Infants' school. A little away along, past Priory Way and almost opposite the entrance to Wood Street is a driveway at the end of which is an imposing large building with mullioned windows and a datestone of 1588. This is 'The Priory' (once known as Geddington House), a former manor house belonging to the Abbey of Bury St.Edmunds. (The other manor of the village, of which nothing remains, belonged to the Crown). From the 17th century, it was in the possession of the Maydwell family (who have brass memorials in the church) for nearly 180 years. One of the surviving outbuildings is almost as old as the house itself.

On the other side of the road as it leaves the village, is an interesting 18th-century thatched house (no.17) attached to a pantile roofed building on its right by an upper 'bridge' of brickwork. Nearby no.9 was once the Quaker Meeting House.

Local crafts: *Book Illustration: Gussie Woods, 19 Skeffington Close, (01536) 742203. *Rural Art: Ian Jones, 19 Newton Road. Tel. (01536) 743612 * Art: Madeleine Weeden, 8 Chase Hill. Tel (01536) 746462.

Snippets:

*The Royal Hunting Lodge: Geddington was once very popular for royal visitors who stayed here frequently (particularly Richard I, John, Henry II and Edward I, who came in 1274, 1275 and 1279) and used this lodge (built by Henry I) as a base for their hunting in nearby Geddington Chase. It was a fine building with separate chapels for the king and queen and several windows, one of which had a painted image of Edward I. The lodge stood a short distance away behind the church. Nothing now remains, though some pieces of masonry from its site are in the church.

An interesting incident is supposed to have occurred whilst King William of Scotland was staying at the lodge one Good Friday, at the invitation of Richard I, who was briefly back in England, from the Crusades (and a spell of imprisonment in Austria) during the spring of 1194. The 'Wat Tyrell' referred to in the poem, is the man who is reputed to have shot William II ('Rufus') with an arrow, whilst he was hunting in the New Forest in 1100. The story was put into poetry in the closing years of the 19th century by Charles Montagu Douglas Scott, as 'The Ballad of Geddington Chace' :

> There rode forth into Geddington Chace
> The Kings of the South and the North Countrèe:
> Said Richard then, "By Goddès grace
> A royal hart soon slain should be.
>
> "King William o' Scotland, bide thou there,
> Behind that trusty oaken-tree,
> And I to that one will repair,
> So may we shoot our arrows free."
>
> And as King William o' Scotland stood
> And mused beneath the greenwood tree,
> He said to himself, "By Christès blood,
> An I mis-shoot when it comes to me!
>
> "And if my arrow should hap to slay
> The King my host, no great pitèe;
> But how should I chance to ride away
> From this false land to my pwn countrèe?
> "In the south Wat Tyrell had many a friend,

*And he could gain the trackless sea;
But how should I fare to this land's end,
Where every man mistrusteth me?"*

*And as King Richard of England stood
And mused beneath the greenwood tree,
He said to himself, "By Christès blood,
An I mis-shoot when it comes to me!*

*"And if my arrow should hap to slay
The King my guest, no great pitèe;
And why should I care what men might say,
Am I not lord of this whole countrèe?*

*Of his liege Wat Tyrell so made an end,
May all such men accursèd be!
But I should be slaying a false-fair friend
Who covets the crown and the realm of me."*

*They waited the morn, they waited the noon,
But never a hart did either see;
They waited the even, until the Moon
Rose up to God in her purity.*

*Then soft to himself said Scotland's King,
"God willed this crime was not to be.
That I should ever so foul a thing
Have thought, may it now pardoned be!"*

*Then low to himself, King Richard he said,
"God's grace this day have savèd me
From killing a man who hath broken my bread.
For the evil thought may I pardoned be!"*

*So the Kings returned to Geddington town,
Where a feast was spread for their revelry;
But or ever they drank the red wine down,
Each at the other oft looked he,*

*And said to himself, "Now God be praised
No hart in the forest today saw we,
Or never thy goblet had been raised
To drink this merry toast with me."*

* An intriguing incident took place in 1576 and concerns Mary Queen of Scots who, whilst imprisoned in Derbyshire, was robbed by two men who fled south to the Forest with money and jewellery. They were captured and taken to London, where they confessed to hiding the jewels in Geddington Chase. With a group of men under Edward Brudenell of Deene, they combed the woods. The results of their search have never been recorded, but it is believed that the valuables still lie buried there.

* Grafton Road was originally known as East Street; Wood Street as Wood End; and The Maltings known variously as Star Lane, Kiln Lane or Hipwell's Jitty.

Walks around the area:

Geddington Chase: one of the last remaining large stretches of Rockingham Forest where you can get a taste of how the forest used to be. You may well disturb a herd of deer silently crossing the track ahead of you. A rabbit will scamper out of your way. A hare may be seen running across an adjoining field. It is a place for a communion with nature, away from the hustle and bustle of traffic and modern life. Two lodges (Upper and Nether) once stood in the Chase. You get there by following Wood Lane to its end where its sealed surface becomes a dirt track and curves (at the Stanion footpath turn-off and old farm buildings) uphill along 'Clay Dick' or Green Lane, an old cattle drovers' road that leads into Brigstock. This is now inaccessible to traffic and requires stout footwear for the rambler to counter the ruts and muddy patches as it progresses, but it is a very rewarding 'long' walk.

* There is another walk to Brigstock, almost parallel to the above, but it can be hard to negotiate at certain times, despite being well-signposted for most of the way. Use of an Ordnance Survey map advisable.

* Stanion. This is an excellent walk with fine views of parts of Rockingham Forest around you en route. Take the track to Geddington Chase, but at the bend and farm outbuildings, leave the track and turn left (signposted) and passing to the left of those buildings, head along the side of the field to the edge of the forest. The route is signposted. There is a lot of wildlife in the vicinity.

Refreshment: The Eleanor House Teashop by the Cross, for cream teas and homemade food.

GLAPTHORN (Glappa's place by the thorns).

The village is virtually in two contrasting parts, Upper and Lower, which are separated by a brook and linked by a road, Brookside.

Church: St Leonard's. Earliest parts: mid 12th-century. 17th-century tower. Medieval paintings include St Christopher, and Doom. Some medieval woodwork. 15th-century font. Communion rail and bench (17th-century). An iron bier can be seen.

Former pubs: the *Crown Inn* (early 19th-century), the *Royal Oak*. There is no pub today.

School: 1847 for 70 children.

Other buildings and places of interest:

Entering Upper Glapthorn from the Benefield Road: the first building on the left is the school (still in use). Many 19th-century buildings line the road, including Kimberley Cottage (just past the school), Rose Cottage next door, and opposite, The Cottage.

Further along the main road, leaving the village, on the right stands the former Manor House, now Manor Farm, whose earliest part dates from c.1538. It was almost entirely rebuilt towards the end of that century by a member of the Brudenell family, Robert (of Deene).

Brookside: entering from the main road the left corner of Brookside (the turning to the right) is the former *Crown Inn* (with the old car park still at the rear). Proceed down Brookside, over the bridge and up the hill.

Entering Lower Glapthorn (from Brookside):

Two thatched dwellings stand on opposite sides: on the left, an 18th-century house; on the right, Rosebank Cottage adjoining 17th-century Melton Cottage. Across the road stands South Farm House and Floral Cottage, both 17th-century. Almost next door are two adjoining early 19th-century buildings: Oak Cottage and the Old Post Office. Almost opposite, on the church side, is The Little Manor, formerly the *Royal Oak* built in the last century on the site of an earlier building. Opposite the church, stands 17th-century Lower Farm, with its outbuildings and wide yard. Near the end of the road on the church side adjoining Laburnum Cottage, is 17th-century Hope Cottage.

Local crafts: Woodgraining/Marbling: John Belcher, White Beams, Benefield Road. Tel. 01832 272181.

Walks around the area:

*Leaving the village, just past the school, a track by a field on the right takes you to a remnant of Rockingham Forest: Short Wood (see below) which lies about half-way between Glapthorn and Southwick. At the end of the path is what is believed to be the former gamekeeper's house, Shortwood, which dates from the mid 1800s.

*A longer walk entails continuing some distance along the Benefield Road, with fine views of the spread-out countryside on the left. A little way past two houses on the right you will see a large thicket. This is **Glapthorn Cow Pastures**, now covered with trees and shrubs, particularly blackthorn which provides an ideal breeding ground for the black hairstreak butterfly. This is one of the reasons why the woodland has been designated a site of Special Scientific Interest, and is a Nature Reserve under the care of The Wildlife Trust for Northamptonshire. There are excellent walks within (at any time of the year), with several tracks criss-crossing your route, glades and a pond. There is a wealth of nature to be seen with a variety of birds and trees. The ground is wet and muddy in many places so waterproof footwear or boots are recommended.

GEDDINGTON: the Eleanor Cross

GEDDINGTON: the Old School and the Eleanor Cross, from Grafton Road

Also at the entrance to the Reserve is a track and a sign marked: Provost Lodge Farm.This building is at the end of the track on the right, and was once Provost Lodge, of medieval origin. You can also turn the track off before the Lodge, taking the public bridleway on the right to Shortwood.

GRAFTON UNDERWOOD (settlement by the grove).

A series of small bridges (18th and 19th-century) cross the stream which runs parallel with the main road, the entire length of this virtually one-street village. Ducks tend to slow any passing traffic down as they cross the road or congregate in the middle of it! Grafton is a quiet village and a conservation area, with many pleasant old buildings (some still thatched) on each side of the stream.

Church: St James the Apostle. Earliest parts: 12th-century. Thirteenth-century tower with gargoyles. Fourteenth century spire. Late 13th-century Priest's Doorway. Memorial brass from the 14th century. Early 18th-century pulpit. Stained glass window given by 384th Bombardment Group of US Airforce, one of the groups stationed nearby during World War II.
Former 'pub': the *Duke's Arms* : 1645 (originally a beer retailer, now a farmhouse. It stands on the corner of Geddington Road).
Former school : 1866 (by Duke of Buccleuch) for 60 children. School House: 1855.
Other buildings and places of interest:
Coming towards the village along the Geddington Road, past Boughton House en-route, you will see a grey marble tablet standing on the left hand side.This is a memorial to the US units that were stationed here during the Second World War. In 1992, Grafton was one of the Forest villages that commemorated the beginning of their association with US bomber groups 50 years earlier. The memorial marks the end of what once was the main runway where Flying Fortresses took off on missions, and here and on both sides of the road to Brigstock are the remnants of the Airforce base with the ruins of its buildings scattered around in secluded spots.
As you continue towards the village, you will see on the right three thatched cottages (nos. 20-22) which are late 17th/early 18th-century in origin. Further along on the same side, before the road junction, stands Spring Cottage opposite which there is a stone well head.
The imposing long, thatched building on the corner as you turn right into the Main Street is 17th-century in origin, and is now known as The Dukes Arms Farmhouse (see above). Some of its outbuildings date from the same period. Proceeding along the street on the left-hand side, you will come to an 18th-century building used today as a shop and the Post Office (here you can also obtain the keys to the church).Between here and the phone box down the street are a string of mainly l7th and18th-century houses, nos. 32-42, many of them thatched, adding a certain old-world charm to the scene. Amongst the group is the Old Rectory (1653), formerly The Manor House. Its barn has a datestone of 1676.
Carry on down the road past the turning on the left to the Village Hall, and cross over to the turning leading off on the right. Along here to the right are two thatched 18th-century houses. Retrace your steps back to the main street and turn left. The building on your left across the plank is the old school. The next track to the left leads to the church and to its right the large Rectory which dates from 1868.
Continue your walk alongside the stream, shaded by the overhanging trees of the grassland behind the long stone wall.At the footpath sign, along the track on the left there are some early 18th-century thatched houses.
Snippets:
* The village became associated with the Montagus of nearby Boughton in 1748, when the manor was bought from the Fitzpatrick family.
* A popular story in the village tells of a schoolteacher associated with a previous building on the site of the old schoolhouse, in the late18th century, and who produced ornate writing with a pen between his teeth, because of his lack of hands and arms.
* There is annual street fair every summer which attracts many visitors.
Grafton Park Wood on the right hand side of the Brigstock road is worth a visit, with a signposted leisurely walk in the shade of the trees, and ample car parking within.

GREAT OAKLEY (clearing among the oaks).

Nestling among trees in a hollow and on slopes around Harpers Brook, the original village has managed to retain much of its identity, despite being encroached on by Corby. Being close to Kingswood and Beanfield Lawn, it was frequently involved in violent incidents involving damage to woodland, or poaching - either actively or in a witnessing role! There are fascinating surviving pieces of the past both visible, and tucked away. The village has lost its thatched roofs, but pantile roofs are very much in evidence on outbuildings at the rear of dwellings.

Church: St Michael's (St Michael The Archangel). Earliest parts: early-13th century. Embattled tower. Unusual low-pitched roof. 13th-century font. Early 16th-century Flemish glass depicting angels' heads. Seventeenth-century communion rail. Hatchments and memorials to the Brooke and de Capell Brooke families of Oakley Hall. Monument to Thomas Brooke d.1638. Many relics from Pipewell Abbey brought to the church by the Brooke family in 1544. These include some medieval figured floor tiles depicting dragons, creatures, crescents and flowers; choir stalls with carved heads at the ends; and four misericords with a crusader monk, a pelican feeding its young, a grotesque head (possibly a 'green man'), and an old man with a scythe and hourglass (either Old Father Time or Death). The church is set in a peaceful position amongst yew trees within Oakley Park.

Former school: built 1867 by Sir William de Capell Brooke (for 35 children). Closed 1957. For many years, prior to its building, lessons took place in a farmhouse kitchen.The schoolhouse next door was built in 1871. The building is now used as an office.

Pub (at Oakley Hay): the *Spread Eagle* dating from 1759 (formerly a coaching inn on the Kettering-Rockingham-Uppingham turnpike road, now the A 6013 Kettering-Corby road)

Former pub: the *Chequers*. It closed around 1870.

Other buildings and places of interest:

Great Oakley Hall. Situated in the park, close to the church, it was built with stone from Weldon, around 1555 by Thomas Brooke for his wife and eighteen children. The Brooke family bacame sole lords of the manor, whose later members included Elizabeth I's 'Master of the Hart Hounds'; a notable magistrate who presided at one of the famous Witchcraft Trials in Northampton in 1612; and an explorer, Sir Arthur de Capell Brooke, who founded the Raleigh Society in 1830, from which the Royal Geographical Society was born. A descendant of the family still lives in the Hall today. It is not open to the public.

The Mound beside the Village Hall: was built by an eccentric vicar during the 1890s, with the help of village children, whom he would reward with sums of money, depending on the size of the contribution (soil, stones, bricks, etc) they brought along. Why he built the mound was always a subject for speculation, with the favourite theory being that he wanted to get nearer to Heaven! The real reason was a long-standing dispute with the local squire. The mound got higher as he began using parts of the Vicarage roof and walls, and he stopped taking services as his comments and behaviour became more unpredictable.The Vicarage never recovered and was pulled down between 1920 and 1921, with the Village Hall being built in its place.

Monks Well: lies partially-hidden in a field close to the brook behind Bridge Farm. Now capped and enclosed in brickwork, it is best seen from the gates to the footpath leading through the park. The well, whose water had a reputation for purity and taste, was formerly used by the monks from Pipewell who came over to Great Oakley to take the services in the church.

Brooke Road: opposite the Village Hall, is the yard and forge of the former blacksmiths. The 19th-century house facing the yard (no.8) stands on the site of older buildings, and contains some of the former stonework and timber. In the gable end overlooking the yard, can be seen two unusual hollow figures in a framed recess, a relic from Pipewell Abbey.

Home Farm Close: Home Farm was originally the main farm in the village (at one time there were as many as twelve, around the Estate), and dates from 1787 with a porch added in 1849.

Woodlands Lane: on the other side of Oakley Park, opposite the old drovers road, 'The Headway'. Originally the site of other houses (on the park side), as well as a farmhouse (the kitchen of which was used as a Nonconformist chapel) and the village poorhouse. The village pub, the *Chequers* used to stand here, as part of Woodlands Farm (the large building on the right). The house with the post box was one of three former post offices, with the village store next door.The small building opposite was the former shoemaker's hut. The end section of the long building by the track on the left, once housed a family of thirteen! Beyond the gates at the end of the road is a field lined with paving slabs. This facilitated access to the railway station, that stood just beyond the top of the field. It was named 'Geddington Station' to avoid confusion with Great Oakley in nearby Bedfordshire.

Snippets:
* The area around the bridge in Brooke Road used to be called 'Duckpaddle' and was prone to heavy flooding. The part of the village on the other side of the park was known as 'The Other End'.
* The windmill which used to stand on the bend at the top of Mill Hill (on the road to Little Oakley) was the scene of a sad event in 1865, when the 16-year-old son of the miller suddenly became ill whilst at

work there. He died a few days later, and the miller left the young man's coat hanging on the door inside the mill, vowing never to remove it. He kept his word until his own death 26 years later. The mill was demolished in 1895. The miller's younger son, James Pain, went on to become a celebrated local benefactor, founding a brickworks in Corby and an ironstone quarrying company in the region.

* Several 19th-century houses around the village have datestones inscribed with a shield and the initials 'WDCB'. These stand for (Sir) William de Capell Brooke, who embarked on a building and rebuilding programme in the village between 1858-72. See how many you can find!

Great Oakley Meadow Local Nature Reserve:

This valuable enclave is the only surviving remnant of what was a larger reserve for a time. Fortunately further erosion via building work has been halted! It is at the eastern end of the village off The Headway, near the Oakley Heights housing development area and BAT plant, and slopes down towards the A 6013 and the *Spread Eagle* . It is a combination of traditional meadow and pasture, and consists of medieval ridge and furrow land, where pottery fragments have been found in the past, and lower grassland, both a sanctuary to a variety of species of plant and wildlife. It is in the care of The Wildlife Trust for Northamptonshire. There is an entrance from The Headway where there is an information board, or from Lewin Road, via the Public Footpath sign and stile near the Brook. Alternatively, take the track past the old claypits close to Harpers Brook. This begins from the stile at the end (left) of Field Cottages (first turning on the right after crossing the bridge on the road towards Little Oakley (almost opposite Bridge Farm).

Pocket Park: close to the City Technology College rugby pitch. Access is from a bend off Lewin Road in the newer part of the village, via a single-track road which becomes a path after passing the Cricket Club. En route you pass a former ironstone quarry, once a favourite spot for bee orchids & butterflies.

Kingswood:

Part of the original Wydehaw Walk of Rockingham Forest, a great deal of the woodland of Old and New Kingswood still survives, despite clearance of parts for agricultural and building purposes over the years, and is now a Local Nature Reserve in the care of The Wildlife Trust for Northamptonshire. There are coppice areas to encourage the growth of trees and two ponds within, as well as excellent short walks through a variety of woodland. In spring and summer there are several varieties of grasses, wild flowers and butterflies to see and the trees are filled with birdsong. Though the deer have now gone, the woods still attract plenty of wild life. Access is available all year round, and there are many entrances, one of which has an information board. It can be reached via the A6003, and A6014, and lies close to Great Oakley (near the supermarket) and the Danesholme area on the edge of Corby.

Walks around the area:

There are four excellent walks.

* One leads to Pipewell, and starts at the end of Field Cottages just past the road bridge over Harpers Brook. En route you pass the old village claypits on the right, where brickmaking was once a thriving trade, the Great Oakley Meadow Nature Reserve and the *Spread Eagle* pub. The field to the left was once the village cricket ground. Alongside the Brook at this point, kingfishers may occasionally be seen. The walk has recently been cleared, re-stiled and signposted.

* The second walk allows you to get to Newton and Geddington. There are two possible routes. The first is to walk up Slab Field at 'The Other End' towards the old station. At the road cross over to the stile on the other side and make your way diagonally across the field towards the railway arch. Pass under this and across the field at the end of which is another stile and a small bridge over a rivulet. Continue uphill keeping the hedge to your right until you see some pylons. For Newton, turn right and follow the hedge down to the road (where you turn left), or for Geddington take a diagonal path (north easterly direction) across the fields, over the farm track and and carry on until you reach the road where you turn left. Both routes are <u>not</u> signposted so you need to be vigilant!

An alternative for Geddington is to take the road to Little Oakley, past the railway bridge and bends (near the viaduct) and look for the Public Footpath sign on the right (the left takes you across fields and through the woods of Oakley Purlieus to old Corby). Go through the gate and head for Oakley Bushes ahead, at the other side of which, you can take up the walk as above.

* For Little Oakley begin at the signpost in Oakley Park, where the track curves round. Walk up the short field, over some stiles and head downhill towards the viaduct which you pass beneath. The walk is more or less straight, with several stiles, fences or gates to negotiate, and is not signposted until you are almost in Little Oakley. If you keep to the right of the hedges, you should have no problems!

* For old Corby, begin as for Little Oakley, but when in the second field past the viaduct, at the farm track, turn left and proceed uphill keeping parallel with the line of pylons on your left. Look out for stiles and gates. Sometimes there is a line marked out across the field to guide you. Head at angle for the north west of the clump of woods (Oakley Purlieus) in the near distance. A rough grassy track takes you through the quiet woods (where you may well see deer) towards the old part of the town. Pass under a small railway bridge and up a slope. Turn left through a small industrial estate (where the old claypits of a former brickmaking works stand). Cross over the main road (A427) into Station Road and on the bend past the bus garages, turn right into the village.

GRETTON ('large settlement').

Originally the third largest village in Rockingham Forest, it is made up of several streets and the views of the surrounding area are nothing short of spectacular. Its streets reveal many surprises architecturally, and walks in the area are extremely rewarding.

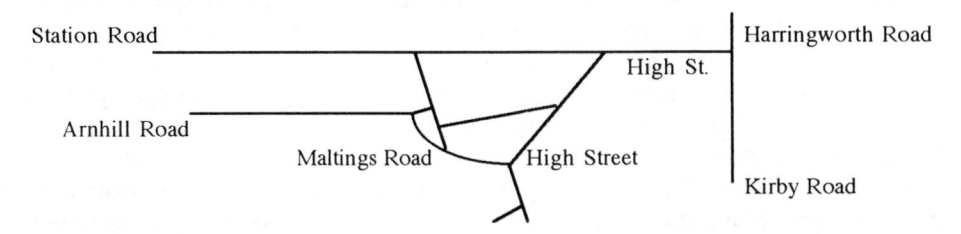

Church: St James (the Great). Earliest parts: 12th and 13th-century. Broach spire. Remnants of medieval wall painting near east window. Medieval niches. Octagonal font. Some 18th-century box pews, choir stalls and pulpit. Some 17th and 18th-century monuments (including the Hatton family). Hatchment above south door. Restored during the 19th century.
Baptist Chapel (opposite the *Blue Bell* in The High Street): 1813 (licensed 1825).
Weslyan Chapel: 1801 (demolished in the 1960s). Connected to four homes in 1925. Craxford Road.
Pubs: the *Hatton Arms*, the *Talbot*, the *Blue Bell Inn*.
Former pubs: the *Fox* (by the High Street and Station Road junction. Now a private house known as The Old Fox); the *White Hart* (32, High Street, now White Hart Cottage/Gretton Stores); the *Crown* (now Crown Cottage, High Street); the *Cat and Fiddle* (now 19-21 Arnhill Road).
Former school: 1853 for 140 children. Now a private house.
Other buildings and places of interest:
Arnhill Road:
The house adjoining the *Hatton Arms* (Corner Cottage) near the corner of Arnhill Road is ancient like the pub, which is believed to be one of the two oldest (15th-century) public houses in the county. The house opposite (originally two dwellings) is from the mid 18th-century. It was a village bakery until December 1970.
Maltings Road:
(On the corner) 'The Maltings' (late 17th-century) with stone mullioned windows, and further down on the opposite side 'Village Farmhouse' which is part 18th and part 19th-century. Across the road from this at the entrance to narrow Hardwick Road, is a pleasant little limestone house (Ivernia Cottage) dating from 1846, with an ornate Gothic porch and plaque. This was once known as 'The Manse' and was home of the headteacher of the village school, during which time the façade was almost entirely covered in foliage. Further along Maltings Lane is the large house from 1700 which once gave its name to this part of the village, 'The Nook'.

Station Road : The 'Old School House' (1853) is next to the church. Nos.4 and 6 (late 17th/early 18th-century) make up a thatched limestone house, with a thatched cat on the roof. Next door, nos.8 and 10 are two dwellings from the same era, as is Stonycroft (no.12) which gives the impression of being a former stone mason's house in its design with some narrow stone mullioned windows, and its large square frame above the front door with variously fashioned and engraved pieces of stonework. The last old house opposite the former station entrance was a wheelwight and carpenter's. Village children used to watch logs being sawn in the sawpit, now covered by the driveway. The long wooden building was one of the navvy huts in use during the 1870's railway construction work.
High Street : a little distance before the *Talbot* on the opposite side, is a long house (nos. 68-72) with

an oval window and a datestone which reads: 1699. A short distance away and set at an angle, is the beautiful L-shaped 17th-century thatched house 'Barn House' with its tall chimney. Another house from the same era, Pear Tree Cottage, stands next to the *Bluebell*. At the other end of the High Street are the stocks, whipping post and War Memorial, all on the Green opposite the church. Unfortunately, the ravages of time have been at work and the stocks and whipping post (both probably 18th-century) desperately need protection against further erosion.

On the right past them, some way along stands Manor Farmhouse, an L- shaped ironstone and limestone building with a circular window and a datestone of 1675. It was formerly known as 'Warren Farm' but was changed by one of its former owners earlier this century because the name was not 'posh' enough! On the left-hand (church) side are long thatched Hall Cottage (nos.15 and 17), and no.13, both dating from the 18th century. Stoneleigh, the next house, was originally from the same century but was partly rebuilt in 1840. It was formerly a parchment maker's: the soaking tanks and drying sheds are still standing. Chantry Cottage (nos. 5 and 7) is a T- shaped house from the mid 17th-century with a well in the garden, complete with handle and chain.

Gretton House and its Coach House appear, dating from the mid18th century (though a small part is thought to be the remnant of a 16th-century farmhouse). An imposing building, it was lived in by a succession of different families including after the First World War, Major D.H.Evans, who was instrumental in the electrification of the lighting in the church, and in providing seating by the war memorial). The house has been used variously at different times since then : at the outbreak of World War II it was requisitioned by the War Office as a Military Hospital for troops stationed in the area ; at the end of the war it was used by Stewarts and Lloyds as a Rehabilitation Centre for convalescent steelworkers, and is now a home for the mentally handicapped. These two buildings mark the end of the High Street.

<u>Harringworth Road</u> (leaving the village). Here stands White Owl Cottage, on the left-hand side - a fine small 18th-century thatched cottage, with a stream running along the front.

<u>Kirby Road</u> : Rose Cottage, is late 17th/early 18th-century, and is part-limestone, part-ironstone.

Pocket Park: a paddock cared for by many volunteer groups (junction of High Street & Kirby Road).
Local Crafts: Handweaving: Elizabeth Palmer, Crown Cottage, 46 High Street (next to the post office/shop).Tel: (0536) 770303.

Snippets:
*Forest corruption affected Gretton in 1251, when a villager named 'William, son of Mary' in jail at Rockingham Castle for offences against the greenery, managed to bribe the keeper for a nightly visit home on payment of half a mark (about 32p) and a promise to be back at daybreak! The visit must have been short as quite a walk was involved between the two villages! The keeper was heavily fined at the court for his goodwill!

* Like Blatherwycke, the churchyard is witness to another burial mystery. James Chappell, a black servant of Sir Christopher Hatton, whom he rescued from a building catastrophe (the rubble of a castle struck by lightning), was rewarded for his deed with a large sum of money and is reputed to have become the landlord of The Hatton Arms in the village. On his death in 1730 he was buried in the churchyard - the mystery is where? His headstone and remains were at one stage removed and reburied elsewhere.Was he disinterred because of prejudice? The puzzle has never been solved!

* In 1840, scandal hit the village when the renewal of a licence for the *Blue Bell Inn* was refused because of the 'bad character of the landlady and the bad reputation of the house'. A petition which led to the refusal had been signed by a clergyman and a group of 'upstanding villagers'. There must have been a lot of drinking in Gretton at that time, since records refer to 20 licences being held there!

* Former street names: Kirby Road was 'Backside'; School Road was The Gap; Station Road was Stoney Lane; Southfield Road was Fullen Road; Caistor Road was Castors Lane; Corby Road was Wood Lane; Hardwick Road was Almond's Lane; The Maltings was The Nook and Pound Lane; Arnhill Road was comprised then of four different parts: 'Cat and Fiddle', West Wells, Little London and 'Town's End'; and part of the High Street was known as Workhouse Lane (giving an indication where this building once stood: believed to be what is now no.57). There was also a Pounds Lane (marking the site of the old village pound) at the Arnhill Road/Maltings Road junction. Clay Lane (between Arnhill Road and Station Road) had what may be a clay pit and building yard at the bottom.

* The former Manor House and its fishponds were sited at the rear (north and north east) of the church, in an area known as Hall Field. An interesting part to walk through. There are a set of water troughs in a wet area at the back of the church, and a bench to sit on to admire the views ahead. Nearby, to the north west, there are three ancient mounds.

* A hoard of ancient artefacts was found along Harringworth Road (OS. SP 910946), including some iron bars believed to have been used for currency purposes (or even possibly for making tools or weapons).
* The former vicarage (partly late 17th-century) is nearby (no.2 Station Road).
* Railway Station: opened to passenger traffic in 1880, closed in April 1966 (though goods traffic still passes through). It lies at the bottom of Station Road on the left.
* Between here and Rockingham stands a **lost settlement**, Coton (Cotes). The area was extensively mined by the Romans for its iron-ore which was transported to the Welland via a specially-built road. The exact site (using an OS map) is SP 876926. It was deserted between the mid 14th- and 15th-centuries.
* Symptomatic of the times we live in: 24 early houses (16 of them thatched) have been demolished in the village since the end of World War II, and another 11 have been converted. More are certain to follow.

Walks around the area:
* There is an excellent walk with fine views, across the fields and the River Welland to Thorpe-by-Water and from there, along the road to Lyddington. Begin at the footpath by the side of the church.
* Rockingham (a walk with sweeping views of hill and dale : see under Rockingham. Begins from a signposted track at the side of a farm on the Corby Road, nearly opposite the Kirby Road turning). It is now part of the Jurassic Way.
* The walk along the quiet main road to Harringworth is rewarding, with fantastic views of the Welland valley to your left. There is now a resting place en route, with benches.
* There is also a 'circular' walk round the back of the village. Walk down Arnhill Road to the very end where it peters out and becomes a track. Walk along this, pass under the railway arch and walk down to the main road. Turning right leads you into Station Road. The walk is ideal for nature lovers who will enjoy the sights and sounds of the countryside in the spring or summer - but watch out for nettles!

Kirby Hall. The Hall was built on the site of a former house in 1570-5 by Sir Humphrey Stafford of Blatherwycke, on whose death it was sold to Sir Christopher Hatton. Two large wide-arched gateways to the Hall, from Hatton's time, stand to the east and west. Various alterations were made to the property by Hatton himself and by Christopher Hatton III in 1638-40. Royal guests who stayed at the Hall include King James I who stayed there three times between 1612 and 1619, and earlier, Queen Anne of Denmark. The Hall stayed in the possession of the Hatton family until 1764.

The extensive gardens have recently been relaid. In their time they were of some fame due to the third and fourth Hattons who were acknowledged horticulturists. There are also remains of a great tree-lined avenue. Today it is under the care of English Heritage and is open to visitors most of the year round. It is remarkably well-preserved in places (such as the Great Hall and Inner Courtyard), and peacocks strut around the grounds which provide an ideal spot for a picnic. There are historical, musical and craft events from time to time. There is also a legend that lights and shadows appear, with ghostly music, singing and dancing audible on dark, windy nights.

Lost village: Kirby village and church stood to the south and west of the Hall, on both sides of the stream that formed the boundary of the property. It was always a small settlement, and by 1584 few houses remained. Both the village and the church had disappeared by 1700.

HARRINGWORTH (people of Hæringa's enclosure).

Harringworth is an attractive village in the Welland Valley, dominated at the Gretton Road end by the magnificent viaduct. The village's irregular shape and earthworks can be seen from the top of Scotgate Hill (the road to Laxton and Deene), an indication that the village was once much larger.

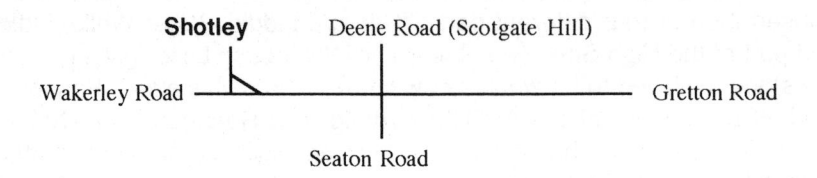

```
                    Shotley      Deene Road (Scotgate Hill)
                       |                   |
      Wakerley Road ───┴───────────────────┴─────────── Gretton Road
                                           |
                                      Seaton Road
```

Church: St John The Baptist. Late 12th/early 13th-century tower. Broach spire (repaired in 1681-3). 13th-century font. Pieces of medieval masonry and rubble in the vicinity. Some 15th- and 16th-century stained glass (bird in a rondel, eagle and head). 17th-century oak pulpit from Barrowden.

GREAT OAKLEY: St. Michael's Church

Bretton House.

KIRBY HALL

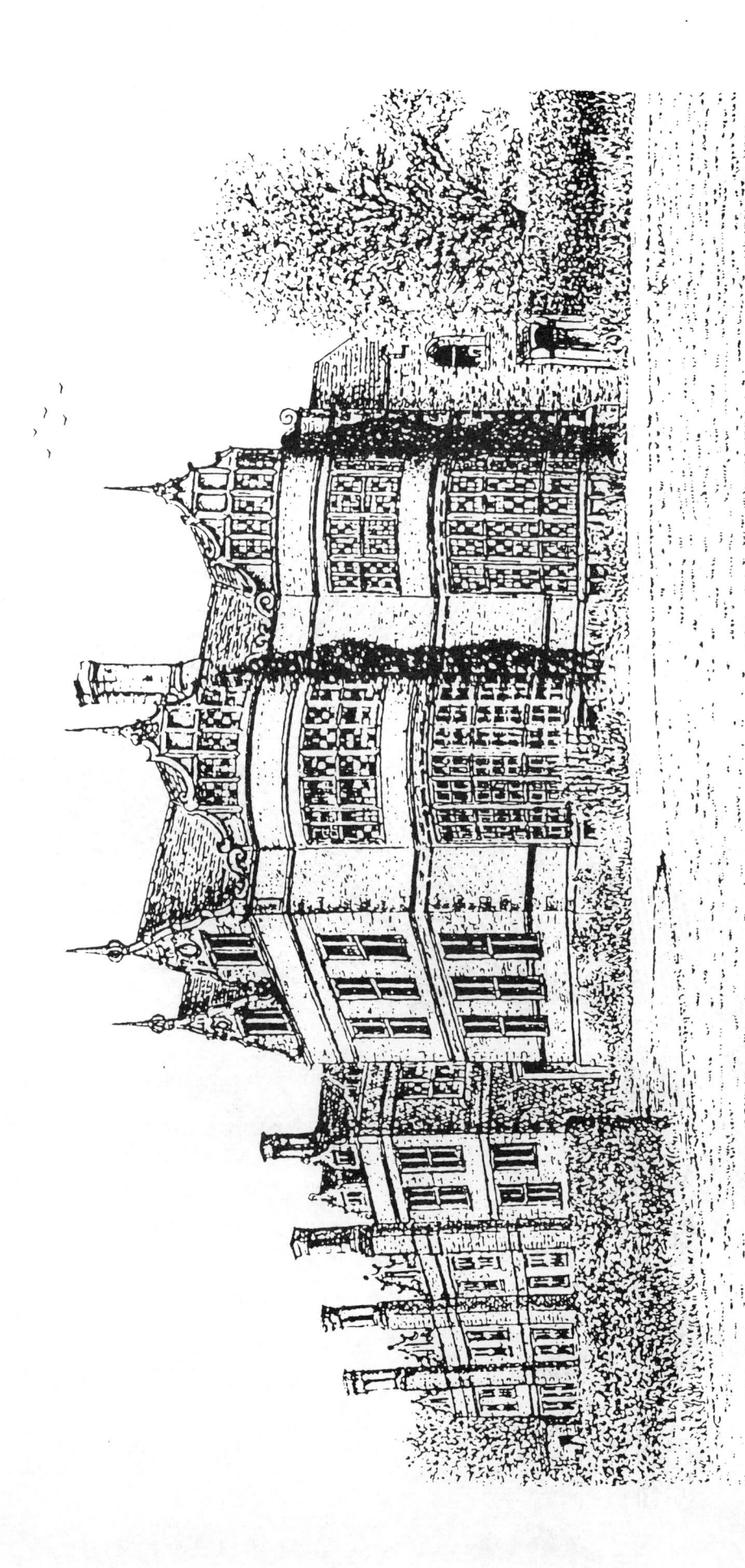

RUSHTON: The Triangular Lodge

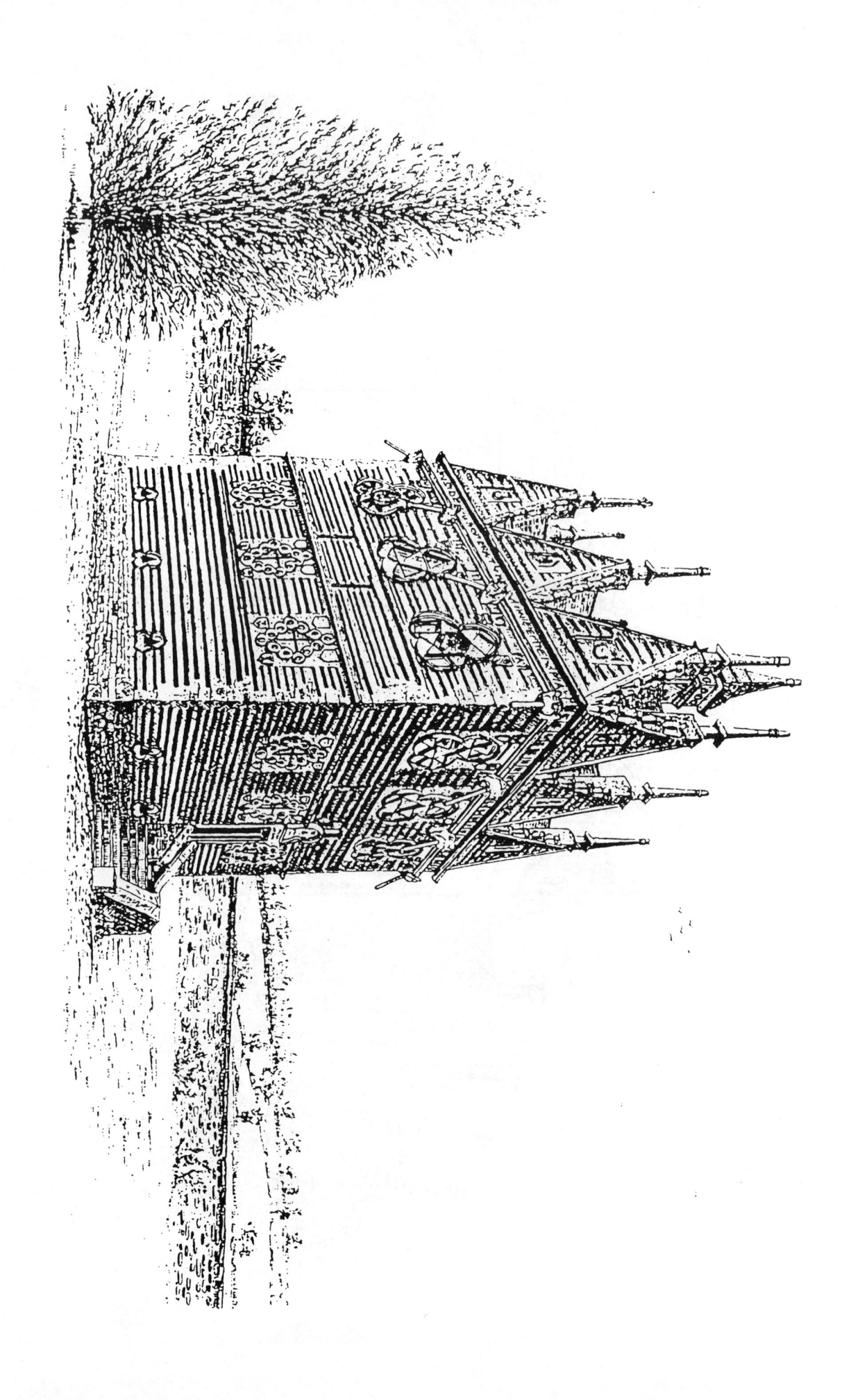

Communion rails (18th-century). Elaborate wall monuments and early 18th-century family vault of the Tryon family (lords of the manor) in an area enclosed with iron railings. Fire hook for removing thatch. The clock was erected in 1877. On the floor of the nave there is a brass and three floor slabs, one of which (currently under carpet) is to a vicar (Matthew Palmer) who died in 1752 at the age of 110 years old! At the churchyard entrance, is a thick-walled Roman coffin, excavated on the edge of the village, and currently containing plants.

Pub: the *White Swan* (built on the site of a medieval inn). It is an early 19th-century building incorporating 16th- and 17th-century masonry from the former inn. Inscriptions from the 18th century are also visible. Apart from re-used items, there are features which imitate those of earlier periods to good effect. It is well worth a visit for a drink and a meal in its fine, comfortable surroundings.

Former school: 1825 for 70 children by one of the Tryon family. Set back a little from the main (Gretton) road. 'The Old School House' as it is known today is used for social functions in the village, acting in the capacity of the village hall.

Other buildings and places of interest:

Begin at Seaton Road by the church. Behind the churchyard, across the field to the left stand Manor Cottages, which contain parts of the former Manor House. The village was the home of Lord John Zouche who fought at Bosworth in the War of the Roses. The family held the manor from the 13th century (via William la Zouche in 1299) but it gradually passed to the Tryon family around 1617. After 1652, on the death of Moses Tryon, the family moved to Bulwick and by 1719 the Manor House was virtually dismantled but some of its remaining parts were later incorporated into the present Manor Cottages. There is a 15th-century upper-floor window. One of the original fishponds of the manor still exists.

Across the road from the church is a fascinating house (no. 25), from where the key to the church may be obtained. It is a thatched cottage, part limestone, part ironstone, in two sections incorporating a small 13th century religious building, perhaps a monastery. It was referred to in 1577 as 'The Hermitage'. The eastern part occupies the former chancel and the later western part (*c.*1800) replaced the nave. Strange happenings have occurred in the house over the years as the long-time owners will testify!

The site outside this house is even more remarkable. In the field opposite, prior to the erection of a farm outbuilding, it is said that a row of skeletons was dug up in 1984, some with their heads missing. They were dated as being 2,000 years old. Unfortunately, there are no archæological records to verify this, but it is interesting to speculate about a major battle or a ritual slaughter having taken place here! What is fact however, is that human bones have continued to be be dug up in the garden of no.25 and in the vicinity.

The Old Vicarage on the other (left) side of the church was rebuilt between 1833-5, incorporating some of the older building, and was extended in 1860. The large manor house in Seaton Road to the right of the church, with hipped roofs and rubbled walls is late 17th-century. The fine old village pub further along, signals the entry to the centre of the village, where four roads meet, marked by the Market Cross. Medieval (14th-century) in origin, a new head was added in 1850. It is believed to be associated with the la Zouche family, in whose time an annual fair and weekly (Tuesday) market were granted in 1387.

The old smithy which faces it is 19th-century and there is an anvil standing outside. Its small ornate chimney top however is medieval (possibly from the former manor house) and was added much later to an earlier house on the site. It is made of limestone and has an octagonal spire.

Cross Farm opposite the blacksmith's was originally 16th-century but was largely rebuilt in the 19th century with some of the original parts. Cross Store, next to the pub, is part of the original Maltings building.

Walk along the Gretton Road towards **Harringworth Viaduct** which was built between 1875 and 1878. This impressive structure straddles the landscape and can be seen from afar. It has 82 arches, each with a 40ft. span, and is three quarter miles in length. The former station stands on a hill to the left as you leave the village on the Gretton Road. Continuing on, past the single railway arch, and just before the bend, set back from the road on the right, is a tombstone marking the spot where a vicar's wife fatally jumped from her carriage after its horse had panicked whilst descending the hill in 1884.

Retracing your steps towards the village, you will see a large thatched building on the right (nos 46-48) from the 17th century. More buildings from the same era appear on the left side (including no.9, The Old School House, at the side of which is a path to the former school which lies behind), and some from the 18th century on the right, as you proceed towards the crossroads.

Continue past the Market Cross, along the Wakerley Road, on the right of which is Lime Farm. It dates from the late 17th-century, has mullioned windows, and does not have a door facing the street. There are modern stables on the other side of the road, ideal for a ride around the fascinating local countryside.

A mixture of houses from different ages mark the end of the village as it almost merges with **Shotley.** This tiny settlement can be seen on the right, a little way down the road towards Wakerley. It is a very pleasant short stroll to the village itself: on the way out of Harringworth you pass Shotley Farm House (17th-century, with later additions) and the thatched Post House which is early 19th-century. Opposite this house is a 17th-century dwelling (no.11). A narrow foot track/holloway leads off on the right-hand side of the road.The village was once much larger and there is evidence of earlier, 'lost' parts lying on either side. As you enter the settlement, the thatched house on right has an old water pump (painted white) in its garden. A former Congregational Chapel from 1867 stands next door. Behind this is Shotley Cottage (1829). A long thatched house (Pear Tree Cottage) which is part 17th-century, stands opposite, at the road entrance to the hamlet.

Walks in the area :
* Harringworth Lodge stands some way out of the village. The former hunting lodge is ancient (part 15th-century with some beautiful windows) with 16th/17th-century additions. It stands in a large former deerpark (stocked with deer from Rockingham Forest in 1232-4, by William de Cantelupe), beside a large fishpond, and a coppice in the background. The public right of way passes close by. The best way to approach it is to the follow the Public Footpath sign at the end of Shotley, and proceed uphill until you reach a road and bridge. At the bridge cross over , make for the Footpath sign and keep going towards the woodland in the distance (Lodge Coppice). Look out for stiles. A lengthy, intriguing walk, now part of the 'Jurassic Way'.
* There is an uphill walk along the road to Gretton with excellent views to the right of the valley and the viaduct. The road to Seaton offers similar rewards, as does the road to Wakerley with its views of white Morcott Windmill on the horizon and the village of Barrowden nestling below.
* Morcott. This is an attractive walk that begins at the Public Footpath sign on the left of the Wakerley Road.This is now part of the Jurassic Way, and it takes you across wetland meadow (near Manor Cottages), along part of the course of the River Welland, over medieval Turtle Bridge (widened in the 18th century and now modernised in brick) and the dismantled railway track en route. The bridleway/lane here is called The Redhill and was a former favourite haunt of gypsies. Straight on for Morcott, or turn right for Barrowden.

ISLIP ('slippery place by the Ise')

It takes its name from the River Ise, near which it once stood, but nowadays it is close to the Nene! The village is connected with its namesake in the USA which is in the county of Suffolk, New York State.

Church: St Nicholas. Late Perpendicular style. Some 12th-century parts, but mainly 15th- century. Pinnacled tower. Very large number of gargoyles with long spouts in their mouths around the roof areas. Medieval font. Tablet to Mary Washington, wife of Sir John, Lord of the Manor of Thrapston, who was great-grandfather of George Washington, first president of the USA. The spire was damaged by lightning during a thunderstorm in the summer of 1900.
Former school: 1862 (opposite the church in School Lane). Extended 1883 & 1894. Closed 1992.
Pubs: the *Rose and Crown* (1691), the *Woolpack* (16th-century origin).
Former pub: the *Bell*
Other buildings and places of interest:
Begin at the High Street (from the Thrapston end): The Forge House (1765) stands on the corner of School Lane. It was still in operation as recently as 1973. Continuing along the High Street, groups of 17th-century houses some thatched, with wooden railings outside, line the right-hand side. Here also are former almshouses from 1706 for 'two poor widows'. Next to the row is the 17th-century Manor House with its mullioned windows. It also has the entrance porch of the former Toll House (which stood at the end of Toll Bar Road).
Further along is the *Rose and Crown* on the corner of Mill Road. The post office is opposite. The corner, where the water pump once stood, was a popular place to gather and gossip! The long house almost opposite is Washington Cottage, which once belonged to Mary Washington (see above).
Along Mill Road, on the left, is an interesting white-painted brick, thatched building, 'The Old Shop'. Mill Road leads into Ridge Road and a nature reserve. Just before Ridge Road, Mill Lane branches off

to the right towards the mill.

Retracing your steps down the High Street, you pass the recreation ground with its ornate gateway, and the Village Hall, before coming to a turning on the right, The Green, along which is one of the entrances to the church. By this entrance, with its gable end facing is an intriguing thatched cottage, St. Nicholas House, half-brick and timber frame, half-stone. It is believed to be the oldest building in the village (after the church) and its site can be traced back to the 13th century. There is a tradition handed down that it once housed stonemasons working on the church.

Continuing along the High Street, the next turning on the left is School Lane (formerly Church Lane) along which are the school on the left, and some buildings of 17th- and 18th-century origin. Opposite the school, adjoining the (other) entrance to the church, are Church Limes and Sexton's House.

Islip Mill (18th-century), was in use until 1960. It stands by the river at the bottom of Mill Lane (off Mill Road). Just pass the Mill, you will come to Thrapston Lakes and the Middle Nene Sailing Club where **sailing** for beginners and experienced sailors is possible. Tel: 01933 317511 (or 460220).

The Rockingham Forest Visitor Centre is based here with an excellent selection of literature and information (including a video screening). It is situated next to the tea room of the *Woolpack Inn*.

Local crafts: *Art: Diana Hudson, 1 Woodford Grange Farm Cottages. Tel. 01832 734057. *Art: Daphne Windsor, 57 Kettering Road. Tel. 01832 733626.

Snippets:

* The village Toll House and its successor 'The Round House' have now disappeared - the former was demolished in 1873, the latter in 1971.
* Chapel Lane which runs down the hill to the *Woolpack* and bridge, was named after what is believed to have been a medieval chapel or sanctuary where thanksgiving was given. It stood near the bridge.
* Also in Chapel Lane is Islip House with an interesting history and a ghost seen during alterations to the building! For the full story read Allan Gray's excellent book on Islip (available for inspection or purchase at the ROFTA Centre at the *Woolpack*).

KETTERING   (origin unknown though, 'settlement of Cytringa's people' has been suggested)

A fascinating town with streets and lanes oozing history. For many years it was nationally celebrated as a centre for boot and shoe-making, as well as religious reform. Some grand buildings from its affluent past are still standing. An excellent place for walking - but the town was never meant for the car!

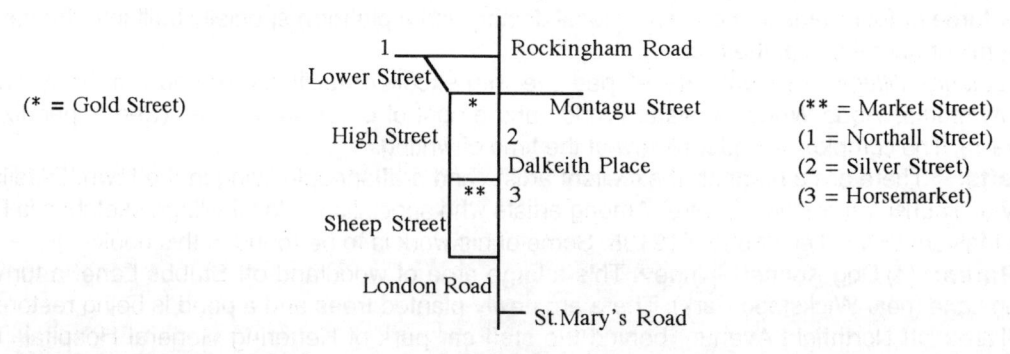

```
                            1    Rockingham Road
                      Lower Street
   (* = Gold Street)              *    Montagu Street      (** = Market Street)
                       High Street  2                      (1 = Northall Street)
                                    Dalkeith Place         (2 = Silver Street)
                                 ** 3                      (3 = Horsemarket)
                       Sheep Street

                       London Road
                                   St.Mary's Road
```

Church: St Peter and St Paul. Earliest parts c1400. Tower:1450. Elegant, well-proportioned spire : 178ft high. Short octagonal turrets. 17th-century brass monument to a former lord of the manor, Edmund Sawyer and his wife, in contemporary dress. Medieval glass. 15th-century porch with three canopied niches: the original statues of St.Peter, St.Paul and Virgin Mary with child, disappeared during the Reformation, but were replaced with new figures in recent times by a retired headmaster and writer whose hobby was stone-carving. Church restored in 1893. The ornate west gates are a memorial to generations of the Roughton family of medical practitioners. 18th-century graffiti on exterior walls. A stone stump, part of the original spire, stands in the churchyard by the footpath.

Fuller Baptist Chapel : 1861 (Gold Street).

Methodist Chapel: 1867 (Silver Street), demolished 1933.

Congregational Chapel: 1893 (London Road).

Toller (Independent) Chapel: 1723 (Gold Street). Restored 1875. Now the United Reformed Church.

Carey Mission House: 1792 (Lower Street). A commemorative plaque in a stone frame is on the wallof the grounds facing the street. The first foreign Baptist missions were inaugurated from here.

Workhouse (1837): now St Mary's Hospital.

Old Pubs (still existing) : the *Periquito Royal* (formerly the *White Hart*, and later the *Royal*. It changed its name after Queen Victoria and Albert stopped by there for refreshment en-route to a christening at Stamford in 1844. It has an oriel window); the *George Hotel* (a datestone from 1659 can be seen inside), the *Cherry Tree Inn* (both Sheep Street); the *Swan Hotel*, formerly *Swan Inn* (Montagu Street); the *Peacock*, the *Three Cocks* (Lower Street); the *Robin Hood* (Northall Street); the *Angel* (Horsemarket); the *New Inn* (Market Place); the *Rising Sun* (Silver Street).

Former pubs include: the *Old White Horse*, the *New White Horse* (High Street); the *Duke's Arms* (1667-1879), the *Sun Inn*, the *Golden Lion* (all Market Street); the *Half Moon* (Market Place); the *Crown Inn* (Gold Street), the *King's Arms* (Northall Street), the *Nag's Head Inn* (West Street), the *Fleur de Lis* (Newland Street); the *Duke of Wellington* (Horsemarket); the *Woolpack*, formerly the *Crown and Woolpack*, now a restaurant (Horsemarket); the *Talbot* (Goosepasture Lane).

Former schools : Kettering Grammar School (Gold Street). Founded 1577. Rebuilt 1856, demolished 1960s; British School: 1834 (in School Lane).

Other places worth seeing/visiting:

Alfred East Art Gallery : (Alfred East 1849-1913). Adjoins the Library. Regular exhibitions by local artists (and photographers) past and present.

Wicksteed Park. (Charles Wicksteed (1847-1931) engineer of bicycles and children's playground equipment. Wicksteed Park opened in 1921. It is a superb attraction offering rides (old and new), food, and crafts (including demonstrations) and is set in vast grounds. Entrance is free, but there is a charge for parking. Playground use is free but many attractions require the purchase of special tickets/wrist bands. Good place for a picnic.

Almshouses (1688) in Sheep Street by Edmund Sawyer.

Market Place (where there has been a market since 1227) was also used for punishments with the aid of a moveable whipping post and pillory. The Sessions House was demolished in 1805.

Manor House: At one time, Kettering had more than one manor. This large 17th and 18th-century building was built on the site of an earlier building belonging to a former lord of the menor, the Abbot of Peterborough. The Sawyer family, whose decline occurred as a result of the general financial crash caused by the 'South Sea Bubble' in 1720, were among later lords of the manor and they lived in the house. The manor of Kettering was later divided between the Montagu family of Boughton and the Watson family of Rockingham. The building now houses The Manor House Museum and can be found at the rear of the library/art gallery and Tourist Office. One of the exhibits is the 'Robinson Car', one of only three or four made in the town. A local doctor had a platform specially built into the car for performing minor operations at the rear!

Kettering Leisure Village. A recently developed site with excellent facilities for sport, a 'Body Tone' gym, beauty studio, 'Aqua World', 'Crystal World', and a host of other attractions. (See appendix for further details). The complex is under review at the time of writing.

Local crafts: * There are a number of excellent artists and craftspeople living in the town. Details at the Library or Tourist Information Centre. Among artists who specialise in local village sketches is Ron Mears, 40 Malvern Drive, Tel: 01536 512135. Some of his work is to be found in this book.

Pocket Parks: (1) Dog Kennel Spinney. This a large area of woodland off Stubbs Lane, a turning off Warkton Lane (near Wicksteed Park). There are newly-planted trees and a pond is being restored.
(2) A small area off Northfield Avenue, behind the staff car park of Kettering General Hospital. The local Fire Brigade helped to develop the site. A haven of peace away from the nearby busy A6.

Snippets:
* Being the largest settlement on the edge of the western part of the Forest area, Kettering was often viewed with suspicion of harbouring would-be poachers. Records exist well into this century of poachers caught around the Kingswood area in particular - in some cases beaten or cudgelled by gamekeepers and their helpers! The most devastating incident however, occurred in 1638 when an order was made for a search by officials of every house within a five-mile radius of Kettering (including that town) for any nets, weapons and even dogs!

* In November 1810, a 'hurricane' (similar to that of 1987) hit the region, and Kettering in particular was badly affected, with virtually every house 'suffering damage' and large numbers of trees blown down 'in all the streets'.

* Thomas Cooper Gotch (1854-1931) was born and raised in the town. He was for a period a Pre-Raphaelite-influenced artist. Several of his works can be seen in the Alfred East Art Gallery, though an appointment is usually necessary to view them. Another (earlier) member of the family, Thomas Gotch, opened the first shoe factory in Kettering in 1788, which encouraged similar operations to start up around the town. (Other members of the family gained success in architecture and publishing).

* The town has historical associations with renowned social and religious reformers: Andrew Fuller

(1754-1815), William Knibb (1803-45), William Carey (1761-1834) and Thomas Toller (1796-1885). Information leaflets available at the Tourist Office.

KINGSCLIFFE (Cliffe - slope/bank of a river).

Originally this was the second largest village in Rockingham Forest. Even now it is of considerable size, with the additon of much newer housing. It had a long association with the Crown from the time William I made it a Royal Manor. It has many streets and alleyways ('lanes'), leading down to Willow Brook and a track up to the Forest (via a sawmill). Kingscliffe was the centre of control for the Cliffe Bailiwick, and a famed wood-turning centre. It invites exploration, which must be done slowly and thoroughly, so as not to miss anything! A day could be easily spent in the area , without any loss of interest.

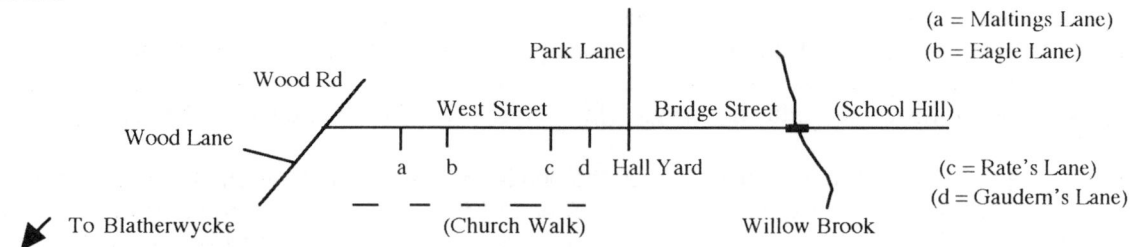

```
                                    |                    (a = Maltings Lane)
                            Park Lane                     (b = Eagle Lane)
              Wood Rd
                    West Street      Bridge Street    (School Hill)
       Wood Lane
                    | |    | |
                    a b    c d  Hall Yard             (c = Rate's Lane)
                                                      (d = Gaudern's Lane)
   ◄ To Blatherwycke    (Church Walk)     Willow Brook
```

Church: All Saints and St James. Earliest parts: 12th-century (the tower). Broach spire (13th-century). The rest of the church dates mainly from the 15th century. The pulpit was made out of 15th-century woodwork from Fotheringhay Church. Glass from the same period (with York heraldic badges) also from Fotheringhay. Interesting monuments in the (north) porch and churchyard, including in the latter, one in the shape of a writing desk to the village benefactor, William Law. There are many gargoyles on the roof. The north porch has a lozenge inscribed with a possible rebuilding date, 1663. Brass plate to Samuel Wyman (1700), a woolstapler, cautions: 'Know Reader that in dust I lie, That as you are, now so once was I, And as I am so must you be, Therefore prepare to follow me.'
Former Methodist Chapel: 1828
Former Congregationalist Chapel: 1846
School: 1881 (in Park Lane). Its future is under consideration at the time of writing.
Pub: the *Cross Keys* (17th-century).
Former pubs: the *Windmill Inn* , the *Wheel* (17th-century, now a private residence 'The Wheelhouse'), the *Maltsters Arms* (17th-century), the *Turner's Arms* (all in West Street), the *Golden Ball* (in Bridge Street), the *Wheatsheaf* (18th-century), the *Red Lion* (both in Park Street). There was also a beer house, the *Eagle Tap* during the early 19th-century off West Street/Eagle Lane.

Other buildings and places of interest:
Hall Yard
A Royal Hunting Lodge ('The King's House') which was favoured in the 13th century, by at least two kings, John and Henry III, was sited nearby, south of the church. It is thought that it went out of use during the 15th century. The name of the yard seems to be connected with the former royal bulding. Hall Farm which forms three sides of the courtyard, has its origins in medieval times and still has part of the original roof. The house was rebuilt and extended in the 17th century. One of the doorways has a datestone 'Anno 1603'.
The small narrow path to the right of the building leads to the former Fire Engine House ('erected by Subscription 1813'), The Rectory (which was a former Millhouse built in 1748 on the site of an earlier cottage) and the Mill, again rebuilt (1815) on the site of an earlier one. Among nearby outbuildings are a granary and a old bakehouse. The small bridge leads into meadowland through which the Willow Brook meanders. This is a charming spot to walk through, containing the Mill Pond, a gnarled old tree at the far end, and horses often grazing nearby.

Bridge Street (School Hill end):
The building on the other side of the road is Bridge House, a 'U' shaped building from 1827. Bearing right, there is an interesting group of inter-related buildings on both sides of the road, known as 'Elizabeth Hutcheson and William Law's Charities'.
William Law (1686-1761) was born in the village and became nationally famous for his religious

writings. When he retired in 1740, he went to live at Hall Farm with Elizabeth Hutcheson and Hester Gibbon (sister of the historian, Edward, who wrote The Rise And Fall Of The Roman Empire), where all three devoted their time religiously, improving the lot of the poor. On the Bridge House side of the road, the first of the group of buildings is a mid19th-century almshouse. This was built next door to a 17th-century cottage which was converted to a school for boys in 1745 by Hutcheson. A plaque above the door (with a sundial) reads: 'Books of Piety are lent to any Person of this or ye Neighbouring Towns'. This refers to a library of nearly 200 books which Law provided for public betterment and which he housed there, in the care of the schoolmaster.The adjoining schoolroom (now no.25) was added in 1749 and also has an inscription above the door ('Deo Adjuvante'). The last building of the set is Hutcheson's Almshouse built the same year, for 'four poor widows', with a panel: 'Vidarum Hospitiam'.

On the opposite (south) side of the road are Law's two contributions: the end building, before the wooded track, Morehay Lane, was his Almshouse (1754) for 'two poor widows or spinsters'. The second building facing it was his School and Schoolhouse, built in 1752, replacing the school, he had founded for girls earlier on the same spot, in 1727. The inscription above the door reads:'Charitati Sacrum'. The old house further along, Calvey Hay Cottage, is believed to be late 17th-century.

Bridge Street: retrace your steps back across the bridge, where just past the small service station on the right stands a conspicuous but charming small early 17th-century house with stone mullioned bay windows and a Tudor-shaped front door. On the opposite side of the road is the old Methodist Chapel (originally 1828). Beside this an early 18th-century house, behind which stands 'Law's Chapel' (also 18th-century), which despite its name was a private house. Further along by one of the entrances to Hall Yard (Law's Lane) stands the 17th-century former *Golden Ball Inn* (now no.2). Opposite is the Market Cross.

West Street
No. 13 is of 16th-century origin; no.21 which is in the grounds of a former rectory, has an 18th-century barn (with triangular air vents) outside and part of a doorway from Fotheringhay Castle in its garden wall; and at the other end, stands a former Congregational Church from 1846 and the late 17th-century mullioned Manor House, which comprises two adjoining dwellings and a set of outbuildings parallel to Eagle Lane which runs down the sides the rear footpath, brook and former quarry.These include a later house and brewhouse (now an art and craft centre, Old Brewery Studios (see below).This was also the site of the *Eagle Tap* (another alehouse), a barn, and a round dovecote.The dovecote is best seen from the bank of the brook at the bottom of Eagle Lane.

The right-hand side of the street is equally as rich in its variety of architecture, and includes no.16, a 17th-century building which has acted as both the village poorhouse, and a pub (the *Maltsters Arms*), no.22, a three-sided building which includes part of a late-medieval hall, and nos.44-46 which are also late 17th-century with mullions, and a later dual-purpose barn and square dovecote at the rear.

Park Lane offers a similar sample of old-world atmosphere at the Bridge Street-West Street end, but is more predominantly 18th and 19th-century.There are some fine buildings of 17th-century origin however: on the right-hand side leading away from the church end, the old School mainly dates from this period, no.12 (with alterations in 1777), formerly thatched and mullioned no.60 (Vine Cottage) from 1659, and no.62 with bay windows and mullions. The 18th-century former *Wheatsheaf Inn* stands close by (nos.54 and 56) and has two sundials. On the left-hand side as the road bends round, you will see Thorpe's Almshouses built in 1668 by another local benefactor, John Thorpe. A little further along stands another mullioned building from the same period, and adjoining this stands a row of houses, the last two of which (nos.39 and 41, The Old Shambles) are also 17th century. The final building of note on this side is the 17th-century former *Red Lion* .

Road to Wansford: Continuing along Park Lane and leaving the village, past the railway arch, there is a turning to the right for Wansford. On the bend here stands the former 17th-century Huskisson's Lodge, recently rebuilt as 'Huskisson's House'. It was one of three lodges standing in the Royal Deer Park.

Local crafts: * Pottery : The Pot Shop at 4, Park Lane, specialises in on-the-premises handthrown domestic stoneware and porcelain .Tel: Gill Meadows, 01780 470239).
* Art and crafts : The Old Brewery Studios, in West Street - entrance at the rear in the yard. There is a shop and popular art classes are held here. Tel: Jane and John Paige, 01780 470247.
* Visual Arts: Sarah Winfrey, 8 West Street. Tel. 01780 470796.

Pocket Parks: (1) A small meadow by the riverside walk (close to the Village Hall and Willow Brook) and wetland area. (2) Originally a railway track, with two kinds of habitat and vegetation. It is attractive to a variety of butterflies and birds.

Snippets:

* During medieval times, as the town grew, there was a flourishing market here, and an annual fair lasting three days which attracted a lot of visitors from around the Forest. One item produced in the village and sold on these occasions, was carved and turned wood, the fame of which spread far and wide. In the 19th century, several turners could be seen in small groups (each person with a different role in the production of the item) in workshops. Different kinds of wood were used according to the product (eg willow for kitchenware, and apple wood for tool handles). Domestic woodcraft products were known as 'treen'.

* The village in the 19th century had as many as nine recorded public houses, but it is known that in medieval times there were even more (unnamed) - if only of a temporary nature! This is because of a quaint custom resulting from the fair: to cater for thirsty travellers and customers, an ordinary house could legally become an ale house by placing the bough of a tree on its doorstep!

* In the 1880s, Kingscliffe was full of shops, including 'several' butchers, grocers, drapers and tailors.Today, all that is left is a small grocer's, a Co-op, a baker's and a post office/village store!

* The village suffered many fires, the worst of which was a great fire recorded in 1462, which destroyed most of the village - 100 houses, including the royal Manor House. It is likely that the village was rebuilt on its present site on the north side of church. The market and fair were suspended during the resulting decline in the town's importance whilst rebuilding took place. They were reinstated in 1604.

* Many springs can be found in the locality, one of which, 'The Spa',was formerly prized for its medicinal properties: its water was supposedly good for rheumatism. It is said to have made awful tea!

* An early 17th-century Rockingham Forest (West Hay Walk) keeper's house, Westhay Lodge stood by the Collyweston Road (almost opposite the bridleway) until 1961 when it was demolished. There is a newer 'Westhay Lodge' in its place. There is also a 'Westhay Farm' close by on the other side. Westhay is one of the most complete fragments of the original forest and may be walked in part (see the walk to Duddington above).

* One of the church rectors (Michael Hudson), with strong Royalist sympathies during the Civil War, carried out successful secret missions on several occasions for the king.He was captured three times by the Parliamentarians, escaping the second time in disguise whilst carrying a basket of apples on his head! He eventually met an untimely end and his corpse was mutilated, part of which was displayed publicly as a warning to other sympathisers and would-be martyrs.

* Much of the former Royal Deer Park on either side of the road to Wansford, became the site of another World War II US Airforce Base in the area. There is a memorial along the road. It is said that Glenn Miller, the popular US bandleader, played one of his last concerts here before his fatal crash.

Walks in the area:

* Blatherwycke (see above)

* Apethorpe. This excellent walk begins in Hall Yard and beside the Mill. Cross over the bridges and stiles to Morehay Lane, the track running alongside the top of the field and back of the village. Turn left and walk along until you see the black Footpath sign. Turn right at this, passing over fields, and the undulating landscape of the former quarries with dramatic plunges and humps. The walk is well arrow marked.

* Wansford Road. This is a short walk round the back of the village, beginning at a stile and black signpost by the bus stop near Hutcheson's Almshouses in Bridge Street. The walk can be muddy and passes across a sloping field, under a former railway arch and through part of the old deerpark. It ends at a farmhouse on the road to Wansford, from which further walks are possible (turn right).

* Duddington (see above). This takes you via Westhay Wood and North Spinney.

* Boundary Cross. This medieval stone marker, which traditionally marked the boundary between Kings Cliffe and Blatherwycke, is well worth seeing, but can be hard to find unless you know exactly where to look! You can get to it by following the road to Blatherwycke, and roughly half-way to the village, just past the turning to Alders Farm on the left, you will see a small clump of trees by the roadside (across the field to the rear is a much larger clump of trees). Boxed in, and tucked away almost behind the clump, is the ancient stone. It is made of limestone and has a cross engraved on its almost round 'wheelhead'.

LAXTON (Leax's settlement)

A charming 'rebuilt' (estate) village, in two parts, with an interesting history, pleasant walks in the area and the Forest still on its doorstep.

Church: All Saints. Early English style. Late 13th-century. Broach spire. Restored & enlarged 1867-8. Reputedly on the highest ground in the county. Unusual iron gargoyles. 17th-century chest tomb. Interesting tombstone at north side of the tower, to Thomas Milley, a publican murdered by the wife of one of a group of gypsies who had not paid for their beer. She was duly hanged. The inscription reads that he "was killed by gypsies in 1687'. The church overlooks the village on the slope of the road leading out of the village to the A43 and Bulwick.

Former school: 1807-8 for 40 children (the schoolhouse was built later in 1833). Lies in the grounds of Laxton Hall. No longer used.

Former pub: the *Stafford Knot* (now Stafford Knot House), opposite the triangular village green. The original building may be of 17th-century origin. The village has no pub at present.

Other buildings and places of interest:

The village is actually in two parts: access to the part known as Upper Laxton, which lies past some fields and backs onto woodland, is via a rough track to the left of the Village Hall (known as Horse Lane, but not signposted), or further along via the narrow foot track (black wooden signpost and arrow markers) between the post office and the last house ('Spanhoe House') as you leave the village on the road to Harringworth. The latter is part of a leisurely circular walk with contrasting landscape and is visually rewarding (one could almost be in an alpine setting!) There are wooden buildings of interesting design at this end of the village, including a large house at the end of Horse Lane, designed by a doctor and made from African shingles.

Laxton Hall lies along a driveway off the triangular green. (Passing through the gates and approaching the Hall, on the left, stands the charming 19th-century thatched Woodland Cottage with rounded overhanging eaves on wooden columns). Set in a park of 250 acres, the present Hall is of 18th-century origin with later enlargement. It has an Ionic portico but its most striking feature is the lofty domed entrance hall. A stable block was added in 1807. Originally the home of the Engaine family, it passed down through other owners including the Stafford family, and the Evans (Carbery) family to whom it passed by marriage with a daughter of the Staffords. The Hall was acquired by the religious Dominican Order for use as a school in 1924 (until 1968). A hoard of about 340 coins from the fourth century was later found in the grounds. The Hall is now in private hands, and is not open to the public.

Main Street (unnamed): As you walk through along the village street, you will notice a similarity about most of the houses. This is because the village was virtually rebuilt by one of the Evans family, George Freke Evans, mainly between 1804 and 1810, using the same local architects. The houses of different designs, were all originally thatched and have the same similar ornate wooden panelling at their gable ends (as can be seen today). In some cases, windows have since been filled with coursed rubble, matching that of the outer walls. Most of the cottages are now named after flowers. Forge Cottage was as the name implies, a former blacksmith's. One cottage facing the green (no.9) has a tablet on its front wall, partly covered by a pipe, inscribed: 'Foundation Stone Laid By Ye Revd. Dr. Bridges May the 29 1804'. The Old Vicarage (1806-7) is set back on the left of the street, almost opposite the wooden Village Hall.

Walks in the area:

The woodland adjoining Laxton is yet another remnant of Rockingham Forest. A walk through Town Wood and Wood Hollow will gradually bring you to Wakerley, passing over some of the runways of an American World War II airfield, Spanhoe (best seen from the Laxton to Harringworth road). The circular black and white Public Footpath arrow markers must be looked out for and adhered to if you are not to go astray! There are also green and gold Bridleway markers. Stout footwear is recommended for these very rewarding walks! The views of the Welland Valley when approaching the road to Wakerley (at which you must turn right) are inspiring. Below, you will see Barrowden and on the horizon, Morcott Windmill. These two woods join onto Wakerley Great Wood and Adam Wood.

LITTLE OAKLEY (clearing in the oaks).

There is no post office, pub, village hall, or shop (the last one closed in 1973). There is little room to park in this quiet, one street village which has been virtually unspoilt by time, but it really is worth exploring.

Church: St Peter's. Earliest parts: 13th-century. 15th-century tower. It has a variety of different-shaped windows: trefoil, round and lancet. There are fragments of medieval wall painting. Recumbent statue of a medieval forester. 16th and 17th-century monuments to members of the Montagu family. The church was restored in 1865-67, and is now partly redundant, with a small section set aside for occasional services. It was recently used as a training place for stonemasons under The Orton Trust.

Former school: 1852 (closed before World War II). Now a private house.

Former 'pub': the *Duke's Arms* (in reality an outdoor beer retailer and off-license). Closed 1953. Now a farmhouse (last building on the left, leaving the village on the way to the A43).

Other buildings and places of interest:

Manor Farm (originally The Manor House), beside the church. The house is 16th-century in origin, with stone mullioned windows. There is a datestone indicating some rebuilding in 1721. It is an interesting building with a chimney-piece said to have come from Boughton House, and a strange keyhole-shaped window believed to be originally from Pipewell Abbey after it was dissolved. Some of its outbuildings are 18th-century, with older work built in. Today the farm produces excellent ice cream.

Opposite gateway to the church: Honeypot Cottage (rebuilt in the 19th century with mullioned windows from the original 17th-century building) and attached to it in the yard, the smaller Primrose Cottage, which has 18th-century origins and has small-paned casement windows.

(Main Street): Sandpit Farmhouse, Moat Farmhouse (18th-century); Moat Cottage, a 17th-century low thatched building with small-paned casement windows; Paddock Cottage, no.7), a thinly-thatched building of early 18th-century origin, one of whose pantiled outbuildings once housed the village blacksmith's. Next to this is the old school and schoolhouse. Nos.20-21 are charming long, low thatched buildings, from the 18th century, some of which overhang the pavement. Leaving the village on the left, past the crest of the hill, is gated 'Featherbed Lane', an old track that once led to Oakley Purlieus and beyond.

The road from the village meets up with the A43. A short distance away, over on the right, stands Rising Bridge which carries the traffic over Harpers Brook. The bridge has been rebuilt or altered over the years. There is a stone in the wall facing the Little Oakley side inscribed with various fading dates, names and the initials of masons who worked on the bridge, among them 'J.Henson 1809' and the date, 1818. The single-arch bridge was widened in 1954 by the County Council.

Snippets:

* Two intriguing incidents occurred during the reign of Elizabeth I. Around 1582, there was a riot in the church, when 15 men from Boughton, Brigstock and Weekley, armed with swords and staves, with the aid of a blacksmith, broke into the church. In the ensuing fracas, one Little Oakley man was killed and another, injured. The incident was brought to court where it transpired that the reason for the attack was a dispute by a new lord of the manor (William Montagu) over a new priest (whom the Crown had appointed), with the men supposedly acting on his behalf!

Ten years later, a messenger of the Queen arrived in the village with a magistrate, to search a house believed to be contravening the nation's religious policy by harbouring 'Jesuytes, Semynaries, Massing priests, Masse books and other superstiticious things' [*sic*]. As a result of the search, some 'offending' items were found, but no human offenders, and the matter was believed to be closed!

* An interesting story still told, relates how a villager walking back from the pub in Geddington late one night lost his way at Oakley Bushes, some way outside the village near the Great Oakley road. On hearing a call of 'Who?' and feeling like an intruder and that the 'voice ' might put him back on the right track, he gave his name, only to hear the voice repeat itself. It turned out to be an owl!

Walks around the area:

* A fine walk across the meadows, via a variety of stiles and gates and passing under the old viaduct leads you to Great Oakley. Begin from Manor Farm: the walk has a black/white arrow marker on a fence of the farm, just before the bridge. (This is the reverse of the walk from Great Oakley : see above).

* An uphill walk to Geddington and Newton is possible via the track at the side of Grange Farm, but be on the look-out for waymarkers. It can be difficult at certain times of the year!

* Similarly, there is another walk to Geddington. This one is parallel with (though some distance from) the main road for much of the way. The small area of woodland which you pass on your right is Newton Spinney, an isolated ancient enclave of the Forest. It exudes its own atmosphere and is a favourite roosting place for rooks which endlessly fly above it, squawking noisily. It is not accessible. Years ago, this walk would have been hazard-free. Today it meets up with the A43, just before it enters Geddington, and one must beware of the traffic for a short distance: there are only grass verges to walk on! Begin the walk just past the bridge (on the left) via the stile and proceed uphill. Signposted and well-marked.

LOWER BENEFIELD ('open land of Bera's people'. At one time, known as Netherthorpe).

Lying at the bottom of a twisting descending road towards Oundle, Lower Benefield forms the other half of Benefield, which lies above. It once had a castle and is comprised of the main road and two offshoots, all worth exploring and offering a flavour of Old England.

Church: St. Mary's. 14th-century. Spire. Many carved heads on the outer walls and inside the ornate porch, and gargoyles on the roof. Chancel rebuilt 1846-7. Brass with wistful inscription to the young Elizabeth Grant who died in childbirth (1608). Misericords from Fotheringhay. Well-preserved 19th-century bier. Private chapel of Watts-Russell family, former lords of the manor. At the entrance to the churchyard, in a fine setting, the lych gate is shaded by a beautiful enormous holm oak of great age. Memorial tablets from the 18th century built into some of the walls of the churchyard.
Former school: 1820 for 110 children (now the Village Hall).
Other buildings and places of interest:
Brigstock Road (ancient Causin Way):
Benefield House (to the left of, and behind the wall of the track leading to the church) is the former 19th-century Rectory. To the right of the track, facing the road are the old schoolhouse and (next door) the old school. Manor Farmhouse (backs on to the churchyard) is 16th-century in origin, with mainly 17th and 18th- century parts. The crowned pillars of the gateway facing the street have a medieval-like appearance. A wooden motte and bailey castle, possibly from 1140, was situated on a moated mound still visible in the grounds, though it is difficult to see from either the churchyard or road. It did not survive long: by 1315, only the site was referred to. On its north side a manor house was recorded in 1445.
Across the road from the track to the church stands 'The Manor House', with two blocked doorways. To its right and with outbuildings leading down to the main road on the bend is Rectory Farmhouse, which was rebuilt between 1877 and 1878. The house has a stone panel with engraved cross keys on its wall facing the road. The walls of its entrance further down, have two charming modern panels engraved with milkmaids, then and now.
Oundle Road. On your right, behind a hedge is thatched no.9, dating from the late 17th-century. Cross over to the other side. The house on the corner, the present 'Messuage Farmhouse' has mid 18th-century origins. Beside this is a thatched house from the same era. Next to the phone box is an L-shaped house (no.14) with a 1730 datestone. Beside this is a long multi-gabled house (Oakdale Cottage). Next door is Berkeley House (with an 'S' wall tie) which is early 18th-century in origin.
Glapthorn Road (leads to a gated, single-traffic track):
Banhaw Farmhouse (on the corner) with stone mullioned windows, dates from the 17th century.
On the left, is the former blacksmith's, which is now the workshop of a woodcraftsman (see below). Next door, tucked away, is a charming, low-ceilinged late-18th century house (no.33) which acts as the village Post Office and small shop.
The end house across the road (no.25) was once a pub. A long time ago there was a fire here, and on renovation, a concealed inglenook was discovered, where some of the villagers would sit with their ale on cold winter evenings. No.38 dates from the late 17th-century. Gradually the road crosses Willow Brook via a stone bridge. Brook Farmhouse, a mullioned-window building from the 17th century, stands on the left, adding to the scene which is very tranquil as the water murmurs and skips over the stones and through lush meadows on its way towards the Nene. A watermill once stood close to the farmhouse.

Local crafts: * Woodcraft : Don Walser, Glapthorn Road. Has been in the village for some time, producing good-quality products in the traditional way. Specialises in pine and hardwood furniture. Tel: 018325 384. *Art : commissions undertaken and painting classes held (including personal tuition). Contact Linda, Manor Farm Studio. Tel. 018325 231.
Gardens: some of the village gardens are open annually to the public as part of a national scheme (see under Aldwincle for details).
Snippets:
* 'Swallow holes' (nine in all) for water are abundant in the fields off the footpath to Upper Benefield.
* Records show that 'craftsmen of Fotheringhay' lived in the Benefields during the 15th century.
* Before 1840, the village could boast three pubs, but now there is just the one - at Upper Benefield.
* Some way out of the village, left of the Oundle Road, close to the Lyveden turn-off, is a driveway leading to Biggin Hall. This is an early 18th-century house with medieval origins, once owned by the

Kingscliffe: the Mill, Rectory and Church

Fotheringhay: Saint Mary's and All Saints Church

NASSINGTON (Manor House and Church)

Abbots of Peterborough, and after the Dissolution by a succession of private owners. Since 1822, it has been in the hands of the Watts-Russell family, former benefactors to Benefield and Oundle.
* Just outside the village on the way to Oundle at the top of the hill is a track leading to the right (marked by a isolated house to its left). This was known locally as The Lane. At the end is a house built of chequered red and black bricks. At one time there was a little community here involved with brickmaking. The track leading off at the end was once Green Lane.

Walks around the area:
* Try walking along the ancient Causin Way as it winds towards Brigstock. Along the way are some interesting buildings such as Fermyn Woods Hall (qv. under Brigstock).
* It is possible to get close to two 'lost' villages from here:
(1) On the main road to the Post Office end, opposite the phone box is a Footpath sign. This will take you to ancient Harley Way, where on reaching the white house at the end of the walk, you turn left along the road to Churchfield Farm, the sole survivor of the former village of **Churchfield,** which stood on the north side of Lyveden Brook. The 17th-century farmhouse is said to contain a small part of the former church that stood close by. In 1960-4, the site was excavated by boys from Oundle School. No public access.
(2) Walking through the churchyard to the left of the church, brings you to a kissing gate, where arrow markers point the way across the small meadow , at the end of which is a stile. Once over this, turn right and head straight towards Banhaw Wood which lies south of the village (the well-worn route is usually marked out). Passing through its muddy interior to the far side, there is an uphill walk across meadow (where you are bound to see rabbits, hares or pheasant), past an ancient moat on the left. Eventually you come to another part of Harley Way close to Lyveden Old Building and the track to Lyveden New Bield (qv. under Brigstock). When Thomas Tresham planned the New Bield, the village of **Lyveden** was removed. The area is rich in other deserted medieval settlements.
* The walk along the gated road to Glapthorn is worth-while. It comes out near Glapthorn Cow Pastures (qv.) and a track which passes Morehay and beyond. This is ambitious and is only recommended for those with time on their hands and a sense of adventure! An Ordnance Survey map is advisable for those going beyond the Pastures!

LOWICK ('Luffa's WIC')

A fascinating village with side streets, and a long road leading up to Drayton House. Its castle-like church gives it a regal appearance.The contrast with nearby Sudborough could not be more apparent - near, and yet so different.

Church: St Peter's. Perpendicular style. Fifteenth-century tower with flying buttresses and octagonal lantern, terminating in pinnacles, gives a fine, striking view from afar as you approach the village, inviting closer inspection. Fourteenth-century glass. Alabaster tombs, one of Edward Stafford c.1499; another of a knight and lady in contemporary dress, c.1419. The church was restored in 1869.
Pub: the *Snooty Fox* (formerly the *White Horse*).
Former pub: the *George* .
A walk around the village: as you enter Main Street from the Sudborough/Brigstock end, there is on the right, a large barn with triangular air vents, from 1788. Behind this is the Rectory which was built in the Elizabethan style in 1855-6. The house has some claim to fame since a former rector with a partiality to literature, entertained English authors like Anthony Trollope and George Eliot here. These two are said to have written some of their work whilst staying at the house.
A track on the left leads to the church, to the right (south) of which stands Manor Farm. Opposite the Main Street entrance entrance to the farm and on the corner of Drayton Road stands the old **School** and schoolhouse, with its engraved scroll above the front door. Itwas formerly called the 'Green Coat School' by its founders, on account of the costume that had to be worn by its pupils. Proceed down Drayton Road, past Mill Lane leading off to the right onto a track, appropiately, to the former mid 18th-century Mill and on to Sudborough. On your right, the thatched Post Office and adjoining 'Little Thatch' have stood together since the early 18th-century. Opposite is another thatched building, Owl Cottage, from the same era.

Go past Robbs Lane on the left, and across the bridge over Harpers Brook, passing some 18th-century farmbuildings, and barns (one with a datestone of 1795) on your right. Further along the road, opposite the byway sign there is a well head dating from 1830. Thatched Sunnybank Cottage appears on the left with another thatched (at present derelict) house opposite it.

The road now leads ahead into the grounds of ancient **Drayton House** which has a main block (and a wall on the south side) from the 14th century, with a wider range of buildings from the 15th. There is a public right-of-way through the grounds, skirting the building. It is not normally open to the public, but special arrangements can be made for a visit.

Retrace your steps back down to near the beginning of Drayton Road. Just before the main street, take the turning to your right, Robbs Lane. It is worth a walk along here because of the diversity of old buildings, some of which are listed. On the left of this lane is Pear Tree Cottage from 1747, and next door (no.20) is another house from 1788. As you round the corner there is a former well head with arched brickwork. On the left are thatched buildings such as Cherry Tree Cottage and Ivy Cottage. The older buildings are on the right however, with Bijou Cottage, Thatched Cottage and nos.16 and 18 all dating from the 18th century. A chapel from 1911 also stands on the right. Nos.1 and 3 by the corner are the oldest buildings in the street and date from the late 17th-century : they were a former pub, the *George Inn*. The end of the lane leads into Main Street, on the opposite side of which is the only surviving pub which is believed to date from the mid 17th-century. A nearby barn is probably even older. A little way to its left, almost opposite the Old School House, are nos.18 and 20 from the 18th century.

Finally, take a walk to the right of the pub and follow the main road to the turning on the left, Aldwincle Road. Here on the corner stands a large house with a datestone : 1731. It is the former keeper's lodge.

Pocket Park: a wildflower area and pond on the edge of the village, alongside the Drayton Road close to the bridge over Harpers Brook and on the right before Alley Farm.

Snippets:
* 'The Lowick Oak' which stood in a field south of the village until 1968 was supposedly one of the largest of its kind in the country , with a 25 feet girth and 90 feet in height . It was considered one of the finest old trees of the Rockingham Forest area.

Walks in the area:
* Sudborough (see under Sudborough). Walk 1: begins in Mill Lane (wooden signpost). Just before the mill entrance cross the stile to the right. Waymarked. Walk 2: begins about halfway down the road to Drayton, signposted (green) by the first farmhouse on the right past Harpers Brook.
* Islip. Begin at the same place as Walk 2 above, but go in the opposite direction (bearing left and following the track). An interesting walk with good views as you near Islip. Be careful though - on one occasion the author had to scramble up a thorn-encrusted muddy bank to avoid wading through a very large deep puddle that had formed across a stretch of the track, like a lake!
* Slipton and Twywell via Drayton Park. Follow the road through the Park, past the manor house, after which you bear left and follow the track which leads past Home Farm and winds down to Slipton. Turn left into the village, and follow the signpost opposite the *Samuel Pepys* pub, across a wet meadow to the other side. Turn left at the narrow road which leads straight into Twywell.

MIDDLETON ('middle settlement' i.e. between Cottingham and Carlton).

Virtually 'twinned' with Cottingham, Middleton is a 'newer' settlement than its sister, and exudes a different kind of charm, with more of its older buildings still intact. Fine views can be had from the top of its two hills. Look out for small tucked-away relics of its past, such as water pumps and wall recesses. The village has never had a church (using St.Mary's in Cottingham), but had a mid 19th-century Independent Chapel.

Pub: the *Red Lion*
Former pubs : the *Woolpack* (near the corner with Ashley Road); the *Exeter Arms*.
Former school: rebuilt in 1856 (datestone above far porch) for 120 children and enlarged in 1869. On the front of the schoolhouse above the doorway is a sundial to the left of which is a stone inscribed 'Edw.Lynchley, Jno Lambert, Sam Birdin' and the date 1766. To the right is another stone with the names 'Wm. Aldwinckle, Wm. Hikon, Bailiffs'.
Other buildings and places of interest:
Main Street:
Many of the buildings are of 18th-century origin, including no.15, which uses the name 'Manor House'

(datestone,1785). On the roof ridge there is a wooden 'lantern opening' for pigeons - all that remains of an internal dovecote that formerly existed here. Across the road stands the iron boundary marker between the two villages. Close to the marker are mid 18th-century Vine House (no.37),The Farriers House (no.35) and next door, The Forge (1868). On the left, just before the former Independent Chapel, which is now a home, stood a former pub, the *Exeter Arms*. Further along, outside the white house (no.38), is one of the many old pumps to be seen around the village, with a datestone on the wall behind, 1854. Further along on each side are more 18th and 19th-century houses, but nestling among them on the right-hand side between Cannam House (early 18th-century) and Home Farm, is Willow Cottage, a more recent house of uncertain date but with a reset datestone of 1616. The large 19th-century Middleton House Farm with a huge gateway and horseshoe-shaped hollow to the left of the entrance, is near the end of the street.

At the head of the T-junction, between The Hill and Ashley Road is 17th-century (with later parts) Longridge, with its attractively creeper-covered wooden panelled porch. It is now a garden nursery.

The Hill: Turn left along the Hill and the large house on your left before the pub has a datestone of 1862. Across the road by the footpath to East Carlton, is a house from 1864. A little way up the hill on the same side, is a stone well head, dating from 1844, the water still gushing enthusiastically into the stone trough and drain below. Opposite is Hill House with an 18th-century square dovecote to the rear. Cross over, walk along the road at the side of that house and turn right into School Hill (note the wall on your right with a reset datestone: 1859). Some19th-century houses line the slope.

Camsdale Walk: Opposite this, by the side of the road, is another of the old village pumps. Walking along Camsdale Walk brings you to the old school (qv. above) with its interesting inscriptions. The track continues, with excellent panoramic views on the left, downhill to Cottingham.

Renaissance music: (Lutenist for recitals): Pamela Coren, 36 Main Street. Tel. 01536 770914.

Snippets:
* The village used to have three places of worship: a Methodist Chapel (1841), a Congregationalist Chapel (1808), and an Independent Chapel (1844).

Walks around the area:
* The path opposite the *Red Lion* (signposted, and popular with dog walkers) takes you uphill to the village of East Carlton, and the grounds of East Carlton Park.
*The stile opposite the school at the top of the hill, takes you across meadow and a minor road, along a bridleway (with a newly-created Nature Reserve - see under Cottingham - at the far end, just before the A427). Cross over and pass through woodland to Kingswood, and nearby Great Oakley. (See under that village for closer detail of this walk - in reverse).
*Going down Ashley Road takes you eventually to an unsurfaced track leading to the River Welland.

NASSINGTON (headland where migrants from Peterborough settled).

A large sprawling village of great importance from medieval times as a centre of high religious office. A large number of listed buildings can be seen as you explore the streets, and the choice of walks in the area is phenomenal! Some of the older houses have walls of amazing thickness: up to three feet (90cm).

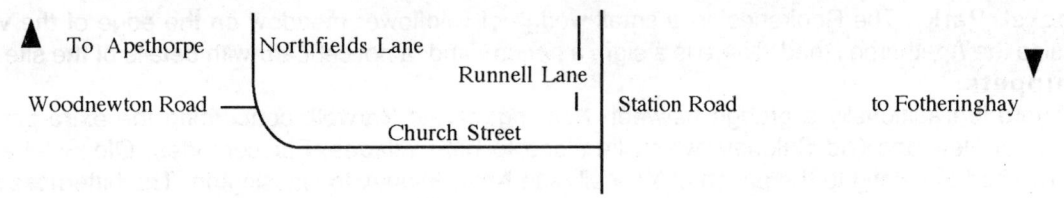

```
        ▲  To Apethorpe   Northfields Lane                                    ▼
                                              Runnell Lane
      Woodnewton Road ──┐                │       Station Road      to Fotheringhay
                         └────Church Street
```

Church: St Mary the Virgin and All Saints. Earliest parts: 11th-century Saxon, with an indication of Norman work. Tower with 15th-century octagonal belfry and crocketed spire. 13th-century font and coffin lids. A cross shaft believed to be 10th-century can be found within. Jacobean pulpit. Despite Cromwellian destruction of the stained glass, and the whitewashing of the church walls, the fine 14th and 15th-century murals have been uncovered (but not restored) at the northern end and above the chancel arch. These include: a Wheel of Fortune, St. Martin on a white horse, and St. Michael weighing souls. The church was restored in 1885. The nearby former Vicarage, now known as 'The Hall', dates from 1880. In 1905, during a heavy storm, lightning struck the spire of the church, damaging the inner stonework in several places. Two of the fissures covered an area of at least two feet, and were nearly four inches deep.

Former Methodist Chapel: 1875 (now a Grain Company.The schoolroom is now the Village Hall).

Former Congregational Chapel: 1839 (now part of the *Queen's Head* in Station Road).
Pubs: the *Queen's Head* (17th-century but remodelled in the 19th), the *Black Horse* (1674).
Former pubs: the *Three Horseshoes*, the *Three Mill Bills*, the *Plough Inn*, the *Boat*, the *Carpenter's Arms Inn*. Others are rumoured to have existed.
Former school: 1862. In Woodnewton Street. Unrecognisable as such, it is now a private house. The later school, from 1894, is still in use and stands in Church Street.
Other buildings and places of interest:
Church Street:
No.35 is 17th-century. On the opposite side stands Nassington House (also 17th-century, possibly with parts from the 16th-century).
Across the road from the church: the **Prebendal Manor House** dates from the early 13th-century, and is believed to be the oldest continuously-inhabited building in the county. Nassington was chosen as the base for a prebendary (member of the cathedral chapter) of Lincoln Diocese and the house when built (on the site of an earlier timber dwelling) was occupied for over six hundred years by many of these high-ranking and influential officials. In the grounds are some interesting outbuildings, among them an early 16th-century square dovecote, a stable/granary and an 18th-century barn. It is now possible to visit the building, which is currently open from June to the end of August, on Tuesdays, Wednesdays and Sundays. Teas are available. There have also been recently-staged historical 'skirmishes' in the grounds, where medieval (or later) costumed characters camp, eat, train, fight and walk around and where *you* can get involved, with the sound of cannon in the background - you can even visit an apothecary! These may well become a regular event.
Another building of interest stands next door, on the corner of the Woodnewton Road. This is the early 16th-century **Manor House** and was for many years associated with the Wolston family of Apethorpe. Note the charming oriel window on the north wall. On the opposite side of the road, stands no.22, an early 17th-century house.
Continuing down Church Street past the church, on the left hand side is the former pub, the *Three Mill Bills*, a thatched early 17th-century building. From this point on and into adjoining Northfields Road there are some 19th-century houses. Among these, on the right, is the former *Three Horseshoes*.

Station Road:
No. 9 on the left is thought by some people to be a former early 19th-century pub, the *Carpenters Arms Inn*, though there is no defiinite evidence for this. A little way down, on the right-hand side, is a group of interesting buildings beginning with the mid 17th-century 'The Nutshell'. Close beside this is a house with a datestone: 1704, and next door, Home Farm (with parts dating to the early 17th-century). 'Greystones' further along on the same side has a datestone of 1698. (Until August 1994 when it was demolished, late-17th century Pear Tree Cottage stood across the road.) The *Queen's Head* pub (on the right) is 17th-century as is Oak Cottage next door. Opposite the latter is another building from the same period, thatched Winford Cottage. There are three more 17th-century houses near the end of the street.

Local crafts: *Art/picture framing: Ann Marriott, 35 Church Street. Tel. 01780 783603.
Pocket Park: 'The Rookeries' is a small wedge of wildflower meadow on the edge of the village, beside the Apethorpe Road. There is a sign, a bench, and a noticeboard with details of the site.
Snippets:
* There is traditionally a grudge between Nassington and Yarwell, concerning the extra-parochial areas of New and Old Sulehay, which lie close to both villages. For centuries, Old Sulehay was considered to belong to the parish of Yarwell, and New Sulehay to Nassington. The bitterness stems from the 19th century when an inspector from the former Local Government Board was sent to meet the overseers of each parish. In 1869, despite protests, both the areas were awarded to Nassington. This obviously did not go down well with the people of Yarwell, as the residents of Old Sulehay attended their church, the men worked on a Yarwell farm and the women gleaned in the fields there. Officially the protests stopped, but when harvest time came, and the first field was ready for gleaning, the women of Yarwell got there first and began working, without sounding the church bell - a traditional signal that the field was ready! When the women of Nassington did get there, the gleaning was practically finished. Still, they claimed ancient rights, ordering the Yarwell women to leave. One of the latter pushed the Nassington 'ringleader' across the boundary ditch, telling all the Nassington people present that they should all return to their own village 'where they belong'!
* Remnants of Rockingham Forest in the vicinity include: Ring Haw, Fair Oak Sale and Great and Little Morton Sale.

*On a hot summer day in 1794, a fire destroyed thirteen buildings in Church Street. It was started by a boy shooting at a pigeon. As a result stacks in a farmyard caught fire. At the time, many of the villagers were away at a feast in Fotheringhay, and therefore were unable to help put out the fire. Some of the buldings were never replaced,with the gaps left still visible today as a testimony to the event.

* The village May Day celebrations are still held.They traditionally included, until well into the 19th century, a May Song, similar in parts to that sung elsewhere around the county. A portion of the song, printed below, gives a charming picture of life in a bygone age:

> *Arise, arise, you dairy maid,*
> *Out of your drowsy dream*
> *And step into your dairy quick*
> *And fetch a cup of cream.*
>
> *A cup of cream, it looks so white*
> *And a jug of your brown beer*
> *And if we live to tarry in the place,*
> *We'll call another year.*
>
> *We've begun our song, we've almost done*
> *No longer can we stay*
> *God bless you all, both great and small*
> *We wish you a joyful May.*

* A large 6th-century Saxon cemetery was unearthed in 1942, south-east of the village, near the river, with at least 100 graves, and a variety of goods, including spearheads, knives, and a range of brooches, keys and rings. One skeleton was nearly seven feet in length!
* Interesting old local place names: Honeyman's Stile, Farthinggreen Piece, Long Shovels, Froghall, Big and Little Framples. Another, known as Hangman's Stile, on a path leading from the Prebendal Manor House to the old Stamford Road, gets its name from an incident when a man with a stolen sheep attempted to cross the stile with the animal tied across his shoulders. In the process of doing this, the load slipped and the man was strangled by the rope which he was unable to remove.
* Nene Viaduct, a landmark from the days of the railway, was demolished in 1981.

Walks in the area:
* An intriguing village appraisal was published for 1989-90, in which 34 Public Footpaths/Bridle Ways were recorded: a vast natural feast for the rambler and the rider! They are well-signposted everywhere: just choose one and walk! Some only lead from one part of the village to another. Others lead to Yarwell, Woodnewton, Fotheringhay, Elton, New Sulehay, Old Sulehay, and beyond. A booklet of walks is available from the village shop in Station Road.
*deres **New Sulehay Lodge:** one of the former official residences of Rockingham Forest (Cliffe Bailiwick) keepers. The buildings lie along, and just off, the road to Apethorpe beside a track, and have been rebuilt.

NEWTON (in the willows) (new settlement)

Formerly two villages (Great and Little Newton), a walk along its quiet lane and through its fields is amply rewarding for such a tiny place. Sleepy it may seem, but it has seen a lot of turmoil and change, which still threatens its slumber.

Former churches:
*St.Faith's. This 14th-century building with a 15th-century tower and spire still stands in a tranquil setting close to a dovecote. At one time it was also a private chapel of the Treshams. It was restored in 1858, but is now no longer used, being a Field Centre since 1978 for naturalists. Its ancient monuments and memorials are now in the church at nearby Geddington.This area was once known as Little Newton, the site of which is believed to have been to the rear (and west) of the dovecote.
*St.Leonard's. This stood at the other end of the village, known as Great Newton. When the two areas were united in 1440, St.Leonard's fell into disuse. Its site is now covered by Manor Barn which faces

adjoining fields, and the patch of grass land outside its rear walls, was the former churchyard. The history of the village and area, and excavations at the site of the house have given rise to the inevitable ghost stories (see 'Snippets').

A short walk: other buildings and places of interest:
At the Geddington end of the village (following a track off the road to the Oakleys and Rushton) stands Mill Farm, one of the oldest surviving farms in the area, though the present building dates from the early 18th-century. The adjoining mill which stood here for centuries was pulled down in 1935. The track becomes grassy as it leads through a gate to into a large field to the left of which is the River Ise and an area of natural interest. To the right stands a large early 17th-century rectangular dovecote, with nesting boxes for 2,000 birds, and two open low entrances. It is inscribed MAURICE TRESHAM, and is the only surviving building of a former Tresham manor house which stood here (in front of the dovecote) until 1667, when it was demolished by the Montagu family who had bought the estate. Only the earthworks of the gardens remain. The track continues past the former church of St.Faith's, and leads into what was Great Newton.
At the end of the track on your right is the rear of Dovecote Farm. You may well see an old fire engine parked in the courtyard as you pass by! In the summer, the farm's fields are full of ripe soft fruit, and are open to the public for picking and purchase. There are also refreshments, donkey rides and a children's play area, with ample parking available. (The front entrance is on the Geddington-Rushton and Oakleys road).
Leaving the track and proceeding down the street, the row of houses on your left date from the 17th-century. Passing by The Old Dairy next door with its long pantiled outbuilding in the yard,the large house facing you ahead is Newton House (once known as Dovecote House) which has a fading datestone of 1792 in Latin numerals on its gable end. (The short turning to the left by the phone box leads to no.5, a fine thatched cottage from the 18th-century and a footpath across the fields - see below. No.11 on the bend on your right, as you walk past Newton House is a long thatched building from the same era, with a hatch in its garden wall. Ahead of you before the road curves round to leave the village is a gateway to the right of which stands The Manor House, a large thatched building whose earliest parts are late 17th-century. There is a stone sundial above one of the doors, and an inglenook fireplace within. Manor Barn on the site of St.Leonard's, stands opposite.

Snippets:
* It was at Little Newton that a thousand peasants from the region, known as 'The Levellers' gathered under a 'Captain Pouch' on 8 June 1607, as a result of losing their land and their traditional livelihood to 'inclosure' by landowners, who were more interested in profitable sheep farming. As a result, disaffected peasants roamed the countryside uprooting the inclosure boundaries of the landowners ('The Midland Rising').The peasants had arrived from Pytchley and Rushton, two other areas badly affected by the practice. They began to undo the work of the Treshams, the result of which led to a massacre by troops brought in by Tresham from Boughton and Apethorpe.Tragically, fifty of the rioters were killed and several wounded.
* In the vicinity of Manor Barn, there have been numerous sitings of apparitions: one in the form of a monk (from the nearby former village of Barford) and the other, in the daytime, of a smiling girl in a long dress, passing through a wall close to the house.

Walks around the area:
* For Geddington, begin from the church/Field Centre, taking a short walk with the dovecote on your left, across the field which is usually full of sheep, toward a gate at the end. The path behind this leads through Mill Farm and onto the road at which you turn right.
* Great Oakley. Perhaps the easiest of the routes to this village is to walk the quiet, winding, undulating road which is well-signposted. A fine walk with good views. To begin this, walk through Newton via the road leading past The Manor House. At the end of the road turn left and then right where signposted 'The Oakleys'.
* For Kettering, turn left at the phone box in the village, down the short cul-de-sac. Cross the stile on your right, and walk over the fields towards the small wooden bridge spanning the river. Once over, turn right and head towards the spinney where there is a stile by the wooden fence. Walk along the earthy track, bear left and at the road, turn left and proceed down the road to the Public Footpath sign on the right.

OUNDLE Both 'Avondale' - (valley of the river) and 'undivided' (not shared between tribes) have been suggested as origins of the name).

A small ancient town on the edge of the River Nene, Oundle deserves its fame and is justifiably an attractive place to visit, steeped in history, with much of its past still intact. Its shops and places of refreshment are worth sampling. A lot of walking will bring its rewards. Another 'gateway' to the Forest.

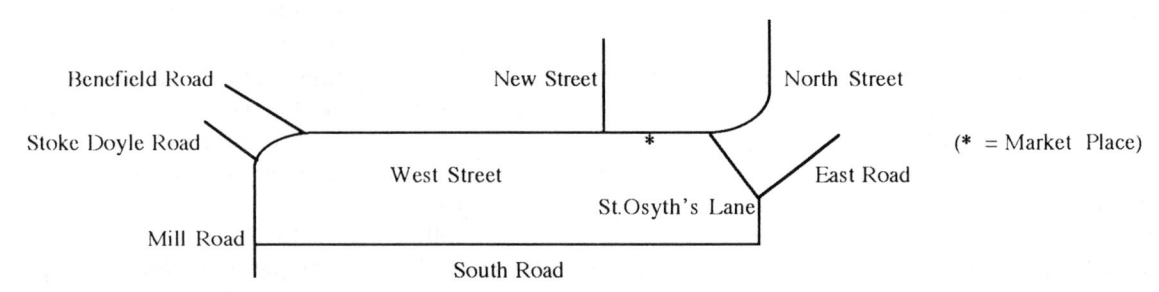

```
         Benefield Road          New Street        North Street
      Stoke Doyle Road                     *                          (* = Market Place)
                             West Street                 East Road
                                         St.Osyth's Lane
         Mill Road
                             South Road
```

Church: St Peter's. Mainly Early English (13th-century),with Decorated and Perpendicular styles. Fragments of Saxon work. Medieval screens, lectern, and coloured pulpit (the latter restored in 1966). The church was restored in 1864. The crocketed spire is 203 feet in height (twice climbed by boys from the school (one of whom put his cap on top of the weathercock) - without permission - and 'rewarded with a sovereign and a caning'!
Catholic Church: Jesus Church (1879) at the western end facing Stoke Hill and Benefield Road.
Former Congregational Chapel: 1864 (on the site of an earler building from 1690), which has been tastefully converted into the Stahl Theatre.
Former Methodist Chapel: 19th-century. West Street. Now used as a bazaar.
Former Baptist Chapel: 1852 .West Street. Now converted into flats.
Pubs: The *Talbot Inn*, in New Street, dates from 1626, and has window casements from Fotheringhay Castle. It has been suggested that a Jacobean staircase was also from Fotheringhay and that it was used by Mary Queen Of Scots before her execution. It has also been said that the inn stands on the site of an ancient hostelry where monks from an adjoining monastery in Saxon times, dispensed food and drink to passing wayfarers, but there is no evidence for this. Other pubs: the *Ship Inn* (West Street); the *Rose and Crown* (Market Place); the *George* (Glapthorn Road); the *Angel* (St. Osyth's Lane); the *Black Horse* (Benefield Road. It has a large model horse outside).
Former pubs: the *Turks Head*, the *Red Lion*, the 17th-century *White Hart* (all demolished, stood in New Street); the *Cross Keys*, the *Green Man*, the *Waggon and Horses*, the *Nag's Head* (all West Street); the *Old Hind* (corner of Market Place and West Street); the *Crown*, the *Half Moon* (North Street/Black Pot Lane); the *White Lion* : 1641 (in North Street); and the *Anchor* (rebuilt in 1637) in St Osyth's Lane, on the corner of East Road. Now no.21, this fine building has a crumbling plaque inscribed 'IM' and still stands proudly, defying time.

Other buildings and places of interest:
North Bridge over the River Nene: rebuilt and widened in 1912-14. Has 11 arches. A stone tablet found during repair in 1835, was inserted in parapet and reads: 'In the yere of oure Lord 1570, thes arches wer borne doune by the waters extremytie. In the yere of our Lord 1571 they wer bulded agayne with lyme and stonne. Thanks be to God'. On the other side of the bridge, just before the roundabout (and technically in Ashton) are two buildings of interest from 1845: the former Oundle Railway Station (now The Old Station House) on the left, and across the road, a former hotel (*Railway Hotel*), later known as the *Riverside* . Both buildings were constructed in Victorian mock-Tudor style. The by-pass makes use of the former railway line to Northampton.
Market Place
The Oundle Improvement Commissioners cleared away old shops and the late 16th-century buttercross here in 1825. The lord of the manor, Jesse Watts-Russell, then built the Market House with the Town Hall above it, using stone from a redundant church at Barnwell.
New Street
Oundle School buildings. Late 19th /early 20th-century. The school was established in 1876, by the Grocers Company. Parts of the school replaced former inns: the extension to the School House replacing the *Red Lion* , and 'The Cloisters', replacing the *White Hart Inn*.

North Street
Laxton Grammar School and Almshouse. William Laxton, a locally-born wealthy grocer, later became Lord Mayor of London, and Master of the Grocers' Company. On his death in 1556, a codicil to his will provided for the foundation of a grammar school and almshouse. The school was initially held in the upper room of the Gildhouse at the corner of the churchyard and North Street. It was rebuilt in 1855 and is now known as the Laxton Long Room. The adjacent school buildings were opened in 1883.
Latham Hospital (almshouses): 1611 'for 16 aged women'. Nicholas Latham was the son of a Brigstock Great Park keeper, who seeing first-hand the problems encountered by the peasants of Brigstock and their rights to commons for their animals, began his resolve to help the less fortunate. Moving to Rushden, he went to Chichele School (founded 1422) in Higham Ferrers. He later became vicar of Barnwell. His vow to help the poor saw its realisation in the form of the almshouses: 'a hospital and abiding place for the finding sustentation and relief of certain aged, poor, needy or impotent people to have continuance for ever.' A coat-of-arms (a cross and a pelican nesting) is on the two gateways along the street. It is still in use as a home for the aged.
Latham's Blue Coat School was founded before Latham's death in 1620, 'for 30 poor men's sons'. It no longer exists, and today, the school buildings and master's house form part of Latham's Hospital.
The Berrystead is a late17th-century building, with a gazebo at its rear (on East Road).
Laundimer House is a boarding house for Oundle School.

West Street
Paine's Cottage (close to the present Stahl Theatre).The long building, with the neighbouring Manse, is basically 15th-century and has mullioned windows. They are linked by a wall, with an elaborate entrance to the street in the form of a three-pinnacled stone doorway which was said to have originally come from Kirby Hall. In the 16th century, both houses were part of a house belonging to Sir Walter Mildmay of Apethorpe. In1801, the eastern wing was conveyed by a local benefactor, John Paine, as almshouses for 'Protestant Dissenters'. They now constitute a private house.
South side of West Street The most important house is Cobthorne. It was built in the 17th century, during the Commonwealth period by William Butler, one of Cromwell's main generals. It is now occupied by the principal of Oundle School. Another building, which dates from 1715 (south of West Street), is now part of Oundle School, and is used for teaching languages.
Stoke Doyle Road. 'New House' (belonging to Oundle School), which stands on the left-hand side of the road, a short distance from the bridge, has a datestone: 1640, but has some medieval parts.
South Road. Bradley's Cottage, 1812.

Snippets:
*There was a medieval deerpark near Oundle, belonging to the Abbot of Peterborough who also owned Biggin Grange, which lies close by. Its southern boundary skirts Benefield Road, on the opposite side to the golf course, and continues up to the bend where a track leads off to Biggin Hall in Benefield parish.
* In 1565, both West and North Streets were known as the High Street; New Street was Bury Street; and St Osyth's (Sithe's) Lane was Lark Lane. South Road and East Road were known as South Back Way and East Back Way respectively. Black Pot Lane was called Dwell (Dowell) Wong Lane.
* In 1666, the Great Plague arrived from London killing 223 people, the majority of whom lived either near 'The Pest House' (Mill Lane), or at an area in North Street which had poor quality housing.
*The Drumming Well: this stood near the back of the *Talbot Inn* in Dob's Yard (now Drummingwell Lane) but it has long been filled in. It was said that a drumming sound 'like a march' could be heard coming from it, whenever a catastrophe was about to befall the land. One observer in the 17th century wrote: 'It beat for a fortnight at the latter end of last month, and at the beginning of this month. It was heard in the very same manner before the King's death and the death of Cromwell, the King's coming in and the Fire of London.' A leading geologist explained the noise as being caused by air expelled from rock crevices into the well, 'through a water seal which was periodically in bubbles'.
* **Museum**: a display of the town's history can be seen at the Oundle Museum (which opened in May 1994) in the Drill Hall Centre. At present it is open on Saturdays and Sundays from 2pm until 5pm. The Drill Hall now also houses the offices of the **Rockingham Forest Trust**, which was set up to conserve, enhance and promote the Forest.

Walks around the area:
* There are excellent walks in all directions. The Nene Way covers the area around the river (1) you can get to Ashton from the bottom of East Road where you take the turning leading off it to the right, Ashton Road, (by the green East Northants Herne Park sign).Then left at the Footpath sign). (2) You can get to Cotterstock from the footpath sign to the left of North Bridge.

* Barnwell Mill and Oundle Marina. From the Market Place, go down St Osyths Lane, past East Road, and turn left into Bassett Ford Road. Cross the field: the walk takes you over stiles, bridges and a lock.
Barnwell Country Park On the site of former sand and gravel pits. Excellent waterside walks: around the park, lake and alongside the river. Some 32 species of birds have been recorded. There is a kingfisher hide. Nature displays can be seen in the Ranger's Office, and there are occasional Family Events. A good place for picnics. It can be reached by leaving the town via South Bridge: the park is signposted on the right of the road. Oundle Marina and Barnwell Mill are found nearby, on the same Barnwell Road.
Cyclists: cycles, trailers, child seats and helmets are available for hire daily (Sundays by arrangement) from Valley Cycles, 5a West Street (Tel. 01832 293511).
Refreshments: The Tea Shop, 75 West Street; Coffee Tavern, 34 Market Place.

PILTON (Pileca's TUN).

An tiny isolated settlement with a tranquil atmosphere, and a relatively quiet history.

Church: St Mary and All Saints. 12th-century in parts, but dating mainly from the end of the 13th century. Restored 1874-5. The porch has the trefoil emblem of the Treshams who once lived in the village. The chancel was rebuilt in 1864. There are interesting 'modern' floor tiles of birds and animals.
Other buildings of interest:
This is a tiny village which is difficult to park in. Begin at the entrance near the phone booth, passing the Victorian wall post box on the way. Towards the end, before the road bends round, are three houses of interest together on the right. The first two are 'The Cottage' and 'Rose Cottage', formerly Grange Cottage and Rose Anne Cottage. Both have 18th-century origins. Next door on the corner, is a much older house, whose original purpose has been a subject of speculation: The Old Watch House, also known as 'The Bede House' and 'The Old Cottage'. It is an intriguing building believed to date from the 16th century and has several ornate carvings, such as human faces, and 'ball flowers' around the roof area. It may have had some religious significance, bearing in mind its possible connection with the Tresham family who were lords of the manor.
Follow the road round across the large area of meadowland beyond. This leads to the church and The Rectory, which lies close by. This was the old manor house of Maurice Tresham and his family. It is of 16th-century origin, with mullioned windows. The former manorial fishpond lies nearby.
Retrace your steps through the village and head back towards the main road along which, you turn left. A little way down is a small green by which a road leads eventually to the Rectory. Turn left along this. On the right there is a cluster of three cottages. The two thatched ones near the road date from the 18th century. Behind them, a third house has a carved human head at its gable end and a datetone of 1851.
Gardens: the gardens of Elmes House are open annually to the public as part of the national scheme (see under Aldwincle).
Local crafts: *Hand crafted wooden toys : C.J. & P.E. Stratford, Bearshanks Lodge. Tel. 01832 272198.
Snippets:
* Nearby quarries were used in the 16th century for building Lyveden New Bield. The village was also once renowned as a tile-making centre.

PIPEWELL (Pippas's stream', i.e. Harpers Brook).

If only history could speak, it would be fascinating to find out more about Pipewell! The village saw a royal gathering and great historic events taking place in its fields, ancient and modern. The original village vanished when the Abbey was built and its estate expanded. Today it is a tiny village lining a short road, with few signs of its past. Worth exploring, but difficult to park in, with a narrow road and some bends.

Church: The original church of Blessed Mary was dedicated in 1311. The present church of St Mary's was restored in 1881 - a small building in a quiet setting off a bend at the edge of the village.
Pipewell Abbey:
Site of a Cistercian Abbey, St Mary's (earthworks in a field by the footpath to Rushton). Its buildings stood on either side of Harpers Brook known as West and East Granges. It was founded in 1142 with 13 monks, and was the scene of Richard I's Great Council in 1189, which was attended by most of the

English nobility and bishops, to raise money for the Crusades. The Abbey received its income from the local rectories (or outgoings from those rectories) of Great Oakley, Barford, Geddington, Great and Little Newton and other nearby villages as well as places in Warwickshire. Eventually it fell on hard times, due to diminishing timber supplies and undergrowth in its woods as a result of extravagant use by the monks, thefts, felling by greedy landowners, sales, the conversion of woodland into pasture for tillage, and the construction or repair of large buildings. It was dissolved in 1538, after which time its masonry and many of its possessions found their way to nearby villages. In the registers at the time of the Dissolution, were listed 'chapells' to St Benett, St Stephen, St Michell and St Nicholas, as well as altars to St Katheryn and 'Trynyte'.

Other buildings and places of interest:
The small church greets you on the left as you enter the village from the direction of East Carlton/Wilbarston. Next to it, on the bend, is the Old Post Office, the building of which dates from 1674. On the opposite side is a row of 19th-century houses, beside which is a stile into a large meadow with earthworks and pits from the ironstone quarrying days of earlier this century. In the field stands a single piece of pointed masonry: a monument to the past.

Further along from the Old Post Office, is the former village **school** which dates from 1880. Two footpath signs stand close together nearby on the left. The second of these, indicates the footpath to Rushton, running to the right of a farmhouse, which leads past the site of the old Abbey.

At the end of the large field on your right, behind the trees stands the large imposing building, Pipewell Hall, the former Manor House. This is of 17th-century origin, and there is a datestone: 1675. There are stone mullioned windows and a Tudor-style entrance arch within. Alterations were made in the 19th century by the famed local architect, Gotch. You pass the entrance to the 19th-century coach house and stables, just past the small bridge over Harpers Brook. Note the fine patterned black and red brickwork (partially concealed) of the building to the left of the entrance.

At the T-junction, turn right. The fascinating small building on the right is the Hall Lodge. It dates from the 19th century, and has a 'Gothic' look with a pointed arch window, lancet windows and a 'fishscale' tiled roof. The thickly-wooded grounds to its left are a favourite birds' nesting and congregating place, especially rooks! A ruined wooden tower among the trees, covered in foliage, conveys an air of mystery!

Some way down the opposite end of the road towards Corby stands Lower Lodge Farmhouse which has its origins in the early 18th-century.

Walks in the area:
* For those wanting to be close to woodland, the walks here are ideal. Try walking along the road towards East Carlton. The trees of Monk's Arbor Wood on the left and Rawhawe Wood on the right, line the road for some way, providing a unity with nature and a scene of tranquillity until some fields give a brief interlude of light and space, before giving way to more forestry in the form of Askershawe Wood, and further away to the right, Swinawe Wood. At the footpath sign on the right, before Swinawe Wood, take the path towards Danesholme and Corby, accompanied by the stream running parallel to the track, within the wood.
* Back in the village, there are the two paths signposted on the left: one to Great Oakley, the other to Rushton. For these two walks, boots or stout footwear are essential, as the way is often muddy or wet.
* The stile into the field on your right, opposite the old school, will allow you to follow a track which skirts farmland on your left and Monks Arbor Wood and Barrowdykes Wood on your right.

The grassland on your left as you cross the stile, is full of earthworks from its iron quarrying days, and a single piece of pointed masonry This is a long, exhilarating walk which eventually leads through a small part of the woodland, across the former wartime Desborough Airfield, and down into Wilbarston.

ROCKINGHAM (farm of Hroca's people).

The settlement which gave the Forest its name nestles in a hollow below the hill on which its castle stands, dominating the landscape for miles around. The original village lay outside the main walls of the castle, but it was resited after the ravages of the Civil War, in its present location.

Church: St Leonard's. The earliest part is 13th-century, but most of the church was destroyed during The Civil War by Parliamentarian forces. The present building was begun in 1650 and was rebuilt again in 1868 and 1873. A tower was added in 1843 by Richard Watson. There is a 17th-century pulpit, but most of the interior is 19th-century. There is a memorial chapel to the Watson family.
Pub: the *Sondes Arms* (1663. Formerly the *Rockingham Arms*).

Former pub: the *Three Horseshoes.* This was run by the village blacksmith!
Former school: 1865 (1842 for 150).School House: 1858. Closed 1946. Now the Village Hall.
Rockingham Castle : During his reign, William I ordered the building of a castle at the top of Rockingham Hill - the same place which the Iron Age tribes and Saxons had found strategically important against attack. With its excellent position, size and situation in fine hunting country, the castle continued a long association with Royalty, and King John in particular was a regular visitor in the early 13th century, leaving behind one of his possessions: an iron chest. The building and grounds eventually passed (on a lease) in 1530 to a local landowner, Edward Watson who rebuilt it into a fine residence, and in 1619 it was bought outright by Sir Lewis Watson. Being a Royalist during the Civil War, he had to suffer a search of the castle by his Parliamentarian cousin from nearby Great Oakley! The castle was later actually occupied by Parliamentary forces in 1643, during time which considerable damage was inflicted and the church was destroyed. In the 18th century, a descendant of the family became Prime Minister on two occasions.

Much restoration has since taken place and it is still in the family today, with Commander Michael Saunders Watson as the present owner. Among the older parts which visitors can see are Walker's House (1655) and The Laundry (1670). Charles Dickens stayed here on five occasions and is believed to have been inspired to write 'Bleak House', as well as dedicating 'David Copperfield' to the owners. An excellent colour guide is available at the castle. There are fine views from the tower and superb gardens to walk around. Two mid 19th-century entrance lodges stand along the road, each with the Watson family coat-of-arms engraved near the porch: the Lower Lodge is a little way to the right as you go up the hill out of the village; and the Upper Lodge, which stands by the visitors' entrance, near the top of the hill, almost opposite the Rockingham Triangle Sports Ground. Open seasonally. Tel. 01536 770240 for details.

A walk through the village:
There is a path leading from the castle grounds to the church which stands closely below. The track continues past the church, down to some stone slab steps by the main road which winds down a steep hill. At the steps, cross the road to the house opposite (dating from 1793). The house next door is The Old Forge and dates from 1792 (it now offers a bed and breakfast facility). A blocked-in well head is in the adjoining wall to its left. The track (with a Public Footpath sign) by the side of the building leads to thatched no.18 on the right which is also 18th-century in origin.Continuing along the Main Street, the next house, no.18a (Paradise House) on the opposite corner of the footpath is generally reckoned to be the oldest house in the village, with a datestone: 1670. A group of buildings from the 18th century now follow: the thatched houses further on (nos.15/16), the two cottages set back from the path, no.13, and at an angle, no. 12 (Pound Cottage), the long Glebe House, and Apple Tree Cottage. The large house adjoining the latter, and opposite the *Sondes Arms*, is Coton Farmhouse. Next stands no.5, which originates from the 17th century. The last house on this side, with the thatched lean-to, is 18th-century.

Cross over to Castle Farmhouse and Castle Farm Cottage. The large house on the corner of the road to Cottingham, with stone mullioned windows, has a datestone of 1674. Among its outbuildings is a barn (round the corner in Cottingham Road) with unusual circular air vents. Continue the walk back on this side. Just past the *Sondes Arms* stands the 14th-century Market Cross, which was rebuilt in 1894 according to the inscription, 'in memory of Laura Maria Watson'. Close by, and set back a little, is the 19th-century former school, now the Village Hall. Next door by the phone box is the village shop (the former school house),which acted as post office for many years. The last building on this side is The Old Rectory with its stone-buttressed front window.

Snippets:
* A Great Council, comprised of nobles and bishops from around the realm, was held by the future king, John, at the castle in March 1095, to help settle a dispute between himself and Anselm, Archbishop of Canterbury.
* Rockingham and its castle was used by the BBC in the early 1980s as the scene of the English Civil War drama serial: 'By The Sword Divided'.
* Charles Dickens on his visits to the castle also produced plays in the long gallery there.The grounds outside are supposed to be the haunt of a Lady Deadlock, whom he saw flitting about the yew hedge. Could he have been inspired by such incidents to have written ghost stories like 'A Christmas Carol' ?
* One of the fields was known as The Tilting Ground, conjuring up the atmosphere of the medieval tournaments that once took place here.
* The village is also well-known for sitings of a ghostly carriage, drawn by horses charging down the hill on certain nights, before vanishing. The hill has certainly been a dangerous place for traffic

throughout the ages with many accidents having occurred. Several people are said to have seen the apparition on various occasions particularly New Year's Eve, though one wonders if a visit to the local inn and a little imagination has had a contributory effect!

* More historically accurate is the order in 1221 by Hugh de Burg, chief justice to Henry III (then only a boy of 14), who ordered a nationwide surrender of any castles held by nobles at that time. William de Fors, Earl of Albemarle, a noble constantly 'changing sides', was constable of two castles one of which was Rockingham. Elsewhere at the time of the order, he rose in revolt, planning to destroy Rockingham. (Needless to say, he did not succeed and was captured and subsequently pardoned - only to join another rebellion against the king two years later!). In true oral tradition, the story of the Earl's intentions was passed down through the centuries and much later commemorated in a poem, 'The Raid of Rockingham' by Charles Montagu-Douglas-Scott:

> *Let my horses be saddled ere dawn of day,*
> *Let my merry men muster all ready to ride,*
> *For I will be over the Welland away,*
> *To harry the Forest of Rockingham wide;*
> *And its towers and bowers shall burn till they fall,*
> *And the owlet shall hoot in the Banqueting Hall.*

(Soldiers chorus):
> *And the warders shall wake,*
> *And the barbican quake*
> *With the thunder of steeds and the rattle of mail;*
> *And our plumes shall arise*
> *And darken the skies*
> *Like the cloud on the uttermost gust of the gale.*

> *And everywhere where the eye can see,*
> *Shall the smoke of a blazing farm appear!*
> *And everywhere where a dwelling may be,*
> *Shall the echo of misery tickle the ear!*
> *And the crops shall be crushed, and the forest be felled -*
> *Not a hut shall be left where a human has dwelled.*

> *And the deer shall be killed; and the flocks and the herds*
> *Shall be swept to the North over Welland away!*
> *With no manner of man will I bandy my words, -*
> *If he fly, I pursue; if he tarry, I slay!*
> *And only some wenches, if pretty they be,*
> *Shall be spared from my fury to wait upon me!*

> *And this shall be told in the ages to come,*
> *How I laid the King's Forest of Rockingham flat;*
> *How I struck at a blow his authority dumb,*
> *How I struck his Verderer down like a rat;*
> *And that Monarch shall writhe for revenge on his throne,*
> *When this deed of my vow and my vengeance be known.*

Walks in the area:
* There is a walk to Gretton from beside The Old Forge, which is now part of the Jurassic Way, more or less straight for much of the way (but needs careful orientation in places for the first part of the journey). A good walk via scrubland, field and meadow passing under the old railway bridge near Gretton, and finishing with a steep uphill walk with devastatingly fine views behind you as you climb, or when you reach the stile at the top. A straight walk across the field from here brings you into Gretton.

ROCKINGHAM

ROTHWELL as it was: the High Street

* A walk to Great Easton is possible from the side of the pub (bridle track) or better, meet it at Cottingham Road. The walk, also now part of the Jurassic Way, passes across meadow and wetland via a bridge over the River Welland. Part of the route is through a conservation area, a project supported by the Countryside Commission, English Nature and English Heritage, protecting traditonal pasture land.

ROTHWELL (red well).

Originally a Viking settlement, Rothwell has grown into a town of substance, with many fine old buildings and a famous traditional annual fair which is still carried on, when the streets become crowded with people from all around. Years ago, surrounding villages would take in visitors as accommodation became scarce in the town. It also had a market of some importance, but this is no longer held.

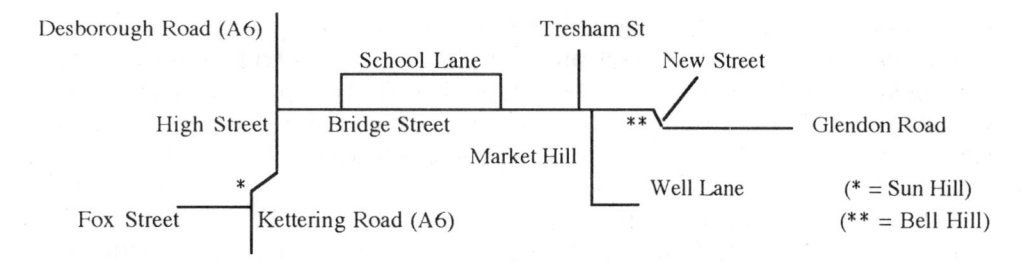

```
Desborough Road (A6)              Tresham St
              School Lane                    New Street
High Street     Bridge Street          **              Glendon Road
                             Market Hill
        *                                Well Lane      (* = Sun Hill)
Fox Street    Kettering Road (A6)                       (** = Bell Hill)
```

Church: Holy Trinity. Mainly 13th-century. with tower. The spire fell down 1657 and broke two bays. It is the longest church in the county : 173 feet. Plaques to members of the Hill family, former lords of the manor. A unique bone crypt, discovered by an 18th-century gravedigger by accident, contains bones of around 1,500 people of unknown origin, despite various unproved theories. It is open for visits on Sunday afternoons during the summer. There are occasional music recitals. At one time the chancel was used for housing the town's fire engine!
Former Congregationalist Chapel: (Fox Street). A building stood here in 1655. The present structure dates from 1735, was enlarged in 1852 and restored in 1893 and 1991. Now known as the United Reformed Church, it was recently restored by English Heritage. A key is available for a visit, from the house opposite. The former Congregationalist School (1885) stands next door.
Former Wesleyan Chapel : 1833 (Well Lane).
Former schools: (1) Free Grammar: 1585 (by Owen Ragsdale) on Market Hill, rebuilt with a schoolhouse 1870, and a classroom added 1893. (2)1886 for 200;
Pubs: the *Rowell Charter Inn* (Sun Hill. Formerly the *Sun*); the *Blue Bell Inn* (Bell Hill); the *Woolpack Inn* (1714), the *Red Lion Hotel* (both Market Hill); the *Old Greyhound Inn*, formerly the *Greyhound* and the *Sexton* (High Street).
Former pubs: the *Bulls Head* (Bridge Street/High Street); the *Crown Inn* (High Street), the *New Inn* (Kettering Road), the *Horse and Groom* (Bridge Street. At present the Co-op chemist's), the *Chequers* (Market Hill, corner of Tresham St. 1734. Also known as the *Old Woolpack*); the *Plough* ; the *George*. There are records of others. A large number was needed to cater for visitors to the market and great fair.
Other buildings and places of interest:
The Market House (1577) was built by Sir Thomas Tresham of Rushton Hall, at what was once known as Rothwell Cross. Stone from the famed quarries at nearby Weldon was given for its construction by Sir Christopher Hatton. Sir Thomas was renowned for his fanatical religious zeal (being imprisoned in 1581 for being a Catholic and being involved with the Jesuits). His other buildings at Rushton and Lyveden also reflect his faith, in their design. The building has 90 coats-of-arms of local landowning families engraved on the exterior walls, many of which are still legible today. It was actually left unfinished until 1895 when a roof was added by a local architect, J.M.Gotch. It has since between restored by the Rothwell Preservation Trust, formed in 1985, who have since worked on other buildings in the town, and who currently occupy no.14 Market Hill. The Market House has been used as Council offices, but it has also acted as a library, a 'pensioners' parliament' and a jail. It is said that one inebriated prisoner, discovering where he was, managed to escape by undressing, and squeezing his way through the metal bars of a door, which he had stretched to make a sizeable gap. Leaving his clothes behind, he made a hasty unobtrusive getaway!
Jesus Hospital : 1585 (behind the Market House) This was built for 26 old people of the town by Owen

Ragsdale, a former teacher at the Grammar School (which he rebuilt and is now the site of the library). A fine plaque can be seen above a doorway across the courtyard. The houses are still lived in today.
<u>Manor House</u>: (near the entrance to the church) is 18th-century. The original was probably built 1575-80. A medieval fish pond stands in the field opposite.
<u>'Nunnery' Cottages</u>:1660 (at the Desborough Road end of the High Street).The original religious establishment, actually a priory founded in 1247, stood on the site of 'The Priory', a house originating from 1631, which lies a short distance away along the road, to the right of the cottages.
<u>Bridge Street/Market Hill area</u>: There are a number of 18th-century buildings, among them no.21 (corner of) Market Hill which currently houses a Chinese restaurant. It dates from 1710 and has also acted as a 'coffee tavern' and a printing works.

Local crafts: *Art (inc. silk screen printing): Gill Clarke, 6 Oxford Street. Tel. 01536 710278.
Pocket Park: a stretch of meadowland and a stream. Near the Community Centre: access via Well Lane Playing Fields.
Nature Reserve: Rothwell Gullet. In the care of The Wildlife Trust for Northamptonshire, it is a former ironstone quarry hosting a vast array of plants such as hart's-tongue fern, enchanter's nightshade, primrose and, in summer an abundance of spotted orchids. The reserve lies close by the top of a hill along the A6 half a mile outside the town, en route to Desborough. Parking is on a broad grass verge, and the entrance to the reserve is on the opposite side of the road, via a stile.
Snippets:
* 'Rowell' Fair: this ancient fair, once famous for its horse trading, was held the day after Trinity Sunday (nowadays for a week from the Saturday afternoon before Trinity Sunday). A charter for a fair and a market was granted by King John in 1204. It is still held and is very popular locally. The annual ceremony begins with the charter being read in traditional costume, outside the church and the pubs.
* In 1251, the Earl of Gloucester, who was staying at Rothwell, was involved in an after-dinner incident when he and some companions (including a verderer) chased and slew a deer in a field near Desborough. As a result, the matter was referred to the king, and the 'whole township of Rothwell' was accused of conspiracy for 'besetting' (surrounding) the beast, and threatened with 'judgement'!
* The town poorhouse once stood in Market Hill where the Conservative Club building now stands.

RUSHTON ('settlement where rushes grow')

An interesting village with the 'centre', old station, school, village hall and shop at one end, and most of the old buildings (the original village) at the other. Many of these (church, houses, walls) have been built of ironstone. The High Street is 'tucked away' and contains the former smithy (1872) and post office/shop.

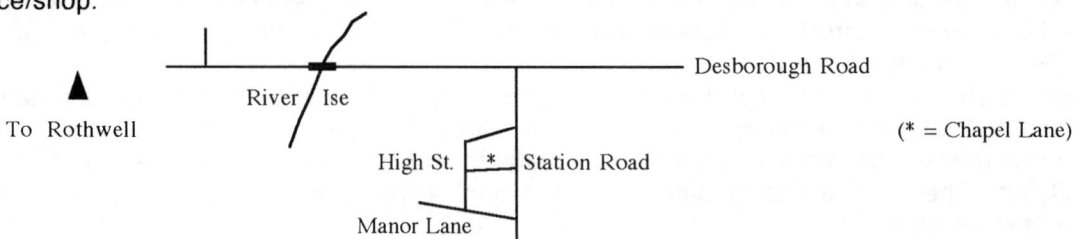

Church: All Saints (14th-century). Embattled tower. Restored 1869. Two outstanding monuments in Purbeck marble can be found within : one is the cross-legged effigy of a knight in mail/surcoat who held land here (died 1296); the other is of Thomas Tresham, Lord Prior of the Knights Hospitallers in the Order's dress (with an 8-point cross, and sword/armour) who died in 1599, and who was lord of the manor of the village. A fire in 1963 damaged the roof. Local talk has it that the clock faces the wrong way, ie. away from the village, where it cannot be seen!
Former church: St. Peter's, demolished in 1799. Had a low embattled tower. It stood on the south side of the outer court of Rushton Hall. The church rubble was used to repair All Saints Church.
Chapel: 1904 (in Chapel Lane. Now the Village Hall)
Pub: the *Thornhill Arms* (named after 19th-century occupants of Rushton Hall).
Former pub: the *Three Cocks*. In the 17th and 19th centuries, different owners of Rushton Hall altered the course of the Rothwell to Pipewell road. When the present road was built, the inn which stood on the former road, ended up in the Hall grounds and became the home of the butler! It is now an outbuilding.

School: 1891 for 120.

Rushton Hall was begun in 1595 by Sir Thomas Tresham, after demolishing a large part of the village that stood in the vicinity. His coat of arms are inscribed on the wall, with additional dates, and the coat of arms of the Cockayne family who later lived here: 1621, 1627, 1629 and 1630. It was built almost entirely from Weldon stone, and has a variety of windows ranging from mullion and transom, casement and canted bay, to tall bow. There is some impressive interior decorative woodwork. It was sold by the Cockayne family in 1810. There are some 19th-century outbuildings and an 18th-century groom's house. The grounds run down to the River Ise. The poet Dryden is supposed to have stayed here, writing 'The Hind and the Panther', whilst 'frequenting' the Hall's 'shades': in the grounds was a moss and lichen-covered urn with a pedestal on which was an inscription recording the event. Today it is a school for the Blind, and is open to the public on special occasions, usually during school holidays. Craft Fairs are sometimes held.

Other buildings and places of interest

The two Entrance (East) Lodges to the Hall, in Desborough Road were built in the Gothic Revival style in the early 19th-century.

Along the main road to Glendon and Rothwell past the entrance is a stone hump **bridge** (the present structure is 1829) over the Ise. When it was built to divert the road away from the Hall, live toads were placed in small slate and cement hatches at the foundations, to see if they could survive for a thousand years! It must have been an idyllic spot once, but today it is difficult to stand there for long - though the narrow bridge acts as a deterrent to would-be fast traffic which has to slow down to avoid self-inflicted damage!

Triangular Lodge: 1593-5 by Sir Thomas Tresham. It was also built with Weldon stone (and alternate bandings of ironstone). The building is in the shape of an equilateral triangle, with everything in three's: 33 feet 4 inches long, three storeys high, with three triangular windows on all the three sides, each topped with three gables. The exterior wall panels have the date 1595 in large black numbers, each with a Christian motto or symbol. In the past it has been known variously as 'Warrener's Triangular Lodge' (from the time rabbits were bred for their meat and skins), 'Three Square Lodge', and 'Trinity House'. Tresham's eldest son, Francis, was one of the conspirators involved in the Gunpowder Plot. The building, now under the care of English Heritage, is a little way outside the village on the Desborough Road. There is limited parking outside on the road.

There is also the usual ghost story attached to such a building. It is said that a tunnel was discovered under the Lodge, which was rumoured to lead to the Hall. A local fiddler volunteered to go into the tunnel to see if this was so, for a financial reward. Playing his fiddle as he went, the sounds got fainter as he made progress until nothing could be heard. A small search party went after him but found nothing except rubble from the collapsed roof. The plan of the fiddler (who had found a hiding place the day before) had misfired, and he was never seen again. Ghostly fiddling sounds are said to be heard occasionally from the area around the lodge at night!

Beech House: situated to the left of the bend of the Desborough Road as it leaves the village. It is mid 19th-century in origin but has a 1641 datestone with the Cockayne family coat of arms on its gable end facing the road. This came from the Cockayne Bridge which stands in the grounds of Rushton Hall, close to the present road bridge, and has cutwaters and two arches. The vicinity of the bridge was once known for its unusual echoing effect: there is a sad story of a little girl from nearby Barford who wanted to talk to the echo, and walked into the river, and drowned. (The bridge has decayed considerably, and is now covered in ivy. In the past it has been noted as a favourite haunt of bats!)

Rushton Hall Farm: (set back off the Desborough Road, between the Hall and Beech House) has a 16th-century square dovecote and a Tudor-arched doorway.

Rectory Cottage (The Old Rectory): is a late 18th-century building facing the church. Behind it stands The Old Coachhouse, and Parish Meeting Hall.

Manor Farmhouse: this fine 17th-century building with some blocked mullioned windows stands a little way back from Station Road, opposite the High Street and Thornhill Arms. It is partially hidden behind trees and a wall. Its outbuildings extend to the edge of a bridleway.

Rushton Manor: dates from 1694 and stands at the bottom of Manor Road, which is at the station/Corby road end of the village. There is a pointed 'Gothic' arch in one of its boundary walls, and a stone 'window' frame in another, near the footpath.

Railway station: now derelict. Despite crumbling away, the waiting room and façade on the rail side still exhibit an ornate mid 19th-century design.

Local crafts: *Art (mainly pastel & watercolours): Joy Norman, 13 Midland Cottages. Tel. 01536 711438.
Snippets:
* The explorer, Baffin had one of his expeditions financed by Sir William Cockayne of Rushton Hall. In return for the generosity he named part of Greenland, 'Cockin's Sound'.
* Two 'lost' villages lie close by: Glendon and Barford. Most of Glendon disappeared in the 16th century as a result of estate extension. **Barford** ('ford by the birches') has only a bridge surviving, as a reminder of its former existence just off the Kettering-Rockingham road. In 1327 there were only 14 inhabitants listed, and by 1515, as a result of conversion of the land to pasture for sheep grazing, the village had all but disappeared. The chapel which had been served by a monk from nearby Pipewell Abbey soon followed. Around 1720 only the outlines of house foundations were reported. The small road leading off towards Newton is strangely quiet and enclosed. There have been many report of road accidents around this stretch of road as a result of the unfounded sighting of a ghostly monk! Part of the area, known as 'The Wedge' is now being developed as a nature reserve by The Wildlife Trust for Northamptonshire.

SOUTHWICK ('south dairy farm'). Pronounced 'suth-ick'.

Though not in the 'centre' of the Forest, Southwick is perhaps (arguably) the best-placed village for access and communications with other communities. It is a small one-street village, situated to the south of a massive chunk of forest area which stretches for miles, and is encircled by a road network which does not encroach on it. Southwick is blessed with a web of walks and bridleways through and around this area.

Church: St Mary's. Earliest parts: chancel arch *c.*1230, and the tower and crocketed spire *c.* 1350. Indents of medieval brasses. 13th-century coffin lid (in churchyard). 17th-century panelling. 18th-century pulpit and communion rails. Several floor slabs to members of the Lynn family (former lords of the manor at Southwick Hall). There is an elaborate marble monument to George Lynn (1758).
Pub: the *Shukburgh Arms* (17th-century).
Former pub: the *Bill and Hatchet*.
Former school: 1872

Southwick Hall : early 14th-century. One of the oldest buildings in the county. Owned successively by three families: the Knyvetts, Lynns and Caprons. The Knyvett family held the manor in the 13th century. It passed to relatives, the Lynn family in 1442, with whom it stayed until the early 19th century. Impressive ornate chimney tops, vaulted undercroft, North Stair turret and 'Gothic Room' with oriel window. The Hall was remodelled in 1872 by George Capron. The grounds include old trees and a giant birch, 'The Elephant Tree' so-named because of its protrusion. Open seasonally to the public: Bank Holidays (Easter to August inclusive) and Wednesday afternoons (May- August).
There is a surviving legend in a poem connected with Southwick Hall, about a hunting incident that is supposed to have occurred at nearby Morehay Lawn during the late 16th-century:

How hushed and holy is the dawn
That wakes the birds on Morehay Lawn,
Where two men stand with weapons drawn.
How sweet with life the earliest breath
That stirs the leaves, and whispereth
Around the twain intent on death.

Up sprang the sun as from a well
Of fairyland invisible,
And one cried out to God, and fell.
The other he turned with guilty speed,
And leapt upon a trembling steed,
And on the flying victor gazed,
"He rideth north, now God be praised!"

*And all the while the birds did sing
As if there were not such a thing
In the wide world suffering.*

*And as they sang above the dead,
Two deer came by with timid tread,
And snuffed the tainted air, and fled.*

*In Southwick Hall the Lady Lynn
Said, as she sat her down to spin,
"Why cometh not my husband in?*

*"He rose betimes, before the dawn,
To hunt the deer on Morehay Lawn;
'Tis noon, nor has he yet withdrawn.*

*"E'en as he rose, he answered plain
To Morehay Lawn he'd ride again,
To hunt the deer with Mildmay Fane.*

*"Young Mildmay fane, a pleasant boy,
Sometimes I think t'would give me joy
If he my husband could annoy.*

*"I like George well, but cold he is,
And perhaps some twinge of jealousy's
Might warm that icy heart of his.*

*"Last Christmas Day I gave a ring
To Mildmay, hoping it would sting
My George well-nigh to challenging.*

*"But no, with slightly courteous air,
He simply said 'The ring is fair,'
'Tis plain for me he cannot care."*

*And as she mused, there came a noise
Of tramping men and clamorous boys:
Said she: "What mean these village joys?"*

*And lo! a crowd came thro' the door,
And four men laid upon the floor
George Lynn, of Southwick Hall no more.*

*"Say who has done this deed? May he
Be thrice accurst, whoe'er it be!
O George, come back! O speak to me!"*

*We know not, lady, tho' all around
We searched the wood; but only found
His ring upon the trodden ground.*

*She sized the ring, and thro' her brain
A flash, as lightning thro' the rain, -
The ring she gave to Mildmay Jane!*

*And all the while the birds did sing
As if there were not such a thing
In the wide world as suffering.*

Other buildings and places of interest:
After visiting the Hall and church, proceed along the main street. An 18th-century house, Church Cottage, stands on the left-hand corner of the Glapthorn road, on the opposite side of which is a barn tastefully converted into a thatched dwelling, 'Cornerhouse'. The village pub which is a short distance away, is part 17th-century : the building became an inn around the middle of the 19th century. Behind it, with its gable end facing, stands thatched Eden Cottage which is from the same era. Across the road from the *Shukburgh Arms* once stood another pub, the *Bill and Hatchet*.. On the left, some way on, is the long thatched Park Cottage which is part 17th-century, and right at the end of the village, on the same side, is the appropiately-named Towns End Farm, another thatched, though later building from the early 19th-century.

Nature Reserve: Southwick Wood: an ancient remnant of a larger tract of forest, is a 56-acre site comprised of woodland, scrub and grassland.There is a specially-created butterfly glade, many old oaks (some over 400 years old) and a great variety of other trees, including the wild service-tree. There are unusual plants associated with ancient woodland. The wood is a favourite haunt of many birds. Situated to the west of the Southwick-Glapthorn Road. A hard verge for parking is available. Walk past the water tower to the entrance, which is signposted. Another reserve (Short Wood) is on the opposite side of the road.
Local crafts: *Art: Susan Bonvin/Andrew Eden, Corner House, tel. (01832) 274141.

Snippets:
* 'Old' forest lodges in the vicinity: Crosswayhand Lodge, Morehay Lawn House, Perio Lodge, Bulwick Lodges, and Stonepit Lodge. Others like Tottenhoe Lodge have now disappeared.
* Interesting local place names: Babholm, Foxholes Square, Langewelsike.

Walks in the area:
Trees are on the doorstep! This is a walkers' (and riders') paradise! There are excellent long walks to Woodnewton, Apethorpe, Kingscliffe, and Blatherwycke through woodland. All four walks begin at the side of the church and cross the field to the forest area which lies ahead.
* (1) Woodnewton. On reaching the forest, take the grassy track to the right, skirting the edge of the woods for some way, before passing through the woodland until you reach a stream (marking the boundary of the woods) Once over the bridge, it's uphill along the track over open countryside and then straight on down to Woodnewton with views of Apethorpe Hall in the distance on the left and the idyllic scene awaiting you of Conygar Farm and the water gushing through the Mill.
* (2) Apethorpe: as for Woodnewton, but at the bridge turn left and follow the edge of the field and course of the stream uphill to Lodge Farm at which you turn right and descend along the track to the village.
* (3) Kingscliffe.On reaching the forest go straight ahead until you come to the rough farm track passing across. Turn left onto this, and when you come to the bend, disregard it and go onto the grassy track ahead. Take the first turning on the right (marked at present by a portable metal watch-tower!) and follow the grassy track down and up for a considerable distance, with tremendous panoramic views of the forest all around you (you will feel quite small!) En route you will see Shire Hill Lodge nestled below on the far left, and you will pass over a wooden bridge spanning a small brook.The route is now arrow-marked. At the top of the hill, you will come to Tomlin Wood, with arrow markers in four directions..You need to follow the edge of wood round to its left. It is now straight all the way with the large village of Kingscliffe visble in the near distance.
* (4) Blatherwycke. This is only for the more ambitious! It is a long but rewarding walk for which a keen eye and an Ordnance Survey Map are necessary, as it is easy to go off-course! As for Kingscliffe but at the four arrow markers at Tomlin Wood, take the sharp left turning up to the narrow rectangular-shaped wood of Morehay Lawn (pronounced 'Morey'). Follow the track past it and when you come to

arrow makers for two directions take the right-hand one, down to more woodland, including Hostage Wood. Blatherwycke lies below. Good luck!

* (5) Another (shorter) walk - though along the quiet Glapthorn-Oundle road for part of the way - will take you past a white water tower to a green signpost marked to Tottenhoe Lodge (this was an early 19th-century building standing in part of the original Morehay Walk). This track leads to a **Nature Reserve:** Short Wood, which is now in the care The Wildlife Trust for Northamptonshire, who purchased the 62-acre site, to counter the threat of clearance for agricultural use. This is a fascinating remnant of the Forest and is open to visitors. It is divided into four areas: Dodhouse Wood, Short Wood, Cockshutt Close and Hall Wood, each offering something different. Thirty-five species of bird nest there regularly and there is a great variety of woodland flora. There is active coppicing within the wood to encourage the growth of new stems, which in turn are used for traditional purposes such as thatching spars and hedging binders. Trees to be seen include hazel, ash, elm, and field maple. It is encouraging to see another vital part of the original forest preserved and tended so well! From here you can also get to nearby Glapthorn Cow Pastures, another reserve (see under Glapthorn). For this continue along the track past the Short Wood entrance towards the trees in the distance.

* (6) Perio Mill. No woodland on this walk - just open fields. Walk past the church along the road to Woodnewton. On your left are fine views of Southwick Hall. Just beyond the bend and bridge, there is a footpath sign on the right. This walk (signposted with black and white arrow markers) takes you past Southwick Grange on the left, across fields (one of which at some time has had an intriguing - and noisy - scarecrow!) and crosses a brook which flows into the Nene a little further on. Soon you arrive at a road, opposite and Perio Mill, the original of which existed in the 12th- century. The mill was in use during the 19th century for both paper and corn milling. It is now a commercial Trout Fishing and Clay Pigeon Shooting concern. **Perio** is yet another 'lost' forest village. Perio Lodge, a 17th-century building is close to the original site. A small medieval 'hospital' (to two saints) stood south of the Mill. (Continuing left past the Mill along this road brings you to a T-junction. Turning right at this brings you, after a mile, into Fotheringhay; however if you go straight over the junction along the single track road you will come to a footpath sign on the left, the track by which takes you gradually into Woodnewton. If you continue along the road <u>past</u> the footpath sign you come to a track that leads on for some distance into Nassington).

STANION ('village of stone buidings').

A small village that had a long connection with stone-quarrying and timber. Harpers Brook runs past the back of the village on its way to Brigstock and the Nene. Remnants of Rockingham Forest can still be seen nearby, forming a fine natural backcloth.

Church: St Peters. Earliest parts: 13th-century (the chancel and north chapel are c.1270). The building was at one time a former chapel to the main church of Brigstock. There is a striking medieval wall painting of a deer and unicorn bowing to a 'human' figure. At the other side of the church there is a gigantic rib 'The Dun Cow Rib' (in reality a whalebone that somehow found its way to the village long ago). Medieval glass fragments. Richly-carved font. Communion rail (17th-century). 18th-century box pews. Outside there are two large gargoyles and 51 heads of men, women, and 'grotesques' - which some say are former benefactors to the church or even villagers living there at the time it was built. The original broach spire was at one time dismantled, lengthened and placed on a newer Perpendicular tower, giving it an un-naturally lofty appearance (it is one of the tallest spires in the county).
Methodist Chapel: 1907 (in Chapel Lane opposite the church).
Former school : 1840 for 72 children. Founded by the Earl of Cardigan.
School House: now demolished, it stood at corner of the High Street and Cardigan Road.
Pubs: the *Lord Nelson* (mid-18th century, despite a 1594 datestone in the wall), the *Cardigan Arms*.
Other buildings and places of interest:
Brigstock Road. Opposite the *Lord Nelson* stands Manor Farmhouse which dates from 1605, but is mainly 18th-century.
Little Lane. Once a thriving 'business' community flourished here including a butcher's, lacemaker's, and timber yard. No.1 was built c1670 on the site of an earlier building. Nos. 5 and 7 were built in 1741 as three cottages, one of which was a shoemaker's. No.11 is of 16th-century origin and was built over a well. No.13 was once known as 'The Alehouse' and was an extension of no.11. No.15 has 16th-century origins, and was formerly a farm and dairy. No.17 once had a pottery kiln at the rear.
High Street. Many 18th-century houses here, among them: no.1 (Heartsease Cottage) on the corner (next to which is a small 'green' with some old millstones and the Post Office. This area was known as

Wade's Yard and once housed a mill and bakery); thatched Tithe Barn Cottage (from the early years of that century); and nearby, a building with a blocked-up medieval (Decorated) arched doorway (no.25). It is said that this house had religious connections at one time, but research has so far failed to find the answer. On the path outside is what is believed to be the stump/base of a medieval stone cross. Opposite the church is no.14 (Ivy House) which was once a bakehouse, and opposite St. Peter's Hall stands no.16 (Greycroft).

Round the bend on the church side, is a tall stone house (no.35) with two dates inscribed on a lower cornerstone: 1727 and 1739. Across the road stand the former 19th-century poorhouses once known as 'Workhouse Row'.

Further along on the left is 'Abbots Cottage' which stands on the site of an earlier house: this has largely been rebuilt in the latter years of this century, with a reset datestone in its wall, c.1540.

Kettering Road (once known as Town End Road): no.3 (The Firs) which is almost the last house in the village, and is late 18th/early 19th-century in origin. A little further on, to your right are the remains of the old Kettering-Stamford road, part of which is still used for access to the rear of a house, but which soon peters out to a grassy footpath. The house by the brook, has a visible clock, once part of a village builder's office. On the corner of Willow Lane stands the 19th-century Grange Farm House.

Local Crafts: Stanion Pottery, 24 Willow Lane. Open Monday to Friday (Sat/Sun by arrangement). Demonstrations available. Tel. (0536) 400334.

Pocket Park: an area of meadow and wetland beside Harper's Brook, to the left of the bridge at the bottom of Willow Lane. Known as Keeble's Field. Favourite haunt of a kingfisher.

Snippets:

* A legend attached to the Giant Rib in the church tells of a giant cow which once provided the whole village with its milk, until the wrath of the local witch was incurred and the cow was milked dry!

* A poem exists about a 'fair maiden' who had a bewitching effect on every male! Unfortunately the poor girl was put in a ducking stool and held in the water of Harpers Brook until she drowned:

> In Stanion town on Harpers brook
> There dwelt a maiden fair to see;
> But every lad on whom she'd look
> Fell into dire calamity.
>
> One broke a leg, one lost a pig,
> One had strange buzzings in his head;
> And one, a giant, danced a jig,
> Nor could he stop till he was dead.
>
> In vain the country gallants swore
> They would not look her in the face;
> Her lively beauty overbore
> Their power of will to their disgrace.
>
> Until one day, one winter's day,
> The village rose with one accord,
> The young of either sex, and they
> Resolved to duck her by the ford.
>
> About her eyes they bound a cloth,
> Lest she bewitched them with a look;
> And then with cries and groans of wrath,
> They ducked her in the icy brook.
>
> They ducked her twice and thrice amain,
> They held her down for minutes three;
> And when they pulled her up again
> All stiff and cold and dead was she.
>
> They took the cloth from off her face,

Oh, she was fair, and passing fair!
But none accounted it disgrace
That he had helped to drown her there.

Had she indeed been innocent,
It stood to reason, so they said,
She would have borne the experiment, -
It proved her guilt that she was dead.

And Jack recovered from his break,
And Peter found his erring pig,
And Harry's noddle ceased to ache,
And no one danced another jig.

* The names of the streets have undergone many changes: High Street was formerly Main Street, Town Street or The Causeway; Little Lane was Top Lane; Willow Lane was Back Lane; Corby Road was Weldon Road.

* There used to be Coffee and Reading Rooms in the village, as well as a Clothing Club in the mid-1800s, which operated via contributions from members, of eight shillings and eight pence. In return they would receive goods to the value of fifteen shillings, the difference being made up by the Earl of Cardigan. The small building is now known as 'Wee Cottage' and stands in Corby Road.

* As is to be expected for a settlement whose history is steeped in quarrying (from which it probably gets its name), Stanion was once well-served with public stone and mortar pits: there were four dotted around the village, and one nearby on the road to Geddington. The church at Brigstock is made from this stone. There was also a flourishing pottery industry during the Roman and medieval periods.

Walks around the area:

* There are excellent walks to Brigstock following the course of Harpers Brook, and to Geddington, via part of Geddington Chase. The former which is way-marked, starts at a green signpost at the top of Willow Lane (the Village Hall end). The latter initially involves a walk uphill over meadow, but the view is spectacular: here you are virtually encircled by remnants (near and far) of Rockingham Forest. As you approach the thickly-wooded Chase, you are bound to surprise a pheasant, deer or rabbit. As you walk along the track through the woods, you will pass the gamekeeper's house. Start at the bottom of Willow Lane where the track leads off over the brook (the footpath is signposted and way-marked).

* You can also get to Brigstock (to a different part than the first walk mentioned above) by continuing up the track for some distance, via Lower Lodge (once known as Stanion Lodge) until you come to Dust Hill Road. Turning right leads you eventually to the Park Walk end of Brigstock.

STOKE ALBANY (place of Willelmus de Albini: Aubignys in France).

The village is divided in two parts: the earlier (Saxon) part around the church (Lower End) and the later (13th-century) part is up the hill (now Ashley Road). Both contain some of the oldest surviving buildings in this part of the county including the Old (Hall) House beside the church.

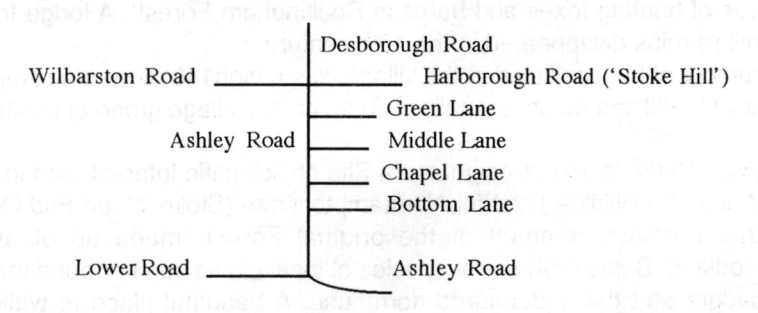

```
                          | Desborough Road
     Wilbarston Road  ____|____ Harborough Road ('Stoke Hill')
                          |____ Green Lane
         Ashley Road  ____|____ Middle Lane
                          |____ Chapel Lane
                          |____ Bottom Lane
         Lower Road  _____|____ Ashley Road
```

Church: St Botolphs. Part 13th-century. Embattled tower. Original medieval roof still intact in the north aisle. A 15th-century monument of Johannes de Ros, a lord of the manor, dressed in armour, used to lie in an arch in the chancel but was removed in 1790, because the wife of one of the rectors found it hideous: at first the lid was overturned and used as a seat, before being broken up and buried under a nearby path! Monument (1683) in porch. Font inscribed: 'Marke Marshall, churchwarden, 1681'. Chancel restored 1872. There are graffiti on the stonework around the main doorway and a sundial above the porch, inside which there is a charming inscription asking men to scrape their shoes, and women to remove their outer footwear before entering. An unique feature of the church is a recently-carved (bespectacled) stone corbel at the base of a window in an exterior wall on the left side (near the tower): it represents the current rector! The church is in an idyllic setting by a green, partly surrounded by chestnut trees, with the former school and oldest house in the village to its left.

Pub: the *White Horse* (thatched, with a datestone: 1706) on the corner of the Harborough and Desborough Roads.

Former pubs: the *White Hart* ; the *Talbot* (now Talbot House opposite the 'White Horse' on the corner of Ashley Road) with interesting secondary front doorway and right-end wall.

Former school (and schoolhouse): 1871 for 60 children. (Lower Road. Now the Village Hall).

Other buildings and places of interest:

Ashley Road: The Manor House (now 'The Manor') on the right-hand side of the hill leading down to the church, was the home of the lords of the manor (de Albini) from whom the village later took its name, and the De Roos family (through inter-marriage). The house still has some original parts from the 15th and 16th centuries. There are almost illegible datestones on the gable end of the house (1682) and above the barn to its left (1683). Above the main door are shields inscribed with the de Roos (Ros) coat-of-arms. Earthworks of 13th-century fishponds are visible behind the building. (A closer glimpse can be obtained, together with a fine view of the surrounding area, by walking along the winding uphill road to Wilbarston (no path), and crossing into the field at the public footpath sign, via a stone stile).

Proceeding down the hill, there are four interesting side streets leading off from the left-hand side of the road: Green Lane, with one of the two village greens; Middle Lane (which has a plaque on the corner thatched house, showing that the 'Best Conserved Area' award was given by Kettering Borough Council in 1982. One of the old village water pumps stands low-down outside the house, facing the road, in a brick-framed recess; Chapel Lane with the old chapel mid-way on the left, and some 18th-century buildings including no.12, with a datestone: 1739, and finally Bottom Lane at the end of which there are two 17th-century houses : no. 8 and no.12, the latter having a datestone at the base of its chimney, 1651.

Ashley Road swings round to the left at the bottom of the hill, where 'The Old House' stands (behind the Village Hall and next to the church). It is well-named and even older than the Manor House: its earliest parts are believed to date from the 14th century, and there are 16th and 17th-century additions.

Lower Road: (another route to Wilbarston) no. 4 has a faded datestone facing the road: 1684.

Desborough Road: no.1 (opposite the pub car park) has an almost illegible early 17th-century datestone at the base of a chimney. The village shop/post office is further along the road on the edge of the village.

Snippets:

* In 1201, William de Albini was given a grant by the king, to enclose a park near his manor house 'to enjoy the privilege of hunting foxes and hares in Rockingham Forest'. A lodge for the purpose stood in the vicinity until its ruins disappeared in the 19th century.
* In 1721, the number of houses listed in the village was a high 140: sizeable compared with today!
* The Village Feast is still carried on annually in June, on the village green opposite the Manor House.

Nature Reserve: Stoke Wood : Designated a Site of Scientific Interest, and in the joint care of The Woodland Trust and The Wildlife Trust for Northamptonshire (Stoke Wood End Quarter), this is a rare treasure: another precious remnant of the original Forest, made up of ancient semi-natural broadleaved woodland. Some of the rarer species of local plants can be found there, and it is a haven for muntjack, badger and the endangered dormouse. A beautiful place to walk in, with an aura of tranquillity, and a feeling of communion with the past. It lies outside the village on the Desborough Road, almost opposite Bowd Lane Wood (which is not open to the public, and is a former deer park which belonged to William de Albini, with a still-visible earthen bank enclosure). By this wood and metal gate there is a short lay-by where there is very limited parking. Access is across the road, via a stile, (post-marked The Woodland Trust) and a farm track leading straight to the wood, part of which is still in private ownership. Stout footwear is recommended: it can get muddy and slippery!

STANION: looking towards the High Street and St Peter's.

Wilbarston at the turn of the century

Thrapston: from the southern end

Walks in the area:
* Ashley. The best walk starts from the track to the left side of the church. Passing through the gate, there is a fine example of medieval ridge and furrow field on your right behind the church. The walk is arrowmarked at the stile and stream ahead, and joins the uphill route from Wilbarston further on.
* Wilbarston, via Lower Road. Either proceed all the way up the hill past the church, or about half-way along, turn right at the wooden Jurassic Way signpost, over the stile, and use the charming old stone clapper bridge over the stream, before walking uphill over grassland to the exit, right of the church.

STOKE DOYLE (holy place of Henricus d'Oilli).

A tiny village running along the main road with a side track (unmarked), Church Lane, leading towards sites of antiquity. Another track, by a black signpost, and traditionally known as Hatchdoyle Lane, (with a turning, Rectory Lane), leads to a dead end! The church, rectory, and site of the manor house and fishponds lie away from the main road. A former chalybeate spring (Sevenwells Spring) lies nearby.

Church: St Rumbold. Tower with pinnacles and balusters. 17th-century wall monument. The church was rebuilt in the 1720s. Sculpted angels (19th-century). Many 17th-century tombs in the yard.
Former school: 1865. 'The Old Schoolhouse' has a datestone of 1874.
Pub: the *Shukburgh Arms* (mid 18th-century).
Other buldings and places of interest:
Howe Hill Farm (formerly Manor Farmhouse): late 17th-century, with mullioned windows, and square dovecote at the rear.
Rectory : 17th-century (but of earlier origin) with 1633 on one bay window, and a gable dated 1731.
Gardens: the gardens of Mill House are open to the public annually as part of a national scheme (see under Aldwincle for details).
Snippets:
* The original village once stood near the river but was moved to its present site along the road.
* The area was disafforested in 1638 by Edward Doyley (whose ancestors had given their name to the village) who had 1,200 acres of land in Rockingham Forest.
* The old manor house (south of church) was pulled down in 1870 and a farmhouse built on its site. A large stone dovecote with hipped roof and lantern survives from the old building, as well as fishponds and moat.

SUDBOROUGH (southern fortified place).

A fine village for a quiet thoughtful walk along its thatched-lined street. Excluded from the 1299 perambulation,Sudborough was involved in confrontations with Forest villages who became extremely wary of its poaching habits. One particularly notorious incident is discussed below.

Church: All Saints. Early English, Decorated, Perpendicular styles. Fourteenth-century pinnacled tower. Late 14th-/early 15th-century brasses to the West family. Fragments of medieval glass. Stone altar tomb with brass effigy of a knight (13th-century).
Former school: 1841 (by the Duke of Buccleuch). Opposite the Rectory.
Pub: the *Vane Arms* (18th-century. Formerly the *Cleveland Arms*).
Former pub: the *Round House.*

Other buildings and places of interest:
Main Street: The long thatched house on the right, opposite the pub (no.39) has a thatched fox and peacock on its roof. It dates, with the adjoining thatched house (no.40), from the 17th-century. The church and Rectory (1826) are over to the right. The Rectory opens its gardens to the public annually as part of a national scheme (see under Aldwincle for details). A long continuous row of houses on the left, beginning with no.17, Appletree Cottage (no.15) and Frog Cottage (no.16) and ending with The Long House (no.10) dates from about the late 17th/early 18th-century. The Manor House, on the same side at the end of the street before the road bears left, is from the same period.
Turning left on the way out of the village you pass on the left, Dean House (datestone1855), Woodbine House and on the bend, the Round House which is considered to have been a former toll house, but was in fact a pub built by the local farming and brewing Coales family in the 17th century. It has a reset datestone on its wall: 1660. The present building is said to be late 18th-century. The house was lived in until quite recently by the renowned county author , 'B.B.' (D.J.Watkins-Pitchford).

Snippets:
* There is a tradition at a nearby place called 'Moneyholes' that the large earthworks to be seen there are the site of a medieval religious establishment, but there is no evidence to support this.
* Local woods have names such as Cat's Head Wood, Lady Wood Head, Snape's Wood. One of the ancient tracks within the parish is in fact closer to Brigstock and lies on a route to Lyveden: it is known as Stephen's Oak Riding, a reference to the medieval king of that name, who is supposed to have shot a deer here. A very large old oak that once stood in the vicinity, and acted as a boundary marker (until it fell down), was said to have been climbed by boys from Brigstock, thirty of whom were able to fit inside the trunk quite comfortably!
* In 1837, a group of men from the village headed along the green lanes to Deenethorpe, on a poaching expedition. A keeper on the Cardigan estate at Deenethorpe, had received advance news of the intended incursion, and posted fourteen assistants at Burnt Coppice to lie in wait. The gang of 25, with their 'bag' of 180 rabbits, were set upon, and after the ensuing mêlée, the poachers fled leaving yards of rabbit netting behind, and three prisoners. The next morning, a gruesome discovery was made when a fourth poacher was found near the scene of the affray, disembowelled. Strangely, in the ensuing post-mortem, the victim was pronounced as having died from exertion, and that no mark had been found on his body! The three prisoners were tried at Northampton, and found guilty, but on account of good character references, and having large families, were sentenced to one year's imprisonment 'in the house of correction to hard labour'. A song was written, 'The Sudborough Poachers Song', in commemoration of the incident:

In 1837 it plainly doth appear,
A bloody scene was felt most keen
Until death did draw near.

Poor Samuel Mayes of Sudborough town
A lad of well-known fame
Who took delight both day and night
To hunt the lofty game.
Mourn all you gallant Poacher men
Poor Mayes is dead and gone
Whilst our hero brave lies in his grave
As ever the sun shone on.

With nets so strong we marched along
Unto brave Deenethorpe town
With nut-brown ale that never will fail
Was many a health drunk round.

Brave lunar light did shine that night
As we to the woods repaired,
True as the sun the dogs did run,
To chase the timorous hare.

Then to the Poachers
The keepers they did start
And in that strife took poor Mayes' life,
They stabbed him to the heart.
For help he cried but was denied
There was no-one that by him stood.

And there he lay till break of day,
Dogs licking his dear blood.
Farewell, dear heart, for I must part,
From my wife and children dear.
Pity my doom - it was too soon

That ever I came here.
Farewell, those dear brave lads,
What'ere revenge they held
That cruel man with murderous hand
Which caused me for to yield.

* A watermill once stood near the bridge, on the edge of the village en route to Slipton.

Walks in the area:
* Lowick (1) The walk begins at the signpost on the bend of the road as it leaves the village towards Lowick and the A6116. You pass through a small farmyard, cross a field, and follow part of the course of Harpers Brook, past a spinney and Lowick Mill and over a stile onto the track into the village. It is arrowmarked (black and white) en route. Do not be afraid of the bulls!
* Lowick (2) This walk begins at the other end of the village from the last walk, on the Slipton Road, at the footpath sign beside Spring Cottage on the left. It goes over Harpers Brook, uphill some of the way (with good views) towards a clump of trees and then bears left, before a slight descent. Follow the arrowmarkers. There are plenty of stiles.
* Aldwincle. Follow the road out of the village towards Lowick. At the main road bear right and walk a short distance before crossing over and following a track towards the woods. At the edge of the woods keep virtually straight on (do not turn left!). The walk is more or less straight. After leaving the wood you will eventually come to a track. Turn right and follow it into the village.

THRAPSTON ('comfort town').

A major town on the river Nene, headquarters of the East Northants Council, and a 'gateway' to the Forest.

Church: St James. Earliest parts: 13th-century. 14th-century tower and spire. Coat of arms of the Washington family (ancestors of the first US President). Restored 1841.
Methodist Chapel: 1885
Baptist Chapel: 1787
Pubs: the *King's Arms*, the *Mason's Arms*, the *White Hart*, the *King's Head*, the *Red Lion*, the *Fox Inn*.
Former pubs: the *Swan Hotel*, the *White Hart Hotel*, the *Woolpack* (all in Bridge Street), the *George Hotel* (now part of the Corn Exchange building).
Former school: 1851
Other buildings and places of interest:
Chancery Lane: Montague House. Sir John Washington, Lord of the Manor, lived here with his family. He was the second son of Lawrence Washington of Sulgrave, and uncle to John Washington who had emigrated to America in the 17th century and who was great grandfather of George, first President of the USA). The building near the entrance to the street, was later used as a private school and is now a solicitor's offices.
'Nine Arch Bridge' (of 14th-century origin) spans the Nene, and the entry to the village from the south end. There was an even earlier bridge here. Another had as many as 24 arches! It was partly destroyed in a great flood (1795) and the area around Bridge Street was often subject to severe flooding.
Local crafts:
There are a number of artists. Details from the Library.

Snippets:
* Oundle Road was once known as Titchmarsh Lane; Midland Road was Denford Road.
* The 17th-century Manor House (in Chancery Lane) was demolished in 1967 and the Tollbar House on the Kettering Road, in 1971.
* The site of the watermill and millhouse is now a campsite, boating house and marina.
* The building which housed the former poorhouse (1836) was until recently used as the Council Offices, which now have new adjoining premises.
* There were once two railway stations: Midland Road Station, and Bridge Street. The latter opened in 1845, and closed in 1964.

TWYWELL (double stream).

A village, mixing stone and brick in its buildings. It was once noted for farm engineering, clock making and its brickworks. Another 'gateway' to the Forest.

Church: St Nicholas. 11th-century. Embattled tower. Ancient urns. Saxon arch. Norman doorways and font. The purpose of an unusual low side-window, has been variously interpreted as being for the use of lepers and ex-communicants, or for ringing a hand-bell (in place of a Sanctus bell). Medieval Easter sepulchre. Quern stone. Restored 1867. Remnants of the bark used to bring the remains of the famous 19th-century explorer David Livingstone back from Africa (see under Rectory).
Pub: the *Old Friar* (a thatched late 17th-century building).
Former pub: the *Masons Arms*.
Former school: 1876 for 120 (closed 1979. Now used by the Girl Guides). It is at the top (Slipton) end of the village.
Rectory: stands south west of the church (built in 1760). It was once lived in by Horace Waller, rector between 1874-95 and African explorer. He was an active campaigner against the slave trade on his return. General Gordon of Khartoum was a frequent visitor. In the house, the rector edited the journals of his great friend, Dr. David Livingstone.
Buildings of interest:
Church Lane: Manor House (Farm) was once connected with the Mulso family, and has 15th-century origins, though the present building has a 1591 datestone and much later additions. There are 17th-century outbuildings visible from the roadside, including a pantiled square dovecote, and a converted barn, part of 'Ayres Rock', with a datestone: 1662.
High Street: Manor Farmhouse (19th-century). Attached is an earlier rectangular dovecote with end gables and lantern.
Lower Street: Home Farmhouse (1663) with mullioned windows. Opposite: Home Farm Cottages (17th-century), including Post Office Cottage: 1660. On the right, leaving the village towards the A604 and close to the pub, is The Old Toll House, or 'Round House', with a curved ship-like wall at one end, a mid 17th-century building, with an older building attached, which once acted as the village poorhouse.
Site of Special Scientific Interest: a newly-acquired site of 135 acres comprising woodland, natural limestone grassland and an ironstone quarry. There are pools with unusual species of plants and invertebrates. At the time of writing this site is still being developed for public access and enjoyment. This will be an excellent place to walk.
Snippets:
* A monastery once stood nearby between Slipton and Sudborough (hence the pub's name) and was closely associated with the village.
*A detached part of the village called Curtley was joined to Slipton in 1885.

UPPER BENEFIELD (field of Bera's people).

Formerly known as Uppthorpe, Overthorpe or Upperthorpe, this is the other half of Benefield, its lower part lying at the bottom of a twisting road (along which is 18th-century Nethertown Farmhouse), though there is a also a choice of two straight walks across the fields to that village: one from beside the village shop; the other on a bend of the road as it descends out of the village. This end has the village pub and shop, and has a different setting and atmosphere to its counterpart.

Pub: the *Wheatsheaf* (1659).
Other buildings and places of interest:
'Druids' (no 13) has a datestone of 1791. To its left is an interesting tall old barn with two elaborate arches and storied hatches, part of Townsend Farm. Next door is long, moss-covered no.15 (18th-century) with an unusual building formation. Across the road is no. 16 (Cherry Tree Cottage) also from the same era. Rose Cottage (no.17) next door has a datestone of 1692. The house with mullioned windows next door (no.18) is even older, dating from the early 17th-century. Further down on the right after a wide gap is the large Ashley Farmhouse, another building of 17th-century origin. Across the road, no.25 (and after another gap) nos.27 and 28, all date from the 18th century.
The village shop on the right, Benefield Stores, part of which was once a bakehouse, is from the same

era. Across the road stands an early 18th-century thatched cottage (no.32). The other thatched cottage nearby (Bluebell Cottage) is of a much later date.

Further along, opposite the 17th-century pub, is a building with mullioned windows, and on its front wall, there is a carved lion and a datestone of 1651. Nearby on the corner of the Glapthorn Road turn-off is Hatfield Farmhouse, from the same era.

Local crafts: Knitting design: Tessa Watts-Russell, no.37 (Main Street). Tel: 01832 5377 (for personalised commissions).

Snippets:
* The name of the village and Lower Benefield is pronounced 'benner' (not bean) field.
* The *Wheatsheaf Inn* was a popular haunt with US airmen stationed nearby during the War. Then it was a typical small village pub. Today it is larger and more commercialised, but offers more facilities and a highly-recommended restaurant.

Walks around the area:
* To the south west of the village three large remnants of the forest can be found: Spring Woods, Cockendale Woods (both along which a public footpath runs) and Blackthorns. To reach them you need to return to the entrance to the village along the Weldon Road. Off the cul-de-sac to the right is a footpath sign pointing diagonally across the field.
* Deenethorpe. The track to this crosses grassland, a stream, a spinney and part of the runways of the World War II US airbase. A long, fascinating walk with a pleasant village at the other end. The footpath starts (signposted) before one of the farms on the left of the Glapthorn Road. (Alternatively, use the footpath signposted on the main road between no.28 and Middle Farm Kennels).

WADENHOE ('Wada's spur of land').

A picture-book village with a Trust to preserve its old buildings, Wadenhoe is a treat to visit and explore. Take your camera and take home memories of this beautiful place. Wander around the riverside, the Mill area, the mound with its church on top, and the quiet streets. Look out for the unusual!

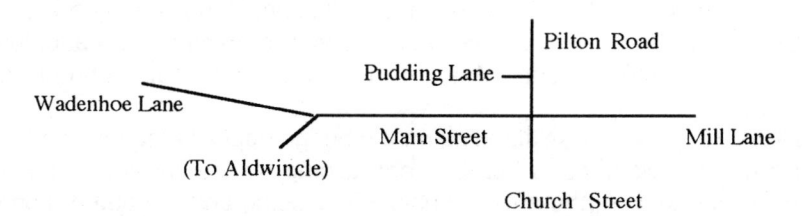

```
                              | Pilton Road
              Pudding Lane ———|
Wadenhoe Lane _____|_____
                \   Main Street    |   Mill Lane
          (To Aldwincle)            |
                              Church Street
```

Church: St Michael and All Angels (formerly St Giles Church). Saddle-back tower (late 12th-century). Evidence of an earlier Saxon church. The rest of the church is mainly 13th and 14th-century, with fertility symbols in the form of a 'Green Man' carved as corbels on the church walls. One bell dates from 1603.

There is a brass memorial on your left as you enter to Thomas and Caroline Welch-Hunt, who after being married for ten months, were 'cruelly murdered' whilst on a belated honeymoon in Italy. The background to the tragedy is as follows: He had recently become the new lord of the manor, and together they looked forward to settling down on their return. Taking a detour from Rome, to see the temples of Poestum, they decided to stay overnight at a small inn in Eboli. However, the innkeeper noticing their wealth, contacted some local banditti, who lay in wait in the temple ruins as the couple made their way to the site early the next morning. When intercepted, the couple handed over money, but being pressed for more possessions, Thomas resisted and was mortally shot (dying that evening). Caroline was also wounded in the process, and she died two days later. Three of the four banditti were captured and guillotined, the innkeeper (who informed on them) escaping justice and carrying on business at the inn for several more years.

There are some interesting 17th-century tombstones in the churchyard, the inscription on one of them is cautionary and begins: 'Reeder art thou in sound Health, So ware I, ...'

Pub: the *King's Head* (formerly the *Duke's Head*) in Church Street. It is 17th-century in origin.

Former school: (now Caroline Cottage) 1839, built for 62 children by Miss Mary Caroline Hunt. Stands near the top of Church Street.

Other buildings and places of interest:
Begin the walk at the bottom of Church Street, where there is parking space. Go through the gate into the field and follow the hard track to the church at the top of the mound. The isolation of the church

from the village, and the earthworks show that, at some time, the settlement that stood here moved to its present site below. It is said that in the 17th century the Great Plague hit the village particularly hard, but this has not been proved. The village windmill also once stood here and the site, with its evidence of defensive fortification, was once known as 'Castle Close'. The area around the church was formerly a deerpark.

Below the church, the stretch of riverside wetland along the River Nene, is a site of Special Scientific Interest with a diversity of plant life. It is a pleasant place for a walk at any time of the year, with winding paths leading up amongst the trees and shrubs overlooking the river. The Nene Walk is one of these tracks and leads to Aldwincle. You might see a boat or two, canoes and even dinghies negotiating the lively river. It is a good place to compose your thoughts before moving on. The village hall, next to the pub, at the start of the walk, often serves teas on summer Sunday afternoons.

Walk up Church Street, passing the first two thatched houses on the left Nene Cottage and its neighbour, both of which date from the late 17th-century. The two adjoining houses, no.32 and Wit's End Cottage, are later, dating from the 18th century. The pub stands opposite, with an adjoining thatched house, 'The Nutshell', to its left, which is early 18th-century in origin. Next to Cergne House on the right are two more thatched houses, nos.28 and 27 both dating from the early 18th- century. Tucked away snugly between the latter and a large tall stone barn, is small white-walled 'Caroline Cottage', the former village school. The barn is part of Mill Farm, the 18th-century house of which stands on the corner.

It is reassuring to know that some villages look after their old buildings and ensure that new ones, whether walls or houses, blend in with their surroundings. Such is the case with Home Farm Close on the opposite corner. A light blue plaque of the Rural Development Commission is attached to the rear wall of the house.

The unusual-shaped building facing you here at the top of Church Street is South Lodge, and it stands at one of the two entrances to Wadenhoe House. It is an attractive, ornate, many-sided building dating from the late 18th-century with different shaped windows, including a 'bull's eye'.

Turn right here into Mill Lane. Wadenhoe Mill at the bottom of Mill Lane, stands on the site of an earlier mill, mentioned in the Domesday Book. The present building is 18th-century with additions in the 1830s. One particularly generous miller, Francis Allen, in the 1840s/50s would send out soup and milk to sick and needy villagers.

There is an air of tranquillity and timelessness standing on the bridge opposite the mill (on the track to Thorpe Achurch). Here a pair of swans can often be seen gliding on the surface of the water, or nestling on the nearby reeds. In autumn, the area is subject is flooding and the author has seen the track to the bridge and beyond, cut off by vast expanses of floodwater, virtually transforming the meadow into a lake!

You can get a glimpse of Wadenhoe House from here, at the small car park to the left of the wall.

It dates from 1657 and was originally built for the de Lacey family who held the manor. The Le Strange family then held it until 1532. Later, around 1800, it was bought by Thomas Hunt of Oundle (whose nephew was the Thomas Welsh Hunt who was murdered whilst on honeymoon). The family held it until well into this century. It is used today as a business centre.

Retrace your steps to the top of the hill, noting as you turn right into Pilton Road, the fine T-shaped thatched building on the corner ('The Cottage'). This is 18th-century in origin. In Pilton Road, The Wadenhoe Trust building stands across the road, and opposite this, in a wooden-gated paddock stands a real gem : an 18th-century round dovecote, with potence and nesting boxes inside. A key is available. The building is in the care of the Northamptonshire County Heritage, whose brown and white plaque is on the gateway. Visitors are welcome, as long as the gate is closed on leaving! Behind it stands Dovecote House which dates from the same era.

Across the road, jutting out on the corner of what is known as Pudding Lane, is a beautiful long thatched cottage (no.21) which has a datestone: 1637. This is part of a row of two other thatched buildings from the same era, lining the small narrow lane (which comes to a dead-end). On a sunny day, it is a 'chocolate box scene' - a charming relic of a bygone age, virtually untouched by time.

Further along the road are two more buildings of interest. On the left is 'Rat Hall', formerly the Old Rectory of late18th/early 19th-century origin. The strange name derives from large numbers of rats that once liked to exist and roam in the vicinity! On the right is North Lodge (1858), the second of the two lodges at the entrance to Wadenhoe House. A black and gold sign outside shows that the house is currently used as a Management Training Centre.

Retrace your steps to Main Street. The large house facing Pilton Road is the 17th-century Home Farmhouse. and turn right. Next to it as you turn right is 'The Thatched Cottage' with a filled-in 'Gothic' window in its gable end. This interesting house existed in the Middle Ages in some form and was rebuilt in its present manner at the end of the 17th century onwards. After the church it may well be the oldest building in the village. It probably has a rival for this distinction, further along on the same side in the shape of Manor House Farm (the former Manor House), which has three datestones: 1593, 1653 and 1670. There is a piece of ancient masonry capping one of its gateposts.

Almost opposite, the Post Office is housed in an early 18th-century building. Continuing along the road past a small field, you come to the large village green: this is the 'newer' end of the village. The War Memorial stands here, and a row of two-tone brick houses with several front gables facing the green show their building date in a diamond-shaped plaque: 1865.

Snippets:
* In medieval times, it was normal for a forester to alert and summon help from nearby villages if a transgression of the forest laws by outsiders, such as poaching, was taking place. Villagers were legally required to answer a call for help. In 1245, Wadenhoe refused, which later resulted in the village receiving a severe reprimand and penalties at one of the Forest courts.
* A gasworks was laid on for the village in 1868-9.
* The Post Office in Main Street is reckoned to have been the first rural telegraph office in the UK.
* John Bridges, the renowned Northamptonshire historian and writer, was for a time, lord of the manor of Wadenhoe until his death in 1724.

Walks around the area:
* Aldwincle (see above). The walk starts from the signpost at the bottom of Church Street.
* Thorpe Achurch/Lilford. The walk starts at the bottom of Mill Lane. Cross over the bridge and head over the water meadow in a north easterly direction towards the river and high bridge. Head towards the church at top of the hill. (For Lilford, go along the track past the church and turn left at the Footpath sign through The Linches).
* Brigstock (see under Brigstock). A good long-distance walk across meadow and through forest.
* Lyveden New Bield. Go along Main Street to the far end of the village and take the first turning (by the green) on the left to the Aldwincle-Stoke Doyle Road. A footpath sign points across a field at the end of which is a single track road. Turn right at this road and left at a signpost further on. Go past Wadenhoe Lodge, follow the arrow markers and eventually cross a field to Lilford Wood, and follow the track through.

WAKERLEY ('watcher's slope').

A tiny sleepy village with a few older houses, some thatched, hugging the sides of the road in the east, and spread out along, and off the road to Harringworth. It is possible that the village was once larger and lay closer to the church than it does now.

Church: St John the Baptist (redundant). Earliest parts: early 12th-century. Late 14th-century crocketed spire. Medieval glass, brass indents, font and piscinæ. 12th-century elaborately carved capitals of interwoven designs including beasts, foliage, human figures and buildings.
Pub: the *Exeter Arms* (formerly the *Red Lion*). Early 19th-century.
Other buildings and places of interest:
Main Road (coming from Wakerley Woods): 17th-century Manor Farm sits back from the road to the right, with a ruined 18th-century square dovecote in a field to its rear. The thatched house by itself on the left of the road is late 18th-century. On the bend, the middle of the three houses on the right (with mullioned windows) originates from the 17th century. The thatched house to its left is 18th-century.
Barrowden Road (opposite the pub):
The site of the former Manor House (built and demolished in the 17th century) lies to the right. Only the earthworks can be seen, some of which mark a once extensive garden. You then pass, on the same side, the site of the old railway station (until recently a caravan site). Ahead is **Wakerley Bridge:** a fine 14th-century stone bridge with a carved head on each side of its walls marking the county boundary and a difficult-to-see datestone on its right (1793 when it was repaired) facing the river. Linger awhile and savour the atmosphere. On the other side of the bridge to the right of the road, is a sign welcoming you to the proud county of Rutland, recently restored to its former status.
Main Road: (towards Harringworth): the former Rectory, 'Copper Beech' (early 18th-century in origin); The Manor House (1769). Both buildings on the left-hand side.

Leaving the village to the right of the bend you cannot fail to see two conspicuous brick towers in a field close to the river. These were begun in World War I and were originally intended as kilns for purifying local ironstone before its transportation to Sheffield or Dudley, via the railway which ran alongside. Originally four were planned, and none were ever used. It is rumoured that German prisoners-of-war from a nearby camp up the hill were involved in their construction. There is an interesting view of the towers from the churchyard of Barrowden just on the other side of the river.

Walks around the area:
Wakerley (Great) Woods. Over 600 acres, the woods are yet another (large) remnant of the Forest, with an abundance of wild life.There are two specially-created walking routes (a short blue trail, and a longer red trail) along which some fine Swallow Holes (collapsed underground caverns, through which water disappears) may be seen.Within the woods there are also limestone workings and an old ironstone quarry. Cycling is also possible as is horse riding. The woods are popular with dog owners. There is also a picnic and barbecue area. Occasionally there are special family events laid on.
*Adjoining Wakerley Great Wood are Adams Wood, Wood Hollow and Town Wood, which also have public rights of way through them.
* Barrowden (see above). The walk is now part of the Jurassic Way.
* Harringworth. Follow the quiet undulating road, and enjoy the views of the river valley, settlements, and the white windmill of Morcott on the horizon. An Anglo-Saxon cemetery was once found close to the road.

WANSFORD (ford by the spring).

Once lying partly in Northamptonshire, partly in Huntingdonshire, Wansford marks the limit of the Rockingham Forest area. It is worth a visit if only to see and walk across its magnificent bridge.

Church: St Mary The Virgin. Perpendicular style. Part 13th-century. Parts of the walls belong to a small pre-Conquest (Saxon) church. Was originally a 'chapel of ease' to the church at nearby Thornhaugh. The Norman font (*c.*1100) is of great interest, not only for its striking design depicting (in 13 arches) human figures in various poses (fighting, holding a book, etc) and the Baptism of Christ, but for its origin: it is believed to have come from the church of the 'lost' village of Sibberton, the site of which lies close by) and which was wiped out by a plague. It was found at Sibberton Lodge and was being used, it is said, as a water trough for cattle. There is also a Communion cup of 1570. A bell of recent origin is named 'Barnaby's Bell' in honour of a legendary character associated with the village.
Pubs: the *Haycock Inn* (17th-century coaching inn), the *Cross Keys*, the *Paper Mills*.
Former pubs: the *Old Mermaid* - later called the *New Mermaid*. (It stood near the church) ; the *Marquis of Granby* (stood close to the *Old Mermaid*); the *Black Swan* (now 'Swan Hill House', the last house in Old North Road before the A47/A1).
Former school: none - the village children walked to Thornhaugh or Stibbington.
Other buildings and places of interest:
The old village is virtually one street running from what is now the Old North Road (Stamford Road, over the crossroads, through Bridge End, and over the bridge into Elton Road. On the left-hand corner of the Old North Road, opposite the church, is a 17th-century house and further along on the same side, past the bus stop, is an ornate former lodge (no.19 or 'Hillside') with scroll and coat of arms. Built *c.*1602, it has a mullioned bay window.
Just past the church along Bridge End are some interesting old houses, including two more from the 17th century. Ahead stands elegant **Wansford Bridge**, the 'showpiece' of the village. This ancient long structure has 10 arches with several cutwaters. Originally it had 13 arches. The bridge was frequently mentioned in the 13th century. In 1234 (Henry III) an oak was granted from 'the forest of Clive' for work on the bridge. Villagers would be granted 10 days religious penance or be allowed 'pontage' (right to tolls for wares crossing the bridge). Early surviving parts date from the last years of the 16th century and the first years of the 1600s: on the first left-hand cutwater (coming from the direction of the church, or Bridge End) are various inscriptions with dates (on the side facing the river), one of which is 160 - (the last figure is illegible). The date,1577, is inscribed on the inside of a pedestrian refuge at the centre, opposite which is an old white metal county boundary marker: Huntingdonshire/Soke of Peterborough.The southern portion was rebuilt in 1795, after ice had severely damaged the surface and made the bridge impassable to traffic.
Leaving the bridge, you see on the left the *Haycock Inn*, which takes its name from an incident that is said to have occurred in the vicinity during the 17th century, when a farmworker fell asleep on a

WELDON: the old lock-up by the Village Green

WOODNEWTON: St.Mary's Church, from the main street.

haycock by the banks of the river one night, only to find when he awoke that the waters had risen and swept him along the current for a considerable distance. He was asked by some men who rescued him near the bridge, where he was from, to which he is supposed to have replied in his confused state, 'Wansford In England!' - a name by which the village is sometimes known. (Another more credible version says that the rescue took place on the coast!) The event was celebrated in verse, in a book by Richard Braithwait ('Corymbæus'), *Drunken Barnaby's Journal,* published in 1716 (though written long before the author's death in 1673), about the character's journeys. On later editions the frontispiece showed Barnaby on the haycock. The scene was also depicted on the original sign of the *Haycock Inn*. This was later sent to Woburn Abbey.

'On a haycock sleeping soundly
The river rose and took me roundly
Down the current: people cry'd
Sleeping down the stream I hyd
'Where away', quoth they, 'from Greenland?'
'No, from Wansforth Brigs in England!'

The main street (Elton Road) is filled with many 19th-century buildings with datestones. One house has a wall plaque requesting motorists to check their car for cats before driving off! Further along on the right, as you leave the village, stands the ornate 19th-century gatehouse to Stibbington House with church/castle-like capped tower, and tall chimney stacks with embattled crowns.

Snippets:
* Wansford was once noted for its papermills. There was also a flourishing barge trade along the Nene.
* In 1836, a year before she became Queen, 17 year-old Princess Victoria stayed at the *Haycock Inn*.
* Wansford Station though not actually in that village, is now part of the Nene Valley Steam Railway. It is also the home of Thomas the Tank Engine!
* On the Wansford to Southorpe road, there is another conservation area under the care of The Wildlife Trust for Cambridgeshire: Southorpe Paddock Nature Reserve. A haven for butterflies and wild flowers. The old Roman road, Ermine Street, can be traced running through the site.

Walks in the area:
* Yarwell. Begins at the church end of the bridge. Signposted & arrow-marked, with variations of route possible. Basically a short, direct and picturesque route, which can include part of the riverside.

WEEKLEY (wych elm wood).

The village lies in two sections, split by the main A43 road.

Church: St Mary's. Earliest parts: 14th-century including tower and spire. Restored 1873. There are several 16th- and 17th-century monuments to the Montagu family of Boughton House.

Other buildings and places of interest:
The roads in the village have no name plates, with mail being delivered by house number.
Entering the village on a bend of the A43, from the direction of Geddington, you will see two large fine cob and thatch houses, on either side of the road leading off to the right (traditionally known in the village as 'Wood Lane'). These are both early 18th-century in construction, but are said to be of earlier origin. Both cob and thatch appear to have been standard in the village, and most of the other thatched houses that can be seen are of the same type and age though smaller. These can be found along the 'main' road of the village (leading off to the left by the small green), and along the turning behind the post office (once known as 'Wet Lane', and later as 'Wash Well Lane'. Sheep-dipping used to take place at the far end).
The turning on the left near Corner Thatch (no.10), and nos. 12 and 13 (all of which have some 17th-century features), contains two remarkably well-kept old buildings, the first of which is a former stone-built 17th-century **school** by Nicholas Latham for the village and nearby Warkton. A plaque above the door, though partly obscured in summer by plants, reads: 'A Free School for Weekely and Wreckton. Founded by Nicholas Latham. Clerke.Parson of Barnewell Saint Andrew To Teach Theire Children To Write and Reade. Anno Domini 1624'. The large building stone building next door is also 17th-century and is the former almshouse, Montagu's Hospital'. There is a large dark red painted square above the doorway in which there is a sundial '1614' (red sundial 1611) and the Montagu coat-of-arms and the inscription: 'What Thou Doest Do Yt In Fayth'. The nearby church at the end of the road completes the

picture. Retrace your steps along the road, passing the Village Hall (1890) on the left with its large grassy enclosure. At one time it stored the Duke of Buccleuch's lending library of 3,000 books which were for the benefit of the residents of the Estate (Weekley, Little Oakley, Newton and Geddington), who were allowed 'free use'.

Snippets:
* Sir Edward Montagu purchased the manor of Weekley in 1528. Many of the villagers helped to develop and maintain the Boughton Estate.
* The streets officially have no names - just house numbers and the name of the village.

Walks in the area:
*By the side of no.30 at the far end, is a track over the fields to nearby Warkton. Go through the metal gates and cross the field in a north-westerly direction. You will come to another metal gate and short wooden fence near the roadside. Cross the road, turn left and go over the track beside the road bridge spanning the River Ise. The village is ahead.

Boughton House

The village of Boughton virtually disappeared when the monks of St Edmundsbury Abbey built their monastic dwelling there. It was bought from St Edmundsbury Abbey in 1528 by Sir Edward Montagu (adding a manor house and courtyards to the existing 15th-century Great Hall) in whose family it remained until the 18th century when it passed by marriage to the Buccleuchs.

There are 365 windows representing each day, 52 chimneys for the weeks, seven entrances for the days, and four wings (for each quarter of the year) geographically pointed. Ralph, 1st Duke of Montagu, was a former ambassador to Paris, at which time he was influenced by French art and architecture, so much so that during the 1690s he made considerable additions to Boughton House. There is a rich array of tapestries and art works, as well as a superb collection of armoury and weapons, including some pieces from the 15th century.

Though it lies beween Weekley and Geddington, the only public access is on the Geddington-Grafton Underwood Road. The house is open to visitors for a very limited season daily from the beginning of August until the beginning of September. The grounds which are extensive and include a large children's adventure playground, a tree-shaded walk and a nursery for gardening enthusiasts, are open for a longer period: from the end of April to the end of September (except Fridays).

WELDON ('hill with a spring').

The village was once known as 'Weldon in the Woods', signifying its position in Rockingham Forest. For centuries, it was divided into two parts, Great Weldon and Little Weldon.

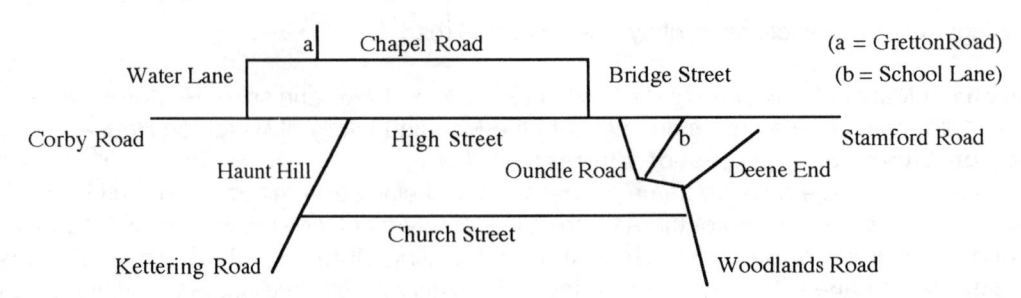

```
                    a   Chapel Road                      (a = GrettonRoad)
      Water Lane  ┌──────────────────┐  Bridge Street    (b = School Lane)
                  │                  │
Corby Road        │   High Street    │  b              Stamford Road
              Haunt Hill        Oundle Road  Deene End
                       Church Street
          Kettering Road                    Woodlands Road
```

Church: St Mary The Virgin. Early parts: 13th-century. The church has an unusual feature: there is a lantern in the rebuilt Norman tower which at one time was lit at dusk (see Snippets). A spire is said to have existed, until it was replaced around 1700 by the present tower. There was once a tomb to one of the Bassett family, who were once lords of the manor. Fifteenth-century font and window. 17th-century and Victorian stained-glass. Until World War II, a 'noonday' bell would ring daily at midday, and at dusk, 'as a curfew'.

Chapel: (1792). Now the Congregational Church. In Chapel Road.

Pubs: the *King's Arms* (replacing an older 16th-century coaching inn which was demolished in 1962 with a number of cottages, to widen the main road); the *Shoulder of Mutton*, the *George*, the *Woolpack Inn*.

Former pubs: the *White Hart* (stood on the corner of Water Lane/Corby Road); the *Nag's Head*.

Former school: 1820, extended 1872 and 1891. Closed 1973. On May Day, a maypole was traditionally placed on the green outside the school and dancing took place.

Other buildings and places of interest:
Coming from the Corby end, it is perhaps best to park along Water Lane, before the bend to the right. This is part of Little Weldon. As you walk round the bend, note the group of 17th-century houses (nos.41,37 & 35) on the left: no.37, Cornforth Cottage, (with green-painted windows) has an outbuilding with the gable end facing the street.Shortly you will come to Gretton Road (now blocked off at the end, but once an important route) off which leads Larratt Road, where the village windmill once stood, not far from 'Hunt's Wood', on the site of even earlier mills. It originally came from Wing until 1839 where it had stood beside another mill!
On the right of Chapel Road, opposite the Gretton Road turn-off, stands an impressive long thatched building with mullioned windows (no.46). This dates from the late 17th-century. Further down the road is a short footpath leading to the Congregational Church. The rear of the Manse which faces the church has a sundial.
Across the road from the church is 18th-century Hunters Manor, which replaced the original manor house (on another site). Approaching the end of the street, there are five houses of note: on the left hand side are no.5 (Pell Cottage) which dates from the 17th century, and on the corner, no 1 (mid 18th-century). On the opposite corner is The Old Farmhouse (once known as Home Farm), a fine late 17th-century building with mullioned windows. Next door to its right, with its gable end facing the street, is a former blacksmith's cottage from the early 18th-century. Next to the pub is another building from the same era, (thatched and white-painted) no.14. To the right of the pub is a 'jetty' (pathway) through to Corby Road.

Chapel Road merges into Bridge Street at the corner. Make your way along this to the end past the Village Hall set back on the right, and over the brook to the T-junction. Turn left into Stamford Road. The building on the corner is the mid 18th-century butcher's shop, with a building from the same era, now the Post Office, next door. Beside this is the *George* , an excellent inn and hotel combined. The restaurant offers good value food and is recommended! There is a cosy inglenook fireplace inside, and this is ideal during cold windy winter days. A story has been told of a pet snake which once escaped and got lost somewhere in the water pipes of the building! The hotel is mainly 18th-century but is on the site of a much earlier building. It adjoins a former shop, dating from the 19th century.
Further along are 'Scotch Corner' and next door, no.11, both of which are 18th-century (the latter bearing a datestone, 1794). Nearby is 'Little Cottage', a charming 'story-book' building with a low-pitched roof, Tudor-style doorway and an old firemark. It has been dated as late 17th/early 18th-century. The *Woolpack* pub is from the same period. Finally, 'Rosslyn' (The Rosary), no 23 with a datestone, 1818, has an elaborately-patterned low porch.

Cross the road and turn right towards the Green. Until 1950 a pump stood here and on the eastern side there was a blacksmith's until the 1930s. Left of the Green is School Lane. A group of 18th-century houses line the left-hand side. The first one is supposed to have marked at one time the boundary between Great and Little Weldon. The next row of houses lining the green as you go round the corner are from different eras, one of which was once the *Nag's Head*. The oldest of the houses is the first one, no.9. At the end of the row on the corner of the Green and next to the former school is a striking, circular limestone building with a ball on top. This was an 18th-century 'Roundhouse', the village lock-up, and is now a listed building. It has an iron-studded solid wooden door, and two metal grills at the top on different sides. Miscreants and drunks would have had a hard job trying to get out!
Walk to the other side of the Green via the former school and adjoining schoolhouse on Oundle Road.This is a charming narrow and twisting road, never intended for motor traffic and must be negotiated with care, but what a feast for the eyes and imagination! As you round the bend, if you can shut out the traffic, you could easily be in a long-lost world.Two early 18th-century thatched cottages Washbrook Cottage (no.8) and Willowbrook Cottage (no.10) lie sleepily on the right. On the opposite side, from the same era, are white painted, thatched no.5, and no.7. Further along on the right, again from the 18th century, is no.16, at the side of which is a narrow thoroughfare to a small bridge crossing the busy Willow Brook. This is one of many such bridges for access to the other side in this part of the village.'Greystones' stands next door, a larger mid 17th-century building with mullioned windows. Across the road, stands the old bakehouse (18th-century), which at the time of writing is under reconstruction.
Cross over to this side for a short diversion along the turning Deene End. This was formerly the outkirts of the village, and as its name implies is the part of Weldon nearest to the village of Deene. A short walk will take you to a set of modern buildings, but two old buildings on the edge still stand defiantly as representatives of the past. On the left is thatched Hatton Lodge (no.10) with 17th-

century origins, which stands beside a stone stile into the cricket ground, and opposite, a little way down, is no.11, also thatched but a little younger in age, being early 18th-century.

Retrace your steps to Oundle Road and proceed round the bend to the stone bridge crossing the brook. The area around the bridge here was where, traditionally, sheep dipping once took place. The imposing old building set back from the road to the left and opposite Church Street (the so-called 'Manor House') is in reality a former farmhouse with 17th-century origins, and was part of an estate. The original two manor houses of Weldon no longer exist (see below, under 'Snippets').

Turn right into Church Street and walk towards the church in its fine setting. (Paths lead off from the road and the brook can be crossed at various places. It is worth trying one or two). Most of the houses line the left-hand side. Opposite the church, is an early 19th-century house (now divided in two, nos.22 & 24) that was formerly a rectory, and was lived in by the Finch-Hatton family at one time. Garden fêtes were once held there, and it had extensive gardens. Next door (no.20), stands yet another former rectory, a building dating from the mid-1700s, which was once the home of Dr.J.Clark, a surgeon who was present with Nelson at the Battle of Trafalgar. Next to this is an even earlier building, the 17th-century Old Rectory Lodge. The last building on the left, is Glebe Farm House, which originates from the 18th century. Finally, the last house on the opposite side (no.1) was once a thatched alehouse.

Turn right at the junction (left leads to the former stone quarries), and proceed down Haunt Hill, so-called because of reports of blood-stained masonry, apparitions, an underground passage and other legends. On the left stands an imposing building, Haunt Hill House (*c*.1636-43), which was carefully crafted by the Worshipful Company of Masons, whose insignia can be seen inscribed above the porch and south gable. The builder was Humphrey Frisby who married Elizabeth Grumbold (daughter of another Weldon mason). There are mullions and a massive central stone-built chimney with fireplace in each of the four lower rooms. The house 'att the towne's end by the quarries' (*sic*) was sold in 1648 for £100 to a William Jones of Gretton. On the right, before you cross the bridge, are earthworks of former stone quarries.

Carrying on, you now come to the High Street. Cross over to the side opposite the newsagent's. No.1 (Willowbrook), has a datestone of 1742. Nearby is a fine house, no.7, which has been rebuilt over the centuries and has datestones of 1587, 1691 and 1844. Further along and set back from the pavement is a 'tall' narrow building with a clockface (no.11). This was formerly a brewery. Nearby, Cheyne House (no.23) has a Georgian appearance, and no.27 has 17th-century origins. Near the corner of Bridge Street is the Oddfellows Hall from 1890.

Retrace your steps along the High Street to the point opposite the green and where Haunt Hill emerges. This is now Corby Road and there are one or two houses of interest at this end of an otherwise ordinary street. No.11, a white thatched building, formerly with a shop, dates from the 18th century. There is a pathway here to Chapel Road. No.23 (25) has mullioned windows, two Tudor-style front doorways and a datestone of 1654, and the initials 'JG' (the stonemason, John Grumbold). Finally, there is Rope House (no.31), a former ropemaker's house with a variety of different windows. With Inglenook Cottage behind it, it was built in the 1630s (Inglenook has a datestone of 1636) possibly by stonemasons working on Kirby Hall. The craftsmanship and design of the houses certainly bears out this theory.

Local crafts: Art (drawings of local scenes): Jeannie Loveday, 34 Chapel Road. (Tel.01536 69998)
Pocket Park: a flood meadow (known as Ley's Field) beside Willow Brook, behind the church. Access via a metal gate, just over the bridge and off the path leading from Church Street towards the *Kings Arms*.

Snippets:
* Both Great and Little Weldon had Norman manor houses which have long since disappeared:
Little Weldon Manor was also known as Hunters' Manor. The manor house was well-placed, being roughly between Geddington Lodge and Rockingham Castle, and acted as the headquarters of the Royal Buckhounds, in readiness for when hunting parties took place. It stood on ground enclosed by the present Larratt Road, Gretton Road, Halls Close and Chapel Road.
Great Weldon Manor was long associated with the Bassett family until 1409, when after further changes it passed to the Hatton family. The manor house stood quite near the church, at the rear of the small group of houses lining that side of Church Street.

* A Roman villa (4th-century), with mosaic pavement and coins, together with other buildings from between the first and third centuries, was excavated in old Chapel Field, 150 yards north of Willow Brook in 1738. A Roman kiln was also found nearby, to the right of the road between Corby and Weldon, by men working in the ironstone quarries.
* Weldon stone was prized and used for building old St Paul's in London, Kirby Hall, Rushton Hall, part of Rockingham Castle (in 1275), King's College Chapel, Cambridge and many other houses.
* Church Street was formerly known as Back Lane; Kettering Road was Stanion Road; Water Lane was March's Hill; Bridge Street used to be Taylor's Hill; Chapel Road was named Little Weldon. Larratt Road was an un-named though important track with one house, which led to the woodland of Larratt Sale and on to Rockingham Castle. (It is now blocked off).
* There is an unsubstantiated legend that the lantern of the church was at one time lit to guide wayfarers through dark surrounding stretches of Rockingham Forest.
* The annual July Fair ceased in the 1960s. As a result of a Charter in 1685, a weekly market and four fairs were granted for the buying and selling 'all manner of Grain, Goods, Livestock and Merchandise'.
*A Market House was built on the village green about 1700, but was demolished in the early 19th-century. It is said that its stone was used to build the village school.
* The village is associated with a composer and organist to Charles I, George Jeffreys.
* An old poem, 'The Witch of Weldon', possibly a folk tune, survives - but whether the story was true, we will never know! :

There lived a young Witch in old Weldon town -
Heyday, and be merry!
Her eyes they were black and her skin it was
brown,
As smooth and as brown as a berry!
Light was her tread and her lips were red,
As ripe and as red as a cherry!
    With a folderol doll and a rumbelow,
    And a folderol dee, doo-day!

Over all the young shepherds she cast her spell -
Heyday and be merry!
Not a woman in Weldon that wishèd her well -
As bonny and brown as a berry!
At the women she hissed, but the laddies she
kissed -
And luscious her lips as a cherry!
    With a folderol doll and a rumbelow,
    And a folderol dee, doo-day!

There dwelt an old Witch in old Weldon town -
Heigh-ho, and aweary!
Her eyes they were black and her skin it was
brown,
All wrinkled and dirty and dreary!
Heavy her tread, not a tooth in her head,
And her haunts and her habits were eerie!
    With a folderol doll and a rumbelow (etc)

The shepherds laughed out when she passed them by
Heigh-ho, and aweary!
Not a woman in Weldon but fearèd her eye -
So black and so wicked and eerie!
She cursed as she went, all crippled and bent,
All withered and tattered and dreary!
    With a folderol doll and a rumbelow,
    And a folderol dee, doo day!

Walks around the area:
*You can get to Kirby Hall, using an interesting route across scrubland and passing the former ironstone quarries. The ground is very waterlogged in places and care must be taken, but the walk is certainly worthwhile. Much of the way it is not signposted, but there are certain 'landmarks' and 'guides' such as following the straight line of the quarry to your right for some distance and then crossing it (before it ends), heading for the spinney, stream and deserted farm buldings ahead. Waterproof footwear advised.
* Brigstock (see above). Walk along the Oundle Road and at the top of the hill, before the bend, turn right at the green signpost, along a rough track. This was once known as Bears Lane, and was associated with a 19th-century travelling showman and dancing bear, who camped there. Excellent forest views and walks.

WILBARSTON
(Wilbeorht's settlement). Pronounced 'wil-BAR-ston', with the stress on 'bar'.

A pleasant village, with a recreation ground and ample parking at the top, modern end of the village (near the A427 Corby-Harborough road).Two roads leading out of the village converge on Stoke Albany which lies just at the bottom of the hill. Some interesting 17th- and 18th-century (ironstone) buildings.

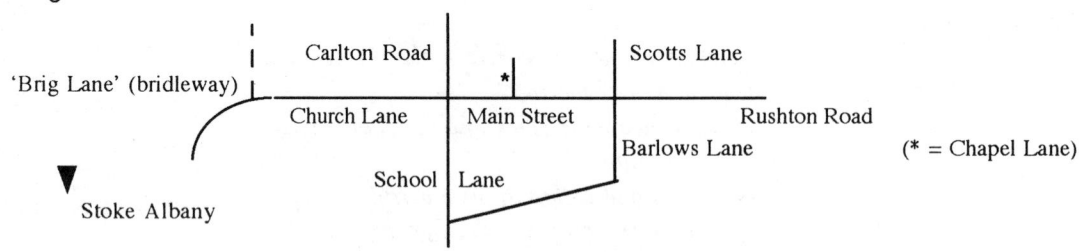

```
                    |     Carlton Road    |         Scotts Lane
'Brig Lane' (bridleway) |_____|*_____
                       /   Church Lane   |  Main Street     Rushton Road
                      /                  |              Barlows Lane        (* = Chapel Lane)
                     ▼                   |    School | Lane
                  Stoke Albany            |
```

Church: All Saints (formerly 'All Hallows'). Blocked Norman doorway. Early parts: 13th- century including the spire. 1654 brass with verse. Restored 1884. It has a unique painted ceiling well-worth looking at. Its spire was struck by lightning in 1982. A cosy, colourful church.
Independent Chapel: 1884 (in Chapel Lane off Main Street).
Pub: the *Fox Inn* (late 17th-century origins, though mainly 18th-century).
Former pubs: the *King's Head*, the *Queen's Head*.
National School: 1845 for 96 children.
Other buildings and places of interest:
There are quite a few 17th and 18th-century buildings in Wilbarston, and one has even earlier origins.
Main Street: Two houses with datestones: one (no. 5, corner of Chapel Lane) from1633; the other (no 8, set back along a path off the road) has a datestone from1634, and mullioned windows. The Old Manor House: late 17th-century.
Rushton Road: no. 24 (1684). The site of the Old Bakehouse is on the opposite side.
Scotts Lane: 2a (The Barn) with datestone: 1637
Barlow's Lane: no 1 (on the corner of Rushton Road): 1655.
Also along here on the left (coming from Rushton Road) stands a late 17th-century building, with ornate time-eroded chimneys. It incorporates even earlier parts (cruck-frame interior) and belongs to Springfield Farm. It is said by some sources to be the oldest surviving building (apart from the church) in the village.
Church Street: 'The Old House' (Pilgrim Cottage) is a 17th-century building (once reputed to be haunted) with a vast garden. The remnants (nesting boxes) of a dovecote joins onto the garden wall of the house. It stands in a small playing field at the rear of the present primary school. Access to this can be gained via a small gate and path in School Lane (opposite no.9).
Carlton Road: Old School House (next to the pub) has a datestone 'EAF 1627' on its gable (with '1731' inscribed on a front wall brick). Next door (no. 3) is a building from 1765 known as The Old Post House.

Local crafts: *Batik and weaving: Frances Lowe, The Old Bakehouse Studios, 7 Rushton Road. Tel. 01536 771484.
Snippets:
 *The village certainly had a rebellious streak! Rockingham Forest villages had in general been relatively unaffected by the medieval and Tudor sheep enclosures that had deeply affected most of

the country. However, they did not escape the 18th (and 19th) century 'Parliamentary Enclosures' which were to change the face of the traditional countryside. Leading local landowners, who had the financial resources for hedging plots of land, could petition Parliament for an enclosure award (for a considerable fee).This usually worked against the smaller landholder and could result in the loss or change of traditional rights of common (like grazing) in open fields - as well as a loss of livelihood. In the summer of1799 there was a riot against such 'inclosure' at Wilbarston, when about 300 people gathered on the hill of what is now School Lane, and lit a large bonfire on the road, to prevent a wagonload of rails and posts (for fencing off a small piece of land allocated to them as compensation) coming through. The local militia were called out and the Riot Act read to the crowd, after which a period of waiting ensued. Some of the more demonstrative 'rebels' were taken into custody, and made to assist in putting up the fencing! Eventually, the crowd dispersed and the work was completed. (Another riot however, took place four years later).

In 1819, a 'Bread Riot' took place at Wilbarston. (In 1815, an National Act had been passed allowing the importation of foreign grain, after home-grown wheat prices had rocketed due to the social and economic upheaval had been cause by the Napoleonic Wars). Again, local militia were called out - from Kettering - to deal with the problem.

Walks in the area:
* Stoke Albany. This is almost on the doorstep. You can either walk down the hill of Church Street - a pleasant, quiet walk - or use part of the Jurassic Way (through the churchyard, down the grassy slope, over a stream via a small stone clapper bridge, and turn left at the road at the bottom. An alternative is to go down the hill of School Lane and follow the bend of the road. If you take this route, look to your right as you pass over the stream: you will see the earthworks of a former watermill. There are fine views as you approach Stoke Albany, especially of the earthworks and pond at the rear of the Manor House.
* Ashley. Follow the bridleway ('Brig Lane') off the bend at the bottom of the hill of Church Street. Arrow-marked. A fairly-long, quiet walk with varying landscape en route.

WOODNEWTON (new settlement by the wood).

With its fertile, well-watered soil, market gardening was once a major source of employment in the village. Even now, it is still a pleasant place to walk, and the newer housing development lining a road parallel to the old main street, does not impinge on the peaceful atmosphere, which is second to none. A feast for those who love old buildings, plus the sight of the fine mill and brook tucked away at the far end.

Church: St Mary's. .Perpendicular style, some Norman. Earliest parts, 12th-century. Enlarged 13th-century. In the porch on either side are 13th-century stone coffin lids. There are two late 13th-century windows and three interesting doorways, including dog-tooth surrounds to the porch (remodelled 1662 with older materials).The tower was rebuilt in the 17th century. There are late 16th/early 17th-century pews, and lectern for chained bible. Carved heads on central pillars (13th-century). Plaque to a US airman whose plane crashed in parish during the Second World War.Thorough restoration in the 19th- and early-20th centuries. Lying on a rare limestone crop, the churchyard has some rare species of wildflowers, and has been designated an important site by The Wildlife Trust for Northamptonshire. It is maintained by the parish councillors, and was awarded the 'runner-up' prize in the 1994 'Conservation of Churchyards Competition'.
Former Methodist Chapel: 1840.
Pub: the *White Swan Inn* (early 19th-century).
Former pubs: the *Hare and Hounds*, the *Horse and Jockey*.
Former school: 1876 for 90 children. Closed in the late1980s. Children now go to Nassington.
Other buildings and places of interest:
At the Apethorpe road end, note the two 17th-century cottages (one of which is called 'Stone Cottage') at the rear of the church. Coming out of the church gates, turn right and cross over the road, turning left at the bend down a narrow lane leading downhill. Here you can float back in time, and linger awhile in the peaceful atmosphere generated by the scene of picturesque Conegar Farm (a former early 18th-century millhouse), its mill and Willow Brook flowing under the bridge.
Retracing your steps back uphill, turn right at Main Street and proceed past the church and the narrow road leading off to the left, St Mary's Hill, on the corner of which stands another 18th-century house.A few doors away stand two adjoining houses, one which is part 17th-century, the other early-18th. Across the road stands Manor Cottage with a datestone of 1688, and an adjoining 19th-century

former Reading Room. Close by is Manor Farm, built on the site of an earlier (possibly 17th-century) building, with the remains of a tithe barn in its yard. Almost opposite is the mid 18th-century Manor House, once the home of the Westmorland family of nearby Apethorpe. Further along, across the road, is the old Methodist Chapel (now a Craft Workshop, see below), with a 17th- century house on either side, and an 18th century dovecote close to the rear. Old buildings continue to huddle close to the sides of the road as you progress along the street: among them on the left, 17th-century Rosedene and the former 18th-century *Horse and Jockey Inn* (now a private house), and on the right, Spinney Farm Cottage (early 17th-century), Bryony Cottage (late 17th-/early 18th-century) and 'The Gardens'.

Facing the triangular green ahead is the late 18th-century Hilltree Cottage and bearing right round the bend, and on opposite sides of the Oundle Road, are the former *Hare and Hounds Inn*, now Willow Brook Farm (late 17th-century), and Meadow View from the same era.

(Bearing left at the triangular green is the Nassington Road, off which leads Orchard Lane round the back of the village. Along here, amongst all the modern houses are some 19th-century buildings).

Local crafts: *Woodcarving, pottery, puppet making, leather working: Woodnewton Craft Studio, The Chapel, 43 Main Street. A small centre (the former Methodist Chapel), housing four local craftspeople. Visitors welcome. Talks and demonstrations (phone first). Courses in Pottery and Woodcarving available. Telephone either Glyn Mould, Rob Bibby, Ken Barnard or Les Theedom on (01780) 470866.

Snippets:
* The village was once the home of Coco the Clown, and every other year (in September) a Clown Festival is held here.

Walks around the area:
*A footpath leads from the church end of the village via Conegar Farm and Mill to Southwick passing through part of a large wood of the Forest.
* Fotheringhay. Just past the green, take the track leading off on the left of the Oundle Road by the Willow Brook Farm. The short walk is pleasant, passing over Willow Brook on the way.
* Elton. Opposite where Orchard Lane leads off to the left of Nassington Road, is a track (signposted) which takes you via Park Spinney and Park Lodge and over the Nene to Elton.
* New Sulehay Lodge. Just past where Orchard Lane leads off the Nassington Road, there is a footpath to the left of the road. This passes between two spinneys and ends past Shortwood Farm.
At the main road turn right and some distance down the road is the rebuilt former forest keeper's lodge (New Sulehay) and further on, Nassington.

YARWELL (either 'spring by the fishing pool' or 'spring where yarrow grew').

Long associated in the past with the Wolston and Westmorland families, this one-street village is ideal for walking, as is the surrounding area with Yarwell Mill, the Nene Walk and remnants of the Forest close by. An added attraction is the placing of items of historical interest, such as ploughs, outside some of the houses by their owners.

Church: St Mary Magdalene. Mostly 13th-century. North and south chapels have been added. Traces of a medieval painting and window in one of the chapels.The plain tower was rebuilt in the 17th century. Several simple floor memorials from the same period. The marble chest tomb in the chapel (1715) of a London merchant, Humphrey Bellamy, is inscribed with a club-wielding 'wild man'. (It is thought that the tale of Dick Whittington is based on his life. As a boy he came, destitute and ill, to Yarwell whilst walking to London. He was fed and cared for by the villagers. In later years he became prosperous and was made Alderman of London). 1790 coat-of-arms of George III.The chancel was restored in1892, which until that date was thatched.
Pub: the *Angel Inn* (17th-century origin).
Former pub: the *Fox Inn* (also a blacksmith's. Now Forge Cottage).
Former school : 1874. Closed in 1981. Children now go to Nassington.
Methodist chapel: 1840

Other buildings and places of interest:
Entering the village from the Wansford road end, you pass two adjoining 17th-century buildings on the left-hand corner of the main street, and the old Prebendal Farm with its many outbuildings, on the opposite side. The street offers several buildings of historical interest which, unless otherwise stated,

Two pre-World War II sketches:
Top: Kingscliffe, the church viewed from the corner of Bridge Street
Bottom: St. Osyth's Street, Oundle

Wansford: the fine ancient bridge over the River Nene

Bulwick: looking down the main street from the Blatherwycke Road end

The Three Horseshoes. Nassington.

ST LEONARD'S CHURCH & MANOR HOUSE, APETHORPE

Wadenhoe: looking down Main Street towards Mill Lane

date from the 17th century. Next to the Prebendal Farm is 'Whitelands'. Opposite, is the 19th-century Vine House, with the smaller, much earlier Vine Cottage next door. The former Methodist Chapel lies almost at the rear of the latter. Jasmine Cottage (opposite the Village Hall has an old washing mangle in its small front garden. 'Farriers' (with its original forge and outbuildings - from a later date) lies across the road, with 'Mullions' from the same era, next door. The former Post Office is opposite. Two interesting buildings stand just before the church: 'Wendmuir' (with a square dovecote behind it) and a few doors away, the late 16th-century 'Ballaugh Cottage'. On the opposite side of the road, to the left of the pub is Sundial Cottage, which was formerly a bakery and still has Victorian ovens at the rear. It has a stone sundial on a pillar and a painted plough in its front garden. A few doors away from here, approaching the bend, is the spread-out Manor Farm which like Prebendal Farm at the other end, has an 18th-century barn with triangular air vents. As the road bears to the right, two buildings face you: Yarwell House (late 18th-century) and the 16th-century Forge Cottage (a former pub). As the village comes to an end, there is a row of 19th-century houses with an adjoining 18th-century building. You are now on Mill Road, one of the two roads to Nassington and from which you can get to Yarwell Mill and its attractions (see below).

Snippets:
* Between the village and the Nene, a large number of Roman relics (particularly pottery) have been found. A building from that period has been excavated to the west of the village at Pound Close.
* The Manor House disappeared in the 16th century. It stood west of the church.
* In the 18th and 19th centuries there were a large number of stonemasons in the village. Many of them had the surname 'Ireson', a family that produced generations of such craftsmen in the region. The last one in the village died in 1971, aged 91. Yarwell stone is mainly colite. In some gardens of the village there are examples of the masons' work. There are also drinking troughs for horses or dogs. Some of the smaller ones are said to have been used during times of plague, and were filled with vinegar to disinfect coins placed therein by visiting pedlars.
* Long ago, the village was involved in disputes with Nassington (qv), and Wansford (over the possession of a church bell). It certainly had a lively past!

Walks in the area:
* Wansford. This short walk across the fields begins at the corner of Mill Road and Main Street (by Yarwell House). The walk is well arrow-marked with variations of route possible, such as 'Lock Walk', by the riverside. Highly recommended, but can be very wet and muddy!
* Just after the last house on the left of Mill Road, as you leave the village, there are two more walks signposted across the fields. The one to the immediate left lets you exlore part of the meadowland around the Nene. The other short walk is part of the Nene Way and leads to Yarwell Mill. The present version dates from 1839, and the nearby Mill house is from the 1730s. It is a picturesque place to wander through (follow the black and white arrow waymarkers), where boats moor, anglers come to fish and holidaymakers come with caravans. The Nene Way carries on along the river and there is a crossing point via stepping stones to Nassington - but beware during heavy rains, when the track can get very muddy, and on one occasion in the author's experience, the waters are so forceful that it is impossible to cross! <u>However</u>, an alternative route has recently been made available and is waymarked! (It will eventually appear on maps).
* Another fascinating walk is at the other end of the village to **Old Sulehay Lodge.** This was one of the former official residences of the Rockingham Forest keepers of Cliffe bailiwick from medieval times and lies in Sulehay Woods, an extra-parochial area. Until the late 15th century this was held by the lords of Yarwell. Therafter it passed into the hands of the lords of Apethorpe via Sir Guy Wolston. The present building dates from the 1640s (there is a 1642 datestone) and was once larger. Part of the building has an interesting blocked three arch arcade in which windows are set. In 1869, the Sulehay area became part of Nassington parish (qv) and led to intense inter-village disputes. Today it is in private hands and cannot be visited, but may be viewed from the road. It is reached from the end of Main Street by continuing straight on for about a mile.
* Apethorpe. A pleasant walk with fine views (looking back). Begins at the Nassington Road, at the green signpost opposite the last house on the left. There is a small stream to jump over. The walk can get complicated, and the use of Ordnance Survey maps141 &142, or 917/918 is recommended.
Visit: Yarwell Mill Caravan Park. Fishing, lakeside picnic area, boating, riverside walks, and of course, caravan site. Tel. (01780) 782344.

PLACES ON THE EDGE OF THE ROCKINGHAM FOREST AREA

The following is a short list of some of the interesting towns and villages close to the Rockingham Forest area: lying just on the other side of the Rivers Nene or Welland.

ASHTON ('settlement where ash grows').

The village was rebuilt in 1900 by Charles Rothschild, who also created the present village green.

Ashton Chapel, School and Schoolhouse: 1706. Unique, in that these were all housed in the same building with the lower floor devoted to the chapel at one end, and a dividing wall separating it from the school at the other; with the upper floor used as the schoolhouse. The original bellcote was of timber, the present one is stone. Benefactor plaque and portrait of the founder, Jemima Creed.
Pub: the *Chequered Skipper* (thatched). Formerly known as the *Three Horseshoes*.
Around the village:
Driving along the one road into the village from the 'main' road, you pass the 17th-century Manor House on the right, which has some medieval parts built into it. As you approach the Green, the chapel (sometimes used for art exhibitions) appears, set back on the left. The large rectangular Green is the scene for the annual autumn World Conker championships which is covered by the international media and is taken quite seriously with three swipes at an opponent's conker allowed.
Throughout the year the scene around the Green is idyllic, with peacocks strutting around, children playing and patrons of the pub opposite enjoying refreshment at the tables provided on the grass. Remember however, that the thatched buildings in the vicinity are not the original ones!
The road which turns off to the left of the Green leads into the grounds of the Ashton Estate Office (formerly Chapel Farm House) which dates partly from 1627 according to a datestone.
Proceeding along the road through the village, a triangular green appears. The turning on the right here leads to Vine Cottage and Thatchers Cottage, both originally 17th-century (the former with two reset datestones, 1659 and 1730) but which were part of the Rothschild modernisation programme.
The road leads out of the village towards another charming, isolated old building which was once 'The Entrance Lodge'. Here the road splits in two: the left fork peters out, becoming a footpath, in the vicinity of which is a rifle range! To the right it becomes a private road (Brickyard Wood).
Back in the village, (on foot) with the chapel on your immediate right, follow the track that leads to the Mill. Set back from the track on the right, stands 'The Cottage' of late 17th/early 18th-century origin which was modernised in 1900.
Local crafts: Clothing Design: Barbara Cottrell, 1 The Bungalow. Tel. 01832 273053.
Ashton Mill and Fish Museum: used late 19th-century machinery for power. Converted by Lord Rothschild in 1900, to provide water for the village.The museum houses a display of thatching and blacksmiths' crafts, and antiquated farm machinery. Opens on Sunday afternoons during the summer months.The house by the museum dates from 1722 and opens as a teashop for visitors to the mill.
Ashton Water Dragonfly Sanctuary: this is actually on the outskirts of Polebrook as you leave that village (en route to Lutton) and is signposted on the left-hand side of the road, where a track leads to a small carparking area. It is situated in beautiful Ashton Wold, a quiet stretch of woodland, now a nature reserve, full of trees old and new, some of which line the roads to Lutton and Warmington. The sanctuary is now home to 16 species of dragonfly, and there is a visitors' centre and an illustrated talk/ guided tour (at certain times). However, it is only open five times a year at present. Details of opening times can be obtained by phoning: (01832) 274333.
Snippets:
* There were once four mills (three for corn, one for fulling cloth).
* The population of Ashton in 1841 was 172.
Walks in the area:
*There are footpaths via the Mill, across the River Nene to Oundle, either direct, or via a picturesque 'Nene Walk' following the course of the river.
* There is also a fine, much longer walk along the track through Ashton to Warmington, passing close by Elmington Lodge en route - the only surviving building (19th-century with 16th-century parts) from the lost village of **Elmington**, which was converted into an area for sheep grazing in the 16th century by the

monks of Crowland Abbey. The 'modern' hamlet of Elmington was added in 1885.

BARROWDEN (hill with burial mounds).

An extensive rambling village of great interest. Many of the older houses are of 18th and 19th-century origin. The centre of the village is around its large green. Some of the newer streets have colourful names such as Cuckoo Close, Cider Close, Dovecote Close and Live Hill.

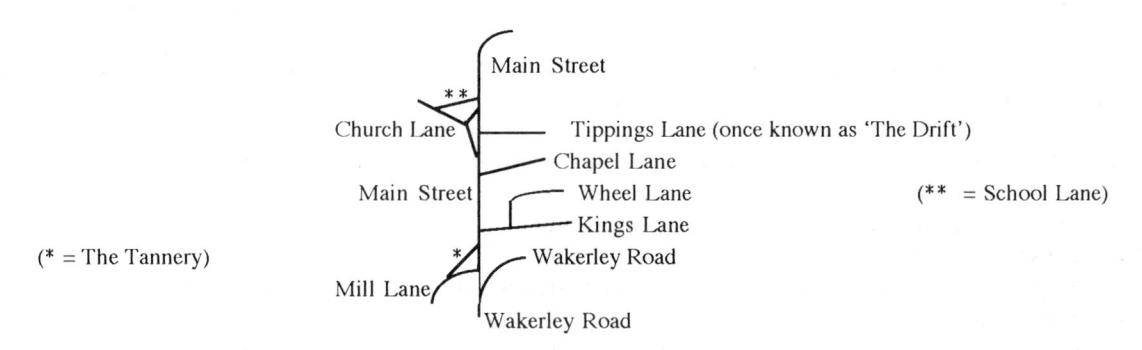

```
                          Main Street
                       **
           Church Lane      Tippings Lane (once known as 'The Drift')
                          Chapel Lane
           Main Street    Wheel Lane                    (** = School Lane)
                          Kings Lane
  (* = The Tannery)      * Wakerley Road
                   Mill Lane
                          Wakerley Road
```

Church: St Peter's. Broach spire. Earliest parts: 13th-century. Wall monument to Rolandus Durant with carved armour, 1588. Picturesque churchyard with fine view of the Welland Valley. The ancient custom of 'rush strewing' takes place on the porch floor of the church on 'the dedication of the festival' (end of June).
Baptist Chapel: 1819 in Chapel Lane. A plaque by the gate records the connection with Thomas Cook (of travel agent fame) who lived in the village for a while.
Pub: the *Exeter Arms* (by the Green).
Former Pubs: the *Wheel* (Wheel Lane), the *Crown* (Wakerley Road), the *Swan* (Main Street. Now 'Stone Cottage'), the *Windmill* (datestone:1630. Corner of Wakerley Road. Now 'Windmil House').
Former School: 1862 for 150 children in School Lane (now a private house).
Other buildings and places of interest:
Wheel Lane: Wheel Cottage, 1797.
Mill Lane: (The mill ceased operating in the 1930s). The Tannery ; Hay Barn Cottage.
School Lane: thatched Pepperday Cottage, early 17th-century, by Church Lane; Durant House, the oldest house in the village - part of the north end facing Main Street (the original house)dates from the 13th/14th centuries, other parts c.1586 and c. 1648.
The Pond at the corner of Church Lane has a duck colony and specially-built shelter. A road sign depicting ducks ,warns motorists approaching the colony!
The Green (the former 13th-14th century market place): The old smithy stands on the green itself (this was one of two in the village, the other being at the rear of the *Exeter Arms*); Dormouse Cottage (a converted farm building); The Old Bakery.
Church Lane: Carey's House (the former Rectory); Church Farm (datestones 1586,1648); Apple Tree Cottage (formerly Church Cottage) has a cornerstone (considered to be a former tombstone) inscribed: WHY LOOKEST THOW, ON MY DYST ON, PASSING BY THOU SE(E), ST NOE WONDER THO, THYSELFE MVST DIE.
Main Street: no. 12 (Wakerley Road end), datestone 1757; no. 38 (far end opposite 'The Maltings'), datestone 1742.
Snippets:
* Thomas Cook (famous for his travel agency, came to the village as a Baptist Church missionary in 1822, but became a woodcraftsman for economic reasons. Here he met his wife, Marianne Mason, daughter of a local farmer. They were married at St Peter's in 1833. They later moved to Market Harborough.

BRINGHURST (wood of Bryni's people).

This small sleepy village stands on an isolated hill about 300 feet above the plain of the Welland. It is conspicuous from a distance at Cottingham, Middleton and East Carlton.

Church: St Nicholas (12th-century). Ironstone and limestone construction. The chancel was rebuilt in the 19th-century. 'Golden' weathercock. Two Royal coats of arms within. Ancient octagonal font. Both Great Easton and Drayton churches were dependents of St. Nicholas.
Former pub: the *Red Lion* (on north west side of the village). It only existed for a very short time in the early 1880s.
A walk around the village:
Manor House (Bryan's House) has a stone doorhead inscribed: 1636, which actually came from elsewhere. Stone mullioned windows and two front doors. The house was restored in 1956 and was divided into two parts.
17th-century houses built of ironstone, clustered round the church including Rose Cottage, some still with thatched roofs, others with Collyweston slates.
Stone Cottage: 1701 (restored 1958) on the west side of the village.
School: 1875 for the children of Bringhurst, Great Easton and Drayton. It lies on the road to Great Easton and Drayton. Still in use.
Home Farm: early parts, late 17th and early 18th-century.
Snippets:
*A lost village, Prestgrave, once stood between Bringhurst and Neville Holt. It disappeared by the middle of the 15th century.
* In earlier days a school was said to be held either at the schoolmaster's house, or in the church vestry.

CALDECOTT ('cold shelter')

Caldecott lies on the north side of the Eye Brook. It is the first village you reach coming from Rockingham, over the Welland: the former Rockingham Railway Station stood at the entrance to the village.

Church: St John The Evangelist: *c.*13th-century. The spire was shattered by lightning in 1798, and rebuilt in Weldon stone.
Pubs: the *Plough Inn* (1868), the *Castle* (formerly the *Railway Inn*).
Former pubs: the *Black Horse* (stood opposite the school); *the King's Arms* (stood in Church Close).
Former school: 1878 for 60 children. Main Street. Closed 1977. Now 'The Old School House'.
Buildings of interest:
Several 17th and 18th-century houses, many of which have datestones. Among them are no.6 Main Street (1646. Rebuilt by Sir Michael Seymour, Rockingham Castle), no.2 Uppingham Road, 'Ye Olde House' (1647), house by the pub at The Green (1684). A datestone,1651, is set in the garden wall of no.5 The Green (towards Mill Lane). A little row of houses in Main Street from 1877 are known as the Independent Foresters' Cottages. The 17th-century Manor House lies at the end of Mill Lane.
Snippets:
*The village stocks vanished in 1835. Two crosses once existed: one at the top of the village where the three roads meet; the other on the Green (still known as Cross Bank).
*The site of the lost village of Snelston lies on the Uppingham Road.

ELTON ('tun' of the æthelings or Æthelheah's people).

Elton lies midway between Oundle and Peterborough. It is in Huntingdonshire and won the Best Kept Village Competition (of that county) in 1994. A fascinating village with various greens including St Botolph Green near the Hall, and Stocks Green at the other end of the village. There are many interesting buildings (some 17th-century), especially in Middle Street which links the two parts of the village, and Duck Lane. There are also two 10th/11th-century Saxon crosses.

Church: All Saints. 15th-century tower. Porch has (now empty) shelved niches left, right and above doorway. Many monuments and memorials to the Proby (Carysfort) family, from the 17th century onwards.
Methodist Chapel: 1864 (corner of Chapel Lane).
School: (founded 1711), 1876 (in School Lane).
Pubs: the *Black Horse* (main road); the *Crown Inn* (a thatched pub in Duck Street close to the Green).
Elton Hall: 1475. Main house completed in 1666, incorporating the medieval chapel and gatehouse, by

Sir Thomas Proby, grandson of Sir Peter Proby, a Lord Mayor of London and earlier incumbent. Excellent collection of paintings ranging form Old Masters to British artwork. Among the book collection is a prayer book of Henry VIII containing his handwriting.Open seasonally in July, August and Bank Holidays.
Mill: 1840. Excellent **walks** from here to Fotheringhay and Nassington. Part of the route crosses land which is currently part of the Countryside Stewardship Scheme, a ten year conservation programme, run by the Countryside Commission with local farmers which allows free pubic access to private fields or waymarked paths. Camping is discouraged. Begins (via a stile) near Stocks Green at River Lane.
Snippets:
Woodcroft Castle, about a mile and a half south of Elton, contains a fragment from an earlier building of the 13th century. There are Tudor additions.
Visit: Entering the village from the A605, are two attractions: on the right, The Old Dairy which includes a restaurant and oyster and seafood Bar. Almost opposite, on the same side as, and adjacent to the Hall, is a plant centre. Here in the old walled garden you can find over 5,000 kinds of plants! There is a regular monthly programme of events including demonstrations and lectures. Open 7 days a week.

GREAT EASTON (until the 19th century, known as Easton-by-the- River, or Easton-upon-Welland).

A fascinating large village well-worth exploring, with picturesque thatched cottages in Barnsdale and Brook Lane. When there is no traffic around, it is an idyllic setting transporting you back to how it once was before the age of the car. The post office/store has a free village trail leaflet, and also sells four booklets by village historian, Ken Heselton: 'The Pubs of Great Easton', 'The Oddfellows of Great Easton', 'Two Wheelwrights of Great Easton' and 'Early Education in Great Easton'. (Tel: 01536 770309 or 770426 for further information).

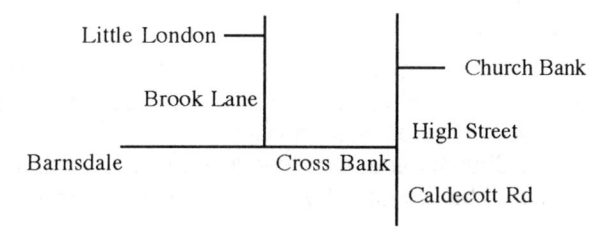

```
      Little London ─┐
                     │        ┌─── Church Bank
         Brook Lane  │        │
                     │        │   High Street
    ─────────────────┤        │
      Barnsdale     Cross Bank│
                              │   Caldecott Rd
                              │
```

Church: St Andrew's. Mainly 13th-century. Built of local ironstone. Many carved stone heads.
Methodist Chapel: 1837 (opposite the present post office/shop).
Congregational Chapel: now demolished. A small burial ground still exists next to its site along the road to Caldecott.
Pub: the *Sun Inn*.
Former pubs: the *Crown Inn*, the *King's Head* (formerly the *Prince Regent* and now 8 Barnsdale), the *Shoulder of Mutton* (now 9 Cross Bank), the *Marquis of Granby* (now Granby House in the High Street), the *Bell* , the *Fox and Hounds*. There were also three un-named 'pubs' in the village for a short time towards the end of the 18th century.
Other buildings and places of interest:
Barnsdale: Furleigh Cottage (believed to be 15th-century) with charming owl feature in the thatch. Situated along Barnsdale (no.16). Also in Barnsdale is thatched no.8 with a datestone of 1774 and the inscription: 'Serve God'. The whole section of the street is a charming composite sight on a sunny day.
Brook Lane:
Brookside Cottage is 17th-century. Brookside House was built between 1630-70.
High Street:
Holme Leigh House (built in 1614 and 1688). 'The Old Post Office' (one of them!) is probably late 17th-century, has a variety of different-shaped windows, and a thatched long-legged water bird on its roof.
Church Bank:
Clock House (19th-century), complete with clock. As the name implies it was formerly a clockmaker's.
Stonewalls : 1694, on the corner of Church Bank and the High Street.
The thatched stone cottage (formerly the *Crown Inn*) on the right beyond the green near church is believed to date from the15th century. It is possibly the oldest building in the village (after the church).

Great Easton Manor, formerly 'Greylands' (1615).
Leaving the churchyard by an iron gate towards Lounts Crescent, you will see a circular stone well head in a field on your right.
Little London : A small lane with its own atmosphere. The origin of the name is unknown: various theories have been put forward, such as it was once the site of 'industrial' activity (ie where smoke was often seen!) - or it was a newer part of the village (spreading out like London).
Snippets:
* There are remains of a windmill on north side of road to Caldecott.
* There is also a flourishing Local History Society in the village, which was instrumental in setting up similar organisations in the area. (see Appendix).

LYDDINGTON ('settlement on the Hlyde' - river).

An interesting village steeped in history, on the road between Gretton and Uppingham.

Church: St Andrew's. Part 13th-century. Broach spire. 14th-century coffin lids. 15th-century rood screen, and 17th-century altar/communion rail). 16th-century brasses. Medieval wall paintings (including a figure of either Edward The Confessor, or St Edmund). Monument to Edward Watson (of Rockingham Castle). 'Sound jars' for enhancing priests' voices above the chancel. Ancient and modern carved corbels, including a 'green man'. Recently restored organ.
Chapel: 1870 (now the Village Hall).
Pubs: the *Old White Hart*, the *Marquess of Exeter.*
Former pubs: the *Swan*, the *Pied Calf*, the *Lord Roberts* (all Main Street).
School : 1870 for 90 children and 30 infants.
Other buildings and places of interest:
Bede House: part 15th-century (1480-96) manor house belonging to Bishops of Lincoln. Converted into almshouses in 1602 by Lord Burghley. The Banqueting Hall has a carved ceiling and oriel window. Under the care of English Heritage. Open seasonally, and well-worth a visit.
Gazebo: (polygonal tower) on the corner of Church Lane, inscribed with the Lincoln coat of arms, was part of the Bede House, and was once known as 'The Bishop's Eye'. This can be entered from the grounds of the Bede House.
The Green: clustered around here are a group of 17th and 18th-century buildings. However, no.1 (facing the Main Street) is believed to date from as early as the 15th century. The *Market Cross* (13th-century) was removed in 1837, but was later returned to near its original site in 1930.
Main Street: the street is dominated by many buildings from the 17th and 18th centuries. Among the older houses however are the 'Priest's House' (no.31) opposite Church Lane, with a wall plaque inscribed 'Coelum Patria Christus via' and 'Richard Rudd, vicar 1626'. Bay House (no.17) has a datestone, 1656, but may be earlier.
Church Street: no.6 has a datestone,1668.
There are also 17th-century buildings in Stoke Road.

MEDBOURNE (meadow stream).

A beautiful Leicestershire village, which lies in an idyllic setting with a stream running through its streets. Another place to explore slowly. A village trail leaflet will shortly be available, at the time of writing (1995).

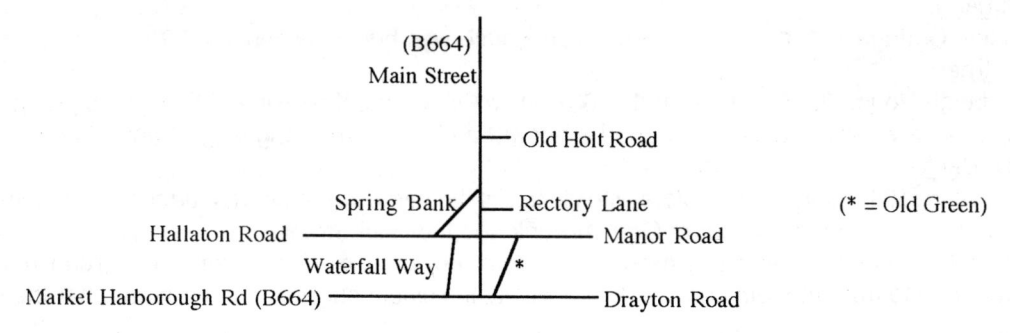

```
                        (B664)
                      Main Street

                                ── Old Holt Road

                 Spring Bank ╲  ── Rectory Lane        (* = Old Green)
   Hallaton Road ─────────────── Manor Road
                 Waterfall Way │ *
   Market Harborough Rd (B664) ───── Drayton Road
```

Church: St Giles (part 13th-century, rebuilt by 1320). Embattled tower. 17th-century furnishings (when the church was renovated). George III coat of arms. Stone coffin lids. The 17th-century transept was a school room until 1868-9. The only remaining gas lamp standard in the village is by the church gates.

Methodist Chapel: 1798 (renovated 1857-8) stood in Spring Bank. Present building, the Mission Hall (1870) stands on Main Street. The gates were forged by the last village blacksmith.

Pubs: the *Neville Arms*. Formerly the *Red Lion*, and rebuilt in 1863, it stands on the site of an earlier 18th- century pub which had suffered in a fire, in 1856. This is believed to have been started by a visiting magician and a blacksmith who struck a horseshoe on an anvil placed on the former's chest. The sparks - or nearby candles - are said to have set light to the thatched roof.

The *Horse and Trumpet* (a pub since 1870. The building which houses it is late 18th-century and is rubble-walled. The original pub was also destroyed by a fire, and stood on the opposite side of the road from the present building, on the site of the old school).

Former pubs: the *Queen's Head Inn*. It was built in 1733 and closed in 1905. Now a private house known as Old Queen House. It stands between Spring Bank and the stream); the *Crown Inn*, built c.1680 was closed around 1927. It is now a private house (25, Main Street).

School: 1868-9 for 100 children. Now 'The Old School Centre'.

Medieval packhorse bridge: spans Medbourne Brook at an ancient ford, close to the church. Dates partly from the 13th century. Its brick paving and handrails are more recent. It is possible to walk over the bridge to the church.

Other buildings and places of interest:

Main Street :

Old houses stand here from about 1680 (nos.27 and 29). The farmhouse opposite Old Holt Road (Pagets Farm) is late 17th-century.

The Old Forge and house beside it: 1875 (closed 1958).This was built on the site of the old workhouse.

The Old Bakery : 1863 (with pink-painted gable end).

The 19th-century station master's house and site of the former railway station lie further along the road.

Old Holt Road :

Cottages at the bottom (Main Street) end, date from around 1700.

New Holt Road :

The Old Hall between New Holt Road and Rectory Lane is mid 17th-century. It was also once known as Medbourne House, and Medbourne Villa.

Manor Road :

The Manor House (on the north side of New Holt Road) has late 13th-century origins. Whilst being restored by the Payne family, wall paintings from the reign of James I were discovered. The kennels and cottages opposite date from 1884, built by Sir Bache Cunard. A former name of the house was Huntsmans House due its connections with the Fernie Hunt.

Lower end of New Holt Road: Dale Farm: a 'H' shaped building with tall chimney stacks. Late 17th-century.

Rectory Lane (a cul-de-sac leading to a narrow footpath):

The Old Rectory : built about 1830, but has at the northern end a crosswing from the 17th century, and an 18th-century addition at the south end.

Spring Bank:

Bridgedale (Farm) : 1709, south end of village. Built on an artificially-raised site to lessen the risk of flooding. 'Burnside' between the farm and brook : 1861, but with a datestone of 1601 and the inscription: 'Robert Smith R.N. Serve God'.

Waterfall Way :

A row of houses (including the Neville Arms) stand alongside a brook, and the area - until five years ago - was subject to very bad flooding as old (and recent) photos show, one of which has the water up to the doorway of the pub! Nearby Waterfall House was particularly badly-hit, with floodwater coming up to its windows.

Manor Farm: mid 17th-century, stands west of the church. Another dangerous fire in the village occurred in its yard in 1857, damaging a few buildings. Further damage was only averted by the timely intervention of rain and a change of wind.South of the farm on the west side of the brook, there are three 17th-century ironstone dwellings: Laburnum Cottage (once a sweet shop), Woodbine Cottage and thatched Saddlers Cottage (once the home of the last saddler in the village).

Snippets:
* A Roman fort/settlement once existed nearby at Mill Hill on Slawston Rd. A windmill which later stood on the site, was struck by lightning. This too, no longer exists.
* There was evidence of a Roman villa, 150 yards south of bridge. It was found in 1721, with a mosaic pavement 41ft. x 22ft, partly in an orchard and a garden. It is now once again covered over.
* The village was originally centred on a large rectangular green, the church being at its north west end.
* Rectory Lane is known locally as Parsons Lane, and Manor Road as Kennel Lane.

STAMFORD (stony ford).

The famous stone-built coaching town off the A1. It stands on the River Welland and is a blend of medieval and 18th-century architecture.

Medieval churches: *All Saints* (13th-century) with brasses. *St George's* (13th to 17th-century) associated with Order of the Garter. *St John's* (15th-century) a small church with roofs of angel carvings. *St Martins* (built in the 1480s). Contains Burghley tombs. Fine glass. Graveyard contains tomb of Daniel Lambert, famous 52 stone man, who died in 1809. *St Mary's*: 13th to 15th-centuries. painted and gilded ceiling. Fine fittings and art work. (Another church, *Holy Trinity,* stood in East Street, but was destroyed during a battle in 1461. There is also a former church, *St Michael's,* still standing in the High Street, near the corner of Maiden Lane).

Old Pubs: among these are the *George* (16th-century coaching inn). It has been said, questionably, that the long sign spanning the High Street, was used as a gallows to deter would-be criminals! *St Mary's Vaults* (a former timber-framed coaching inn in St.Mary's Street); the *King's Head* (in Maiden Street); the *Millstone* (in All Saints Street. Has painted lettering: 'Good Stabling and Loose Boxes'); the *Crown Inn.*

Other buildings and places of interest:
St Leonard's Priory : Norman architecture. A church founded by Benedictine monks. Early 12th-century remains have been found.
Browne's Hospital : 1475 almshouses, built by William Browne, a wool merchant who also helped rebuild *All Saints.*
Brazenose Gate and Knocker : 13th-century gateway. The original knocker is now at Brazenose College, Oxford.
Greyfriars Gate : an early 14th-century entrance to a religious institution where the wife of the Black Prince (and mother of Richard II) is buried.
Norman Arch : a postern gate in the former town walls. Entrance to St.Mary's Passage, off St. Mary's Hill.
Former St Paul's Church : 12th and 13th-century remnants, now part of the chapel of Stamford School.
Stamford Castle : 13th-century remnants can be seen between the bus station and Bath Row.
Burghley Hospital : 16th-century with remnants of the 12th-century 'hospital' on whose site it was built. A long building facing Station Road, and the River Welland.
Brewery Museum : a Victorian steam brewery in mint condition, which can be visited.
Tolethorpe Hall: at Little Castleton: 16th-century manor house (with 18th-century alterations). Birthplace of Robert Brown, founder of Congregationalism. Open air Shakespearean Theatre in the summer.
Burghley House: This grand building, with its gardens and deer park, stands on the edge of the town. Built between 1565-1587 by William Cecil, Chancellor to Elizabeth I, it has been home of the Cecil (Exeter) family ever since. Open to visitors from the beginning of April until the beginning of October.

Snippets:
* The town was used by the BBC for filming a 'period' serial version of George Eliot's 'Middlemarch'.
* For walkers, six thematic town trails, as well as countryside rambling leflets, are available from the Tourist Information Centre.

TANSOR ('Tan's bank').

Essentially a one-street village, Tansor is a quiet attractive place, with a lot of hidden history. It lies on the other side of the Nene from Cotterstock and other Forest villages. There are many houses from the 18th century, some with datestones.

Church: St Mary the Virgin. Earliest parts: 12th-century. Tower. Medieval brass to a rector.Thirteenth-century piscina. Screen and poppyhead benches (15th-century). 17th-century pulpit. Seven stalls from Fotheringhay with misericords, including images of heads, angels, a falcon, a rose and musical instruments. Some medieval painting. The church was restored 1886-7.
Former pubs: the *White Horse Inn*, the *Black Horse*. There are no pubs in the village today.
Former school: 1866 (closed 1970). Currently houses the Tansor Playgroup.
Other buildings and places of interest:
(Coming from the A605 end): immediately on the left stands The Lindens, a large imposing house, formerly a rectory, now a residential Home. A little way along on the right, is the site of the disused railway. Further along on the same side, some way past the bridge, stands Tansor House (1721), opposite which is the former *Black Horse* pub. Facing the road to Cotterstock and Oundle are the former *White Horse* pub (17th-century) and the Old Post Office, which once had a bakehouse at the back.
Facing the church, behind the high wall is a huge complex of buildings associated with the former Rectory which burned down in the mid-1800s and was rebuilt in 1860, with later additions, one of which has a datestone of 1869. It is now a private house. The (currently blue) door in the wall facing the church was the exit from the site of an underground passage leading from the Rectory for the priests going to church.
Just before the road bends to the right you will see an open driveway on the left: this is one of the entrances to Tansor Manor (earliest parts 16th-century, and originally associated with the Westmorland family of Apethorpe), and Riverside Cottages.
On the same bend, immediately on the right, is one of the entrances to the former Rectory. This is a striking piece of masonry, with an inscription in Latin above its Gothic arched doorway, carved heads and the coat of arms of Peterborough Cathedral, with scallops. The road leads on to Fotheringhay.
Walks in the area:
* It is possible to walk the length of the grassy former railway track for miles each way! (Fotheringhay, Elton, Nassington and Yarwell one way ; and Oundle, with its walks along the Nene, the other).

UPPINGHAM (settlement of the upland people).

A scholarly market town, (second largest in Rutland) with lots of narrow passageways leading to interesting tucked-away shops, and old buildings. A pleasant, old-fashioned service and welcome in many shops.

Church: St Peter and Paul. Mainly 14th-century. Some 13th-century Norman figure sculptures (two above the doorway inside). Elizabethan pulpit. The church was enlarged and restored in 1861.
Public School: The original public school founded by local benefactor Robert Johnson in 1584 still exists at the rear of the church, some distance from the 'modern' 19th-century buildings, many of which are listed, and which lie mainly in High Street West. The school was developed and its reputation firmly enhanced during the term of office of Edward Thring who was Headmaster from 1853 until 1887. Distinguished former pupils include Donald Campbell and Boris Karloff. There are guided tours available on Saturday afternoons in July and August. Tel: either (01572) 822672 or 822216.
Pubs: the *White Hart* (originally 16th-century), the *Vaults*, the *Falcon Hotel*, the *Garden Hotel*, the *Crown Hotel* (17th-century with large gold-painted sundial), the *Exeter Arms* (coat of arms 1868), the *Waggon and Horses* (thatched), the *Cross Keys*.
Some of the former pubs: the *Horse and Trumpet*, the *Chequers*, the *White Swan*, the *Unicorn*.
Other buildings and places of interest:
Set back from the High Street, are the Hall (part of which is inscribed 1612 and was remodelled in the 18th century), and The Manor House. The High Street has several old buildings, some of which have datestones from 1616, 1729 and 1734. The 'Tudor House' on the north side of the High Street is believed to be late 16th/early 17th-century. Several interesting alleyways lead off the High Street on both sides, among them Hopes Yard, which has exterior wooden beams in the roof of the entrance way, a medieval oak-mullioned window set in the wall of one of the houses, the Old Bakehouse, Old Cottage, Old Coach Houses and the 'Little Crooked House'.
'Cromwell House' at the corner of Queen Street (formerly Horn Lane) & Station Road is an old dwelling (rebuilt 1895) where Oliver Cromwell is supposed (like so many other houses) to haved stayed one night.
Snippets:
*There was once a Town Hall in the Market Place. It was already dilapidated when in 1587, it was said by

the Elizabethan writer, Leland, to be 'in a very greate Ruyn and Decaie'.

WARMINGTON (Wyrma's farm).

One part of this large village (the Church Street area) was originally called Southorp(e): the other (towards Eaglethorpe) was known as Mill End.

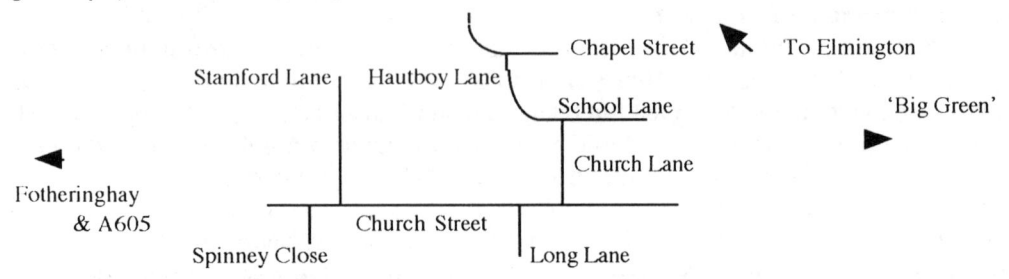

```
                          |
          Stamford Lane   Hautboy Lane  ── Chapel Street   ◤  To Elmington
                                         School Lane                  'Big Green'
   ◀                                                                   ▶
                                         Church Lane
 Fotheringhay
   & A605              Church Street
          Spinney Close            Long Lane
```

Church: St Mary the Virgin. Early English style. Earliest parts date from around 1180-90. Much 13th-century work including the tower, octagonal broached spire, and rare, exceptional carved 13th-century wooden vault over the nave with elaborate bosses depicting foliage and human faces. Medieval coffin lids, spare masonry, glass and door decoration. 15th-century tomb chests. 17th-century seating. The church was restored in 1850 and 1876.
Pub: the *Red Lion Inn* (17th-century coaching inn. On the A605).
Former pub: the *Hautboy and Fiddle* (now a thatched house, The Old Hautboy) in Hautboy Lane. Earliest part: 1648.
School: 1830 (enlarged, and the schoolhouse built: 1873). In School Lane.
Former Methodist Chapel: 1881 in Chapel Lane (opposite the Manor House) now 'The Old Chapel'.
Other buildings and places of interest:
(Begin from the entrance to the village at the Fotheringhay road end). On the corner of Spinney Close and Church Street is the 17th-century Malt House, with the adjoining Oast House. Note the original triangular air vents of the former barn. An 18th-century house adjoins The Malt House in Church Street.
Church Lane: On the right, opposite the church, you cannot fail to miss the three ornate Almshouses built in 1860 by members of the Proby family. Opposite, sitting snugly behind (south of) the church is the late 16th/early 17th-century Old Rectory with two bay windows and low mullioned windows.
Hautboy Lane: on the left of the bend is the late 16th-century Glebe House (formerly The Vicarage House). Just past the butcher's and the shop, is the former *Hautboy and Fiddle* pub. 'The Old Bakery' (or Martins House) from 1848, is further along on the corner.
Chapel Street: On your right stands the Manor House (the former Berrystead), once the home of the Elmes, Proby and Sapcot families. There is a datestone inscribed 1677 and the house was restored in 1962 by Richard Proby.
On the opposite side of the road stands 'The Old Chapel'. On the same side, as the road curves round, stands The Hollies, an early 19th-century house with an added 1696 datestone. A little further on is a pair of 17th-century cottages with mullioned windows.
Eaglethorpe ('Eagwulf's settlement', though 'village by the oaks' has also been suggested). This 'satellite' settlement lies at the other end of Chapel Street, on the other side of - and close to - the busy A605. It was once known as 'Mill End' and is nowadays much smaller than it was long ago. It began to change in the late 16th-century and now consists of just a few houses which line the path to the river and its ancient water meadows. The large house on the right, is Eaglethorpe House (late 16th/early 17th-century) which was rebuilt by Sir Thomas Proby, and incorporates an early 16th-century door and frame from Fotheringhay Castle and which has carvings associated with the House of York.
Walk down the track with the large Eaglethorpe Farm (1646) and its interesting outbuildings on your right, among them (a short distance away from the farm and ahead of you) a round 17th-century dovecote with the original ladder to the nests within. The building makes a fine photograph.
As you approach the former Mill (recently repaired), the old early 19th-century Miller's House lies to your left. Entering through a gate, you come into an area used by Elton Boat Club and the East Midlands Angling Federation.

Walks around the area:
* Fotheringhay: begin at Eaglethorpe. Turn right at the Mill, and follow the arrow-marked route over water-meadows and the river. The lantern-towered church of Fotheringhay stands out clearly on the skyline, as you walk across the fields. Just before you enter the village, you pass the earthworks of the former castle on your left and a small deer park.
* Ashton (and Oundle). Walk down pleasant Long Lane (off Church Street) , turn right and follow the signs. It is a lengthy walk along a track for much of the way, and the view is mainly one of open-countryside. You pass close to the lost village of Elmington.

TOURIST OFFICES IN THE AREA

ROFTA: Rockingham Forest Visitor Centre, The Woolpack Hotel, Islip. There is a video presentation, displays, and a large selection of leaflets and booklets on aspects of the Forest. The ideal starting point with everything you need to enjoy a stay in, or visit to the Forest region. Open seasonally from Easter to September 30th. Refreshments available in the adjoining tearoom, or pub.
Corby: Civic Centre, George St., Corby NN17 1QB.
Oundle: 14 West Street, Oundle PE8 4EF
Kettering: Coach House, Sheep Street, Kettering NN16 0AN
Market Harborough: Pen Lloyd Library, Adam & Eve St., Market Harborough, LE16 7LT
Rutland Water: Sykes Lane Car Park, Empingham, Oakham LE15 8PX
Oakham: Public Library, Catmos St., Oakham LE15 6HW
Stamford: Stamford Arts Centre, 27 St Mary's St., Stamford PE9 2DL

MUSEUMS

Although Rockingham Forest does not have its own museum, there are some good ones in the vicinity. It is encouraging that two villages (Brigstock and Weldon) have thought of having a museum of their own.

Kettering: Manor House Museum, Sheep Street, Kettering, Northants (Tel. 01536 410333). Open Mon-Sat, 9.30am to 5pm. Excellent displays of town and local history, including a section on Rockingham Forest, with sound effects, and posters created from medieval documents. This innovative museum is a joy to wander around, with an open "touch" policy which allows interaction with the exhibits. Special thematic events throughout the year, especially for children. Well-stocked shop. Free admission.
Market Harborough: The Harborough Museum, (Council Offices & Library building), Adam & Eve Street, Market Harborough, Leics LE16 7LT (Tel. 01858 432468) . Open 7 days a week. Entrance varies according to day of week. Free admisision.
Normanton Church Water Museum: on Rutland Water. History of the site. Open seasonally. Small admission charge.
Oakham: Rutland County Museum, Catmos Street, Oakham, Leics. (Tel. 01572 723654).Housed in former riding school. Displays of local archæology, town and country history. Good areas on farming and military history. Open 7 days a week. Free admission.
Oundle: (recently opened). Town and area history. The Drill Centre, (First Floor), 1 Benefield Road, Oundle. (The building is also HQ of the Rockingham Forest Trust). A promising new venture. At present it opens at weekends, 2-5pm. Free admission but voluntary contributions welcome. (Tel. 01832 272055).
Stamford: Broad Street , Stamford, Lincs. (Tel. 01780 66317). Open 7 days a week. Opening times vary. Mainly town history and archæology. 'Middlemarch' Trail leaflet available. Small admission charge.

WALKING IN THE FOREST AREA

For reasons of space, the walks in this book have not been described in great detail. The purpose has been to show what walks are available in the Forest, and their starting point. However a separate book dealing with the walks in detail, with maps, is planned for the near future. The author is not responsible for the maintenance and diversion of the footpaths/bridleways, or any mishap that may occur en route! For many of the walks, Ordnance Survey maps are highly recommended: the two covering the Forest are the Landranger Series, 141 and (to a lesser degree)142. The Pathfinder (Second) Series nos. 917 & 938 are very useful (also 918 & 939).

The Ramblers (Corby & District Group) have a programme of walks throughout the year, varying in length and difficulty. The short walks are usually in the evening (Spring/Summer), on Tuesdays, or Wednesdays and are between 3-6 miles in length. The longer walks are between 8-15 miles, (usually on Sundays), last all day and require a packed lunch and drink. Contact Paul Mortimer, 01536 261196, or Tony McCay, 01536 645327 for details.

Northamptonshire Countryside Services issue an **'Enjoying the Countryside'** programme which includes various activities and (free) guided walks of varying duration or difficulty, though most are leisurely and family-orientated. Three issues are brought out for April-June; July-September; October-December. Some walks start from the Country Parks (Brigstock or Barnwell), others from the smaller woods of the Forest such as Southwick or Short Woods. Past activities have included 'Exploring the Nene Valley', 'Dormouse Monitoring', 'Nature Detective Day' and 'Strange Lights and Tall Tales'.

Forest Enterprise (part of the Forestry Commission) produce an annual programme **'What's On'** of walks with a nature theme such as deer watching, a moth evening, a children's activity morning, fungi hunting and bat watching.The programme is available from Top Lodge, Fineshade Wood. Those woods of Rockingham Forest which are covered are Fineshade, Wakerley, and Bedford Purlieus (off the Kingscliffe-Wansford Road). A small charge is made for some of the walks. Fineshade also offers an excellent wood-carving course, which is open to anyone, regardless of experience. Details in the programme.

Blue Badge Guides: a programme of leisurely guided-walks. These are led by local specialists, approved and specially-trained by the Tourist Board. There is a charge for these walks.

WALKING LEAFLETS

Countryside Walks:
A series of over 30 leaflets, produced by Northamptonshire Countryside Services, which cover a circular walk around a village/town or villages in the county, and show points of interest en route. The following leaflets are of relevance to the Forest area:

17: Nassington
19: Fotheringhay & Elton
20: Oundle
22: Yarwell
23: Bulwick
25: Aldwincle & Wadenhoe
27: Apethorpe
28: Easton-on-the-Hill, Collyweston & Duddington
29: Thrapston
30 : Brigstock
31 : Rothwell

Jurassic Way:
A series of three leaflets produced by Northamptonshire Countryside Services, covering a newly-created walk, 88 miles in length. Section 3 (The Hermitage to Stamford) 'Forest and Flow' covers the Forest area, starting from near Stoke Albany. The underlying rocks are, as the name implies, from the Jurassic era. The route has the usual black & white arrow-markers, with the addition of a white shell symbol. Wooden signposts are deeply routed with the lettering: JURASSIC WAY. Highly recommended.

Nene Way :
A set of leaflets in 5 sections, produced by Northamptonshire Countryside Services, which cover a walk approximately 70 miles in length, along the River Nene. Sections 4 (Islip to Oundle) and 5 (Ashton to Wansford) are of interest to the Forest area. A supplement on local accommodation, refreshment and transport is included. The route is well-signposted and arrow-marked.

The Tresham Trail:
Though this is not specifically a walk, and is unmarked, it is possible to follow the route through the Forest area, from Rothwell to Pilton - a considerable distance! The 'trail' was designed to give information about various sites connected with the Tresham family, and how to get to them by road. Small charge. (Northamptonshire Libraries and Information Service). A more detailed booklet: 'On The Tresham Trail' is available from the writer, Lewis Stanley (Tel. 01536 712521).

Rambles In Rockingham Forest (ROFTA).
These leaflets have been designed by the author for ROFTA (Rockingham Forest Tourist Association). The walks are periodically monitored for any changes or diversions (temporary or otherwise).

1. East Carlton Park
2. East Carlton Park - Wilbarston- Middleton
3. Great Oakley - Corby Village
4. Geddington - Great Oakley
5. Geddington - Brigstock
6. Geddington - Stanion
7. Fotheringhay - Eaglethorpe - Warmington
8. Oundle - Cotterstock
9. Wadenhoe - Achurch - Lilford
10. Wadenhoe - Aldwincle
11. Great Oakley - Pipewell
12. Pilton Circular Walk
13. Bulwick - Blatherwycke
14. Southwick - Woodnewton - Apethorpe
15. Kingswood - Cottingham - Middleton
16. Wakerley Woods (Fineshade Wood- Wakerley Wood-Wakerley-Barrowden)
17. Twywell - Cranford
18. Wansford - Yarwell
19. Gretton - Welland valley
20. Ashton - Barnwell
21. Weldon - Brigstock area
22. Duddington - Kings Cliffe - Apethorpe

THE WALKERS' CODE

With over 100 Public Footpaths, Bridleways and other rights of way, the Forest area has a lot to offer : varying landscapes - hills, dales, hollows, waterside, wetland, meadows, fields, scrub, woodland - and atmosphere, flora, fauna, tranquillity, even isolation if you so wish. It is important therefore to protect this precious heritage. Make the most of the routes, but please help to safeguard the environment for the Forest community and for future users.

1. Always wear suitable clothing and footwear for the season, and remember to allow plenty of time to complete your walk.
2. Look out for any waymarking signs (usually black and white arrow markers, timber signposts, or green metal signposts). There are many in the Forest area, but sometimes there are not and you will have to be on the look-out for 'landmarks' (like church steeples, gaps in hedges or stiles) and other guides. In a number of cases, an Ordnance Survey map might be useful.
3. Remember to close gates behind you. Straying stock can cause damage or even spread disease - and carelessness may lead to tragedy.

4. To avoid harm or distress to farm animals and wildlife, it is best to leave dogs at home or in a safe place. If you have to bring them, they should be kept on a leash.

5. Always keep to the path to avoid trespass. If the path is obstructed you are allowed to seek a reasonable way round the obstruction, taking care to avoid causing damage. Please report the obstruction (such as a fence) to the Rights of Way Authority (01536 524100) with information about location. By law, a footpath can be ploughed up (except round the edge of a field) but must be restored within 14 days.

6. If your route takes you onto a road, keep right, facing oncoming traffic - and use the verge if one exists.

7. Remember that every piece of land in the Forest area belongs to someone, so please treat it with respect and other walkers will be made welcome.

HORSE RIDING IN THE FOREST AREA

There are bridleways everywhere, all signposted and of varying length: use the OS maps as above.
Forest rides and tuition are available at Manor Farm, Sudborough. Tel: 01832 733208.
Full day rides and tuition are available at Harringworth Manor Stables, Wakerley Rd., Harringworth. Tel: 0157287 400.

CYCLING AROUND THE FOREST AREA

Guided bike rides are available and appear in the **Enjoying the Countryside** programme which appears three times a year. See the 'Walking around the Rockingham Forest area' section above.
Cycle hire is available at Oundle (Valley Cycles, 5a West Street) and, on the periphery of the Forest area, at Rutland Water (near the Whitwell entrance).

Northamptonshire Cycletours leaflets for independent cycling: a joint Northamptonshire County Council/Kettering Borough Council venture. There are currently 4 leaflets available (no.1 is entitled 'Moots, Moats and Manors' and covers the periphery of the forest: Harrington, Thorpe Underwood, Braybrooke and Arthingworth). The following two are of interest to the Forest area:
No.2:   Nene Valley, Thrapston and Oundle.
No.3:   Cliffe Bailiwick and Willow Brook.   No.4: Oundle to Wadenhoe.
Biking Round The Borough (Country Towns and Countryside) a leaflet produced by Kettering Borough Council Leisure Services, with a suggested family cycling tour encompassing Rothwell, Desborough, Stoke Albany, Wilbarston, Pipewell and Rushton.

THE CYCLISTS' CODE

1. Ride only on tracks and Forest roads.
2. Keep out of Nature Reserves and designated shooting areas.
3. Do not make any undue noise, or frighten wildlife - deer, badgers, birds, etc.
4. Give way to walkers and horses, travel at a moderate speed and avoid bunching if riding in a group.
5. Always tell someone where you are going - many areas of the Forest are very isolated.
6. Do not ride on waymarked walking trails, public footpaths or picnic sites.
7. Take care not to start fires.
8. Minimise damage and erosion by avoiding muddy or well-worn tracks.
9. Follow the country code.

DRIVING AROUND THE FOREST AREA

Although the best way to see the real Forest is to walk or ride, there is also an excellent road network. Care must be taken on some of the roads which are narrow, or single track, and tend to have a series of bends or concealed entrances. As might be expected there is a fair amount of farm traffic. Watch out for horseriders, and don't forget to slow down if a horse is approching!

Although some villages have had the main traffic routes diverted away from them by modern wider roads, there is a growing tendency in others, for traffic to pass through at an unnecessarily high and dangerous speed. (Please show concern for the inhabitants!) In some of the smaller villages parking is limited or virtually impossible. Try to park outside where there may be a lay-by, or some other space. More of these are being provided. In others, where there is plenty of room, please respect 'No Parking' signs and driveways. For example the parish councillors of Southwick have a sign outside the church gates requesting motorists to park in another less-obstructive area.

A recommended **'Rockingham Forest Leisure Drive'** (Welland Valley) guide has been produced by Northamptonshire County Council, which maps out a route with points of interest along the way together with some potted facts about the area.

THE RIVERS AND STREAMS OF THE FOREST AREA

There are many streams, rivulets (many un-named) and rivers flowing through the Rockingham Forest region. The following are of special interest.

Harpers Brook (probably named after the 'le Harpur' family which settled near the brook in Norman times): rises from small springs north of Desborough and flows 15 miles in an easterly course. It joins the River Nene one and a half miles down the river from Thrapston, where the old Roman Gartree Road bridged the river. Other smaller streams join Harpers Brook en route. It passes through the villages of Pipewell, Great and Little Oakley, Stanion, Brigstock, Sudborough, Lowick, and Islip. At one time the brook was wider and deeper in places, and was the habitat of freshwater eels and fish. Kingfishers can still be occasionally seen in the vicinity. It is still a favourite with ducks, large numbers of which can be seen nesting and congregating at various points along its course. Recent months have seen a resurgence of the otter. Old mills at Stanion, Brigstock and Lowick.

River Ise: rises near Naseby and flows into the Nene at Wellingborough. Has been the habitat of crayfish. It flows by Arthingworth, Desborough, Rushton, Newton, Geddington, Warkton, Weekley and Kettering.

River Nene: Forms the southern boundary of the old Rockingham Forest. It has two sources, rising from near Daventry, and Naseby, and flows into The Wash. It is 184 kilometres (115 miles) in length. In the Rockingham Forest area, it passes by the villages of (in order) : Islip, Thrapston, Thorpe Waterville, Achurch, Aldwincle, Wadenhoe, Pilton, Oundle, Cotterstock, Tansor, Fotheringhay, Elton, Nassington, Yarwell, Wansford and on to Peterborough and beyond. Downstream of Thrapston its name is pronounced 'Nenn'. There are fine old surviving mills at Yarwell, Ashton and Islip.

River Welland: Forms the northern boundary of the old Rockingham Forest. Rises near Sibbertoft (Naseby area) and flows into The Wash. It is 112 kilometres long and in the area flows close to Ashley, Drayton, Bringhurst, Cottingham/Middleton, Rockingham, Gretton, Thorpe by Water, Harringworth, Barrowden, Wakerley, Tixover, Duddington, Collyweston, Ketton, Stamford and beyond.

Willow Brook: A true 'completely' Rockingham Forest waterway! Very lively, it has miniature falls in places. Rises in Corby, and flows through or near Deenethorpe, Bulwick, Blatherwycke, Kingscliffe, Apethorpe, Woodnewton, and Fotheringhay where it flows close to the Nene, before joining it at Elton. In the olden days it was affectionately known in many areas as 'Withybrook'.

LOCAL NATURE RESERVES

(Further information listed under the relevant village/town in the gazetteer. Leaflets for most of the reserves under the care of The Wildlife Trust for Northamptonshire are available at Tourist Offices in the region. Leaflets for woods under the care of The Forestry Commission are available at the relevant woods themselves, or at Country Parks).

Barford Wedge	between Corby & Kettering (see under Rushton)
Collyweston Quarries	Collyweston
Eyebrook Reservoir*	Stoke Dry
Fermyn Woods	Brigstock
Fineshade Woods	Fineshade Woods

Glapthorn Cow Pastures	Glapthorn
Grafton Park Wood	Grafton Underwood
Great Oakley Meadow	Great Oakley
Kings Wood	Corby
New Coppice	Cottingham/Middleton
Northfield Avenue	Kettering
Rothwell Gullet	between Rothwell & Desborough (see under Rothwell)
Short Wood	Southwick
Southorpe Paddock	Wansford (care of The Wildlife Trust for Cambidgeshire)
Southwick Wood	Southwick
Stoke Wood	Stoke Albany
Tailby Meadow	Desborough
The Plens	Desborough
Titchmarsh	Aldwincle
Twywell Gullet	Twywell
Wakerley Great Wood	Wakerley

There are also Nature Reserves at Rutland Water: Birdwatching Centre and Egleton Nature Reserve (Tel. 01572 770651), Lyndon Hill Visitor Centre and Nature Reserve (Tel. 01572 85378) and The Butterfly & Aquatic Centre, Sykes Lane entrance (Tel. 01780 86515).

WILDLIFE GROUPS

The Wildlife Trust for Northamptonshire has several local groups with a programme of events such as illustrated talks, orienteering, walks, folk concerts, and woodland crafts. Groups in the Forest area are: Desborough (contact Nigel Lingley, 01536 760435), Geddington & District (Colin Berrisford, 01536 746246), Gretton (Linda Moore, 01536 770469), Kettering & District (Celia Burdett, 01536 723536), Nassington & District (Judy Stroud, 01832 280837) and Oundle & District (Ioan Thomas, 01832 272741).

A full programme of events can be found in the Trust's **Wildlife Diary** (What's On Where You Live).

Country and Pleasure Parks

Barnwell	Oundle	(excellent walks, nature displays)
Brigstock	Brigstock	(excellent walks, nature displays)
East Carlton	East Carlton	(with Heritage Centre, craft workshops)
Wicksteed	Kettering	(amusements/rides)

POCKET PARKS

The number of these is constantly growing. Listed are those in existence in the Forest area in April 1995. See under the village or town in the gazetteer except those marked *)

Aldwincle	King's Cliffe (2 parks)
Brigstock	Lowick
Corby*	Nassington
Cottingham	Rockingham
Easton-on-the-Hill	Rothwell
Great Oakley	Stanion
Gretton	Weldon
Kettering (2 parks)	

(*William Mawdsley Pocket Park, close to Kingswood Community Centre).

CONSERVATION GROUPS

The Wildlife Trust has two active groups, Sunday Conservation Volunteers, and Wednesday Conservation Volunteers. Lifts are given (free) from Northampton, or you can make your own way and meet up at the site. Tasks include woodland management, coppicing and hedgelaying. Details in the Trust's Wildlife Diary. If you want to help with any of the tasks on either day, phone 01604 405285, in advance. A packed lunch and stout footwear are essential.

There are also local conservation groups, affiliated to the British Trust for Conservation Volunteers, such as The Barnwell & Brigstock Conservation Volunteers, whose tasks include reedmace clearing, tree planting and an 'Operation Springclean' (contact Ian Gemmill, 01536 373625, or Chris Gaines, 01832 273435).

LOCAL HISTORY SOCIETIES

Many of the groups below have a programme of events running throughout most of the year. These can be found on the noticeboards of local libraries, or by contacting the relevant members listed, to find out what's on. Some advertise their programme in Northamptonshire Local History News. In addition, Oundle has an Archaeological Society, the Nene Valley

Brigstock (Carl Hector. Tel. 01536 373377). Meets in the Village Hall on the second Wednesday of each month. The society publishes a magazine, *Bygone Brigstock*.

Cottingham/Middleton (Sue Hall. Tel.01536 771127 or Peter Bloomfield, Tel.770077). The society usually meets in the Methodist Chapel (sometimes the Schoolroom) on Mondays of the last week of the month with a good programme, but will be concentrating more fully in the next few months on recording the history of its villages. Some events will however will take place: phone for details.

Gretton (Ann Craske. Tel.01536 771102). Meets 5 times a year in the Village Hall every two months, on the third Thursday. The society publishes an annual magazine (in December), *Taking Stock*.

Oundle (Julia Moss. Tel. 01832 273415). Meets every two months, on a Friday, usually at the Palmer Block, Glapthorn Road.

Stanion (Marjorie Strongman. Tel.01536 204872). Meets 2nd Tuesday of month. Location varies.

Thrapston (Margaret Idle. Tel. 01536 82119). Meets every two months on a Thursday in St.James Sunday School Hall. The society publishes an annual magazine, *Strapetona*.

Weldon (Ron Sismey. Tel. 01536 204951 or Peter Hill (01536 741439). Meets in the Village Hall on the third Tuesday of the month, Sept-May (except December). The society publishes an annual magazine (in December), *Weldon-in-the-Woods*.

Willowbrook (Nicky Parr. Tel.01780 782155) (covers Nassington, Apethorpe, Woodnewton and Yarwell). The group have published some excellent booklets of relevance to the area. (see Reading Interests section). There are occasional informal meetings.

Societies on the edge of the Forest

Great Easton (Ken Heselton. Tel. 01536 770426) (meets last Friday of every month. Village Hall).

Market Harborough (Ann Paul. Tel. 01858 464547) (meets second Wednesday of each month, in the museum). The society publishes an annual magazine, *The Harborough Historian*.

Medbourne (John Cooper. Tel. 0185 883 202). A booklet/trail on the village has been printed.

Rutland (Local History & Record Society). Tel. 01572 723654. Meetings at Rutland County Museum, Oakham. The society publishes an annual magazine, *The Rutland Record*.

THE TRADITIONAL LANDOWNING FAMILIES OF THE FOREST

Unusually, most of the big estates of the Forest are still privately owned by families long associated with the area. These are listed below, together with other families who also once had a long-term influence.

Brooke : Great Oakley, and part of Cottingham. John Brooke from Warwickshire, settled in Great Oakley in 1472 as part of a marriage arrangement and an exchange of land deal (that also included Rushton). His descendants, through purchase, became sole lords of the manor in 1546. The male line died out in 1762, and a new line, through inter-marriage, (de Capell Brooke), began in 1782 which continues to this day.

Brudenell (Cardigan): Deene, Deenethorpe, Corby, Stanion, Glapthorn, Weldon, part of Bulwick. Sir Robert Brudenell, Chief Justice of the Common Pleas to Henry VIII, purchased Deene in 1514 and it is still with the family today. The family continued to accumulate land in the Forest area through purchase and lease during the 16th century, Glapthorn coming into the family's hands in 1574. They acquired Corby during the 17th century, as a result of an exchange of lands with the Hatton family. The same century saw Thomas Brudenell created first Earl of Cardigan.

Cecil (Exeter): Kingscliffe, Wakerley, Collyweston, Easton-on-the-Hill. William Cecil, a wealthy Northamptonshire squire, began building Burleigh House near Stamford in 1553. His son, also Thomas, (1542-1635) became Chief Minister to Elizabeth I and organised a group of agents to root out any conspiracy against the Queen. He founded Lyddington Bede House, and acquired Easton on the Hill in 1584. He was made first Earl of Exeter in 1605. His son, Richard, bought the manor of Wakerley in 1618. The family acquired Collyweston in 1800, and Kingscliffe in 1812.

Hatton (Winchelsea): Kirby, Gretton, parts of Pipewell and Corby. Sir Christopher Hatton, dubbed Elizabeth I's 'favourite' was from Holdenby Hall, near Northampton. He was from a family in the south of the county, whose ancestors had lived in Cheshire. He had held various high-ranking posts such as Lord Chancellor and Captain of the Queen's Bodyguard and was, with Thomas Cecil, ultimately responsible for the execution of Mary, Queen of Scots. Through purchase and Royal favour he acquired lands in the Forest area and the Hattons were made 'hereditary bailiffs of Rockingham Forest'. He also undertook the completion of Kirby Hall, which he acquired on the death of Sir Humphry Stafford in 1575. The (direct) male line died out in the middle of the 18th century and a nephew, Edward Finch-Hatton became heir. His descendants (the Earls of Winchelsea) still retain the Estate.

Mildmay (Westmorland): Apethorpe, Nassington, Yarwell, Newton. Sir Walter Mildmay, Elizabeth I's Chancellor of the Exchequer (d1580), acquired the manor of Apethorpe (with Nassington and Yarwell) in 1550 and Woodnewton (formerly belonging to Fineshade Abbey) in 1551. By marriage with a daughter and heiress of that family, it came into the hands of Francis Fane in 1617, who was created the first Earl of Westmorland in 1623. The properties remained with the family until 1904.

Montagu (Buccleuch) : Boughton, Geddington, Newton, Little Oakley, Grafton Underwood, Weekley, Warkton, parts of Kettering and Brigstock. In the 14th century the Montagu family lived at Hanging Houghton, near Lamport. In the 15th century, a descendant, Thomas, acquired Hemington. The family purchased the (now lost) village of Hale, near Brigstock and began to gain influence in that area. A son, Edward, was born at the royal manor of Brigstock, rising in wealth and position, becoming Sir Edward Montagu, Lord Chief Justice to Henry VIII. He bought Boughton and Weekley in 1528. The manor of Barnwell came into the family's hands shortly after. Other lands were later acquired in the Forest area. In the 18th century, when the male line was extinguished, the estates passed by marriage into the Buccleuch family, who still hold possession of most of them today.

Stafford : Blatherwycke, Laxton. In 1542, Humphry Stafford of Blatherwycke, a descendant of the Earls of Stafford, acquired the manor of Kirby and began the building of Kirby Hall, in 1570-75. In the 18th century, when the male line died out with William Stafford, his two daughters shared the family seat: Laxton going to Ann (married to George Evans, with whose family it stayed until the late 19th century), and Blatherwycke to Susannah (married to Henry O'Brien, with whose family it remained until the 1940s).

Tresham: Rushton, Rothwell, part of Pipewell, part of Great and Little Weldon, part of Brigstock, Lyveden, Pilton, Newton. William Tresham of Sywell, who was Attorney-General to Henry V, acquired one of the manors of Rushton in 1438. The family then began building up a number of estates in the area and reached the height of its power (and subsequent decline) under the third Thomas Tresham in the late 16th century with grandiose buildings reflecting wealth, or religious fervour . It was this adherence to Catholicism which led to frequent imprisonment and fines. Disaster continued with the execution of one son, Francis, for involvement in the Gunpowder Plot, and the financial losses incurred by another son, so that by 1645, the decline was complete. The other local branch of the family (at Newton, and then Pilton) finally faded from the local scene in 1715. Decendants emigrated to the Low Countries and the USA.

Tryon : Bulwick, Collyweston, Harringworth. Moses Tryon, son of a Dutch merchant, bought the manors of Bulwick and Harringworth c1620. Some of the family moved from Harringworth to Bulwick which became the main home in 1676. Peter, son of Moses, who had bought the manor of Seaton in 1646, then bought the manor of Collyweston in 1650, which stayed with the family until 1778. A descendant of the Bulwick line, William, who lived in the USA, became governor of North Carolina in 1765, and later, New York. Other members of the family lost their lives during various wars.

Watson (Saunders): Rockingham, Coton, Wilbarston, Stoke Albany, Little Weldon (1638-1837), part of Kettering. In 1544, Edward Watson of Lyddington, a prosperous landowner who was Surveyor General to the Bishops of Lincoln was granted a lease of Rockingham Castle, which the family later bought outright in 1619. A member of the family, through marriage with a daughter and heiress of the Sondes family in the late 17th century, was created Earl of Rockingham. Twice during the 18th century, a relative became Prime Minister. The Saunders Watson family still live at the castle today.

THE MEDIEVAL (DEER) PARKS OF THE FOREST

Although deerhunting was strictly the prerogative of the king, and the animals belonged to him, special licences could be obtained by landowners to impark their land, subject to a number of conditions. On being granted a licence, the landowner could receive a number of deer from the king to keep in the park, on condition that an internal ditch and some form of fencing (eg.hedge, earthbank or wall) was erected at the owner's expense and rigorously maintained by him. If this was neglected, Forest officials could take punitive action. Deerleaps - a device which allowed the king's deer to get into a park, but not get out - were forbidden (except in the case of the Archbishop of Peterborough*, since the Church was exempt from certain laws).

*Biggin (Oundle)	: recorded 1327.
Blatherwycke	: 1270.
Boughton	: 1473.
Brigstock (Great and Little Parks)	: believed to be early 13th-century (possible earlier).
Collyweston	: 15th-century.
Drayton (Old Park)	: begun in 1328.
Easton-on-the-Hill	: 1229.
Fotheringhay (2)	: 'Little Park' (at least 13th-century); the 'greater' park, c.1230.
Grafton Underwood	: begun in 1343.
Harringworth	: early 13th-century.
Kingscliffe	: recorded in the early 13th century.
Lyveden	: 1328
Rockingham	: c.1256 (enlarged 1485).
Stoke Albany	: 1201.
Wadenhoe	: 1298.
Wakerley	: 1228.
Weldon	: 1306.

(Apethorpe was created in the 16th century ; Deene c.1550, extended 1587,1612 & 1642).

THE 'LOST' VILLAGES OF THE FOREST

This list details those villages or settlements which have been 'lost', ie become deserted for some reason eg. sheep grazing, estate expansion, and in one known case, plague. In addition, at least two villages (Stoke Doyle and Wadenhoe) are believed to have been relocated from a nearby site. Other villages: Harringworth, Shotley, Bulwick (Henwick), Blatherwycke, Lower Benefield, Pipewell, Warmington (Southorpe) are a 'shadow' of their former selves, having shrunk to what we see today.

Barford	Hale
Biggin	Hale (near Brigstock): site not definitely identified.
Boughton	Kirby
Churchfield	Lyveden
Coton	Perio
Glendon	

MONUMENTS AROUND THE FOREST

The region abounds in ancient and more recent monuments (or parts of them), including well heads, market crosses (and stumps), milestones, boundary markers, water pumps, and sundials. There are few windmills still surviving and with one notable exception (Morcot) are incorporated in houses or standing in ruins. Watermills can be found, but are now unused.

There are dovecotes that may be visited and entered, as well as stocks, the Eleanor Cross (at Geddington) and the Bocase Stone (near Brigstock). These are listed under the appropiate village.

Many churches need a key (usually obtainable from a list of keyholders in the porch, on a noticeboard, or by inquiring at the post office, shop or rectory). Some double as 'museums' (eg Fotheringhay and Geddington) or have added attractions seasonally (eg. the Bone Crypt at Rothwell). Others hold music festivals in the summer.

There are a few craft workshops/shops, farms/farm parks and a Herb Farm (Brigstock) that can be visited. These are to be found listed under the appropiate village in the gazetteer.

The following buildings may also be visited, and are also listed with further details, in the village or area in which they stand. Most are opened only seasonally and even then, in some cases, of very limited duration. There is an excellent 'general' leaflet "Out and About In Rockingham Forest" published periodically by ROFTA, with current admission prices and opening times of places of interest.

Building:	see under:
Ashton Mill	Ashton
Bede House	Lyddington
Boughton House	Weekley
Burghley House	Stamford
Deene Park	Deene
Elton Hall	Elton
Kirby Hall	Gretton
Lyveden New Bield	Brigstock
Prebendal Manor House	Nassington
Priest's House	Easton on the Hill
Rockingham Castle	Rockingham
Rushton Hall	Rushton
Southwick Hall	Southwick
Triangular Lodge	Rushton
Uppingham School	Uppingham

Earthworks (castles and manorial) in the area

Some of these can only be viewed from the roadside (*), whilst others are close to a footpath and offer closer inspection.

Benefield Castle (Lower Benefield) *
Braybrooke Castle
Fotheringhay Castle
Great Oakley Fishpond
Hallaton 'Castle' (Leics)
Harrington Fish Ponds

Newton Manor Gardens (little left)
Pipewell Abbey
Rothwell Manor Fishpond (only one survives)
Stoke Albany Fish Ponds
Wakerley Manor Gardens*

OTHER LEISURE INTERESTS

For **Cricket, Football or Rugby** fans, there is usually a match close by, wherever you are.

Athletics:
Lodge Park Sports Centre, Corby. Tel: 01536 400033.

Fishing:
Aldwincle: Elinor Trout Fishery, Lowick Lane. (Fish Farm & Hatchery). Tel: 01832 720786.
Perio Mill, near Fotheringhay. Trout Fishing. Clay Pigeon Shooting. Tel: 01832 6241.
Also available at Brigstock Country Park, Eyebrook Resrvoir and Rutland Water.

Golf:
Corby Public Course, off the A47, near Weldon. Tel : 01536 60756.
Corby Golf Range, Corby Rd., Cottingham. Tel: 01536 403119.
Kettering Golf Club, Kettering Golf Links. Tel : 01536 511104.
Oundle Golf Club, Benefield Road. Tel: 01832 273267.

Keep Fit:
The Rockingham Forest Keep Fit Club meets at Rockingham Triangle, Rockingham Road, Corby. Tel. 01536 400033 for details.
Desborough Leisure Centre, The Hawthorns. Tel: 01536 761239. (Indoor sports also available).

Swimming:
Corby Pool Complex. Tel : 01536 400085.
Kettering Swimming Pool, London Road. Tel : 01536 410253.
Kettering Leisure Village. Tel : 01536 414414.
Rothwell, Greening Road. Tel: 01536 710151.
Thrapston Swimming Pool, Market Road. Tel: 01832 733116.

Tennis:
Corby Indoor Tennis Centre, Rockingham Triangle, Rockingham Road. Tel : 01536 407851.
Kettering Leisure Village (qv).

Ten Pin Bowling:
Rock n' Bowl, Rockingham Road, Kettering. Tel: 01536 414004.

For Railway Enthusiasts:
Nene Valley Railway. (Wansford Station, nearby at Stibbington). A chance to ride on old steam trains along stretches of the River Nene. Tel: 01780 782854. Talking Timetable: 01780 782921.
Rutland Railway Museum, Ashwell Road, near Cottesmore. Resting place of locos and railway memorabilia. Some days are set aside for short steam train excursions. (Signposted when operating).

Theatre:
Stahl Theatre, West Street, Oundle Box Office, Tel: (01832) 273930.
Tolethorpe Hall (north of Stamford): Open-Air (summer) Theatre with Shakespearean productions.
Uppingham Theatre, Stockerston Road. Box Office, at the Minerva Craft Shop, Tel: (01572) 823955.
Recently, there have been open-air (summer) productions at Rockingham Castle, and Lamport Hall.
In addition, Corby, Kettering and Oundle have flourishing amateur theatrical groups for most ages (libraries have details), as do some of the villages like Kingscliffe.

Markets in the area:
Corby : mainly Thursday, Friday, Saturday (both in Queen's Square in the town centre). A larger market is held outside the town, near Corby village, and the Asda supermarket, every Sunday.
Kettering: Tuesday, Wednesday, Friday, Saturday. Annual Charity Market in June with entertainment.
Market Harborough : Tuesday, Saturday.
Oakham : Wednesday, Saturday.
Oundle: Thursday.
Rothwell: Monday.
Thrapston: Tuesday.
Uppingham : Friday.

Annual events:
Like other places around the country, Rockingham Forest offers flower festivals, village fetes/carnivals and fairs every summer. May Day is still celebrated at Nassington. The country parks also offer seasonal events throughout the year, many of them family-orientated. Some of the Forest area churches like Rothwell (during May) offer music recitals/festivals. Details of these are available from tourist information offices, libraries, notices, or in quite a few cases, being in the right place at the right time! Oundle has a celebrated International Festival of music, every summer.

Refreshment:
Since the Forest is mainly full of villages, teashops, cafés and restaurants are relatively few and far between (and are to be found only in great numbers in the towns of Corby, Kettering, Oundle, Thrapston, Stamford and Market Harborough). However there are superb restaurants in the inns and public houses, some celebrated and highly commended. Booking is essential in some cases. Some village halls provide teas and snacks seasonally, as do the 'stately homes'. Where there are teashops in a village, this facility is entered under that village's name in the gazetteer.

Bibliography

Bridges, John:	History and Antiquities of Northamptonshire Vols 2-3 (1721, pub.1771).
Baker, John:	History of the County of Northamptonshire Vol 1 (1822).
Gover. J, et al:	The Place Names of Northamptonshire (CUP, 1933).
HMSO:	An Inventory of Archæological Sites in North East Northamptonshire (1975).
HMSO:	An Inventory of Archæological Sites in Central Northamptonshire (1979).
HMSO:	An Inventory of Architectural Monuments in North Northamptonshire (1984).
Leland, John:	Leland's Itinerary (1534-1543, published 1710).
Northamptonshire Notes & Queries:	(Vols 1-6, 1889-94).
Morton, John:	The Natural History of Northamptonshire (1712).
Pettit, Philip:	The Royal Forests of Northamptonshire - A Study In Their Economy 1558-1714. (NRS, 1968). An excellent, pioneering book for the more academically minded.
Scott, Charles Montagu-Douglas:	Tales of Old Northamptonshire (1904-06, 1936).
Serjeantson, R. (ed):	The Victoria History of the Counties of England : Northamptonshire, (Vols 2,3:1906, 1930).
Turner, G.J. (ed):	Select Pleas of the Forest (Proceedings of The Seldon Society, Vol. XIII 1901. (An invaluable book, with translations from the Latin of various Forest Court records, as well as more detailed information about Forest Law and its officials).
Wise, Charles:	Rockingham Castle and The Watsons (1891).

The serious student, wishing to pursue further research is recommended to visit the Public Records Office, Chancery Lane, London, who have many documents relating to Forest matters. There is further material available at the Northamptonshire Records Office, Wootton Hall, Northampton, and at the Northamptonshire Studies Collection at the Central Library, Northampton.

READING INTERESTS

The reader wishing to find out more about the Forest ,will find a detailed list of practically every book connected with the Forest, including the growing number of village histories at present available, appended below.

Some of the older books are still in print; others can be found in local libraries. The rarer ones are available either at the library of the relevant town, the Northants Records Office at Wootton Hall, Northampton, or the Local Studies Collection at Northampton Central Library.

Natural History

* A book on the wildlife of the Rockingham Forest area is in preparation at the time of writing.

Best, Jeffrey	The Past, Present and Future of Rockingham Forest (The Wildlife Trust for Northamptonshire, 1994). Highly recommended.
Best, Jeffrey:	Kingswood, Corby - Description, History, Explanation of Habitats and Wildlife (Nene College, 1983).
Peterken, G.F:	Long Term Changes in The Woodlands of Rockingham Forest (article in the Journal of Ecology, no. 64,1976).

General Forest History

Bellamy, Burl: Geddington Chase - The History of a Wood (1986). Privately published.
Bellamy, Burl: The Rockingham Forest Perambulation 1299 (Northants, Past and Present, Vol 6, No 6, 1984). Highly recommended 'translation'- used by the recent perambulation group (see chapter 1).
Grant, Raymond: The Royal Forests of England (Alan Sutton, 1991).

Individual Village/Town Histories

Alexander, A.W: The Foundations of a Steel Town: Corby 1880-1920 (Corby Hist Soc. 1969).
Bagshaw, E & H: Great Oakley Cricket (privately published, 1965).
Coales,Tony : They Walked by Night (privately published. Tel: 01832 733212).
Gilbert, John L: Wansford and Its Church (privately published, 1972).
Gilbert, John L: Wansford's Paper Mills (privately published, 1974).
Goodwin, J.Martyn: The Book of Collyweston (Spiegl Press, 1987).
Goodwin, J.Martyn: The Book of Easton-on-the-Hill (Spiegl Press, 1989).
Gordon, C: The Parish and Manor of Nassington-cum-Yarwell (A.King, 1890).
Gray, Allan: Islip - 150 Years in Photographs (privately published, 1993).
Hill, Peter: A History of Great Oakley In Northamptonshire (PH Publications, 1991).
Hill, Peter: Memories Of Great Oakley (PH Publications, 1992).
Hill, Peter: A Portrait of Great Oakley (PH Publications, 1994).
(ed) Hopkins, M.L: Geddington - A Diary Of A Village, 1086-1914 (privately published,1986).
Howe, Bob: Now and Then: The Life and Times of Bulwick,Blatherwycke, Laxton, Deene & Deenethorpe (2 volumes, 1986, 1987) (Library or phone: 01780 450285).
Markham, C.A: The History and Antiquities of Geddington (1899).
Mawdsley,W: Corby's Elizabethan Charter, 1585   (privately published, 1981).
Moore,J.R: The History of Desborough (1901, republished G.Coe, 1982).
Nassington Appraisal Group: Nassington Village Appraisal (1989-90).
Pursey, A: Kirby Hall, The House In The Hollow (Auvis, 1988).
Raynes, Monica: Geddington As It Was (Stryder, 1991).
Rhodes, Philip: Wakerley (Spiegl Press, 1994).
Rotary Club (Oundle): Old Oundle (1985).
Sismey, Ron: Corby, A Pictorial History (Phillimore, 1993).
Warren, Bill: Thrapston - A Glimpse Into the Past (Rotary Club, 1987).
Willowbrook Local History Group: booklets on various aspects of Nassington (Tel: 01780 782155).

Legends

Pipe, Marion: Northamptonshire Ghosts and Legends (Countryside Books, 1993).

General

Stanley, Lewis: On The Tresham Trail (published by the author,1994.Tel: 01536 712521).
Tonks, Eric: The Ironstone Quarries of the Midlands: Pt 6 - The Corby Area (Runpast, 1992).
Tonks & Scholes,J: Ironstone Quarrying at Easton on the Hill (Rutland Railway Museum, 1983).
Worledge, J. & V: Wanderers In Northamptonshire (Meridian, 1992).

Education Pack

Rockingham Forest Trust has produced an excellent education pack for use in schools and colleges. It contains information on the wide range of resources available in the Forest area, for practical work and experience. Tel: 01832 274278, for further details.

GLOSSARY OF TERMS

broach spire	an 8-sided spire, rising from a tower without a parapet.
buttress	a projecting stone or brick support to a wall or building.
chancel	the part of the church containing the altar and choir seating.
chimney breast	a projecting side wall surrounding a chimney.
clapper bridge	a simple stone footbridge consisting of slabs laid on pillars.
cob	a building material (usually) of compressed clay and straw.
coppicing	the traditional cutting down of a tree just above ground level to encourage new shoots for timber and other purposes.
corbel	a small stone support projecting from an internal wall.
crockets	(a row of) small carved ornaments, eg. cones, buds, or leaves.
cutwater	a projection from a bridge to divide the current of a river.
embattled tower	a decorative, fortified (castle-like) tower of a church.
lucarne	a small gabled window in the spire of a church.
misericord	a decorative carved projection under a hinged seat in the choir stall. This supported the occupant whilst standing.
mullioned window	a window with a stone framework.
nave	the long, central part of the church leading to the altar.
oriel window	a projecting upper window, with at least three sides.
parapet	a low (often decorative) wall on the edge of a tower or bridge.
pedestrian refuge	a space set back in the wall of a bridge for avoiding 'traffic'.
pinnacles	small slender stone turrets topped with an ornament.
piscina	a basin near the altar, originally for draining water at Mass.
pollarding	like coppicing but the tree is cut down higher up the trunk, away from grazing animals.
potence	a ladder-rest for reaching nesting niches in a dovecote.
sedilia	a stone seat set in the wall of a church, near the altar.
transepts	in a cross-shaped church, the arms leading off the nave.
turret	a small tower projecting from the wall of a building.
wall tie	metal plates supporting weak, or leaning, external walls.
well head	the opening of a well where the water is drawn out.